Political and Lite

Basque Classics Series No. 14

Series Editors

William A. Douglass
Gregorio Monreal
Pello Salaburu

Political and Literary Speeches

Arturo Campión

Introduction by
Roldán Jimeno Aranguren

Translated by
Cameron J. Watson

Center for Basque Studies
University of Nevada, Reno
2019

This book was published with generous financial support from the Basque Government.

Basque Classics Series, No. 11
Series Editor: William A. Douglass, Gregorio Monreal, Pello Salaburu

Center for Basque Studies
University of Nevada, Reno
Reno, Nevada 89557
http://basque.unr.edu

Library of Congress Cataloging-in-Publication Data

Names: Campión, Arturo, 1854-1936, author. | Jimeno Aranguren, Roldán, author of introduction. | Watson, Cameron, 1967- translator.

Title: Political and literary speeches / Arturo Campión ; introduction by Roldán Jimeno Aranguren ; translated by Cameron J. Watson.

Other titles: Discursos políticos y literarios. English

Description: Reno : Center for Basque Studies, University of Nevada, Reno 2018. | Series: Basque classics series; 14 | Summary: "A translation of the book Discursos Politicos Y Literarios, a collection of speeches on poilitcs and literature."-- Provided by publisher.

Identifiers: LCCN 2019054970 | ISBN 9781949805215 (paperback)

Subjects: LCSH: País Vasco (Spain) | Spain--Politics and government--1886-1931. | Regionalism--Spain.

Classification: LCC DP302.B46 C3413 2018 | DDC 320.540946/6--dc23

LC record available at https://lccn.loc.gov/2019054970

Contents

Introduction

The Political and Literary Speeches of Arturo Campión

Roldán Jimeno Aranguren

Presentation

Arturo Campión (Pamplona-Iruñea, May 7, 1854–Donostia-San Sebastián, August 18, 1937), one of the most prominent Basque intellectuals of his time, left a prolific work in the form of historical studies, literary creation, speeches and lectures, and press articles. We are publishing in English his *Discursos políticos y literarios* (Political and Literary Speeches), a book published in 1907 that includes a total of sixteen short talks that the author gave between 1891 and 1906, principally in different political and cultural acts,[1] which allow us to observe the evolution of his thought throughout those years of intense foralist activity.

These speeches and lectures, for which Campión has been considered "one of the cultural fathers of Basque nationalism,"[2] encompass the critical years in which the Navarrese scholar witnessed the breakdown of what had been the pillars of identity in his native land: Basque-Navarrese law and institutions (the fueros) and the Basque language. He had to shore up the edifice that was collapsing. The battle would not be fought in the trenches, as in the two previous Carlist wars. It had to take place in the political arena, but also by creating public opinion, disseminating

1   Arturo Campión, *Discursos políticos y literarios* (Pamplona: Imprenta y Librería de Erice y García, 1907).
2   Stanley G. Payne, "Navarra y el nacionalismo vasco en perspectiva histórica," *Príncipe de Viana* 45, no. 171 (1984), 104.

among the public what had been the historical evolution of the Basque people, underscoring the importance of their language and cultural expressions, and reinforcing, in sum, an identity of being from Navarre and the Basque Country as a whole that had been dismantled progressively since the end of the Second Carlist War. Arturo Campión put his intelligence and knowledge to the service of this cause, and devoted his political life and intellectual work to the defense of the political freedoms of his land.

Campión was considered, in the Basque Country of the first third of the twentieth century, to be an intellectual authority, and as such he received throughout his life numerous tributes and honors. Some contemporary authors of his, such as Julio Altadill and José Zalba, came to analyze his work.[3] Admiration for the Navarrese polymath was reflected in a bust made of him by Fructuoso Orduna in 1930. It was exhibited at the Círculo de Bellas Artes in Madrid and the Navasal department store in Pamplona-Iruñea; and Eusko Ikaskuntza (the Society of Basque Studies), which commissioned the work, ended up placing it in its library, in order to have "the prestige of his figure, severe and classically modeled and that would serve as an example for future generations of Basques who devoted the best of their efforts to their country."[4]

After Campión died on August 18, 1937, his memory and legacy were practically hidden for the four decades of the dictatorship. There was no follow-up to exemplary words in his memory that appeared in the first volume of the journal *Príncipe de Viana*, as a nexus of union between this new institution and its predecessor the Commission for Historic and Artistic Monuments, presided over by Campión himself. That first volume of the journal also included the reprint of one of his articles on Father José de Moret.[5] It was a politically iniquitous article that, in passing,

3   Julio Altadill, "El espíritu de Campión. Su labor anímica," *Euskalerriaren Alde* 20 (1930), 247–257; José Zalba, "El maestro en su taller. Cómo trabaja Campión," *Euskalerriaren Alde* 20 (1930), 258–262.
4   José Javier Granja Pascual, "Arturo Campión y la Sociedad de Estudios Vascos," *Oihenart. Cuadernos de lengua y literatura* 5 (1985), 85–86.
5   Arturo Campión, "El P. José de Moret," *Príncipe de Viana* 1, no. 1 (1940), 34–37.

reclaimed the figure of the first chronicler of the kingdom, which in no way reflected the legal and political thinking of Campión in relation to Navarre and Basque nationalism.[6]

There are scarcely any references to Arturo Campión's historical work in the historiography undertaken during Francoism. His abundant literary output was also ignored. In this regard, the considerations that José María Corella writes in his *Historia de la Literatura Navarra* (History of Navarrese Literature) are telling, when he argues that Campión was "the most eminent figure produced by Navarre in the entire nineteenth century and one of those on the very first row throughout its entire literary history," yet also someone that "today is not exactly valued or discussed."[7] This contrasts with the Basque nationalist world, in which Campión continued to be a highly regarded author, both in the Basque Country itself and among the Basque exile community.[8] As regards the latter, it is especially significant that the first book published by the Ekin publishing house in Buenos Aires in January 1942 was *El Genio de Nabarra* (The Genius of Navarre). That work by Campión, of which a thousand copies were printed,[9] went into a second edition in July that same year and with the same number of copies. Andrés María de Irujo, who ran this emblematic publishing house, recalled in 1954 that from the outset a photograph of Campión presided over the Ekin office, on account of him being an example and "a high prince of our letters."[10] It was also in Buenos Aires that the theatrical piece *El*

6   Roldán Jimeno Aranguren, "Las revistas jurídicas navarras (1940–1977)," in *Los juristas y el 'régimen'. Revistas jurídicas bajo el franquismo,* ed. Federico Fernández-Crehuet and Sebastián Martín (Granada: Comares, 2014), 313–14.
7   José María Corella, *Historia de la Literatura navarra* (Pamplona: Ediciones Pregón, 1973), 200.
8   As regards the former, see for example the works of Carlos Clavería, "Un recuerdo a Don Arturo Campión," *Vida Vasca* 32 (1955), 167; Fausto Arocena, "Los seis grandes," *Boletín de la Sociedad Vascongada de Amigos del País* 14 (1958), 455–57; and Gregorio Múgica, *Los titanes de la cultura vasca* (San Sebastián: Auñamendi, 1962); as regards the latter, see Gabino Garriga, "En el centenario del nacimiento de don Arturo Campión," *Boletín del Instituto Americano de Estudios Vascos* 5 (1954), 85–89.
9   Arturo Campión, *El Genio de Nabarra* (Buenos Aires: Ekin, 1942).
10   Andrés María de Irujo, "La editorial vasca Ekin de Buenos Aires," in *VIII Congreso de Estudios Vascos (8. 1954. Baiona, Uztaritz)* (Donostia: Eusko Ikaskuntza, 2003), 113–15.

bardo de Itzaltzu (The bard of Itzaltzu), with words by Víctor Ruiz
Añibarro and music by Madina, premiered in 1948.[11]
With the end of the dictatorship came the beginning of a
clear recovery of Campión and his work in the Basque Country
itself, with such standout landmarks as a reprint of his *Discursos
políticos y literarios* in 1976,[12] and the publication of his complete
works, *Obras completas*, in fifteen volumes by the Mintzoa publishing
house between 1983 and 1985.[13] Such appreciation for his texts
gave rise to a noteworthy historiography on his work from the
early 1980s on. Among the many studies dedicated to him are,
in chronological order, those of Vicente Huici Urmeneta;[14] José
Javier Granja Pascual;[15] José de Cruchaga y Purroy;[16] Ricardo
Cierbide;[17] José Ignacio Tellechea Idígoras;[18] Koldo Mitxelena;[19]
Elías Amézaga;[20] Jose Mari Satrustegi;[21] Idoia Estornés; Enrique
Miralles;[22] Santiago Cunchillos y Manterola;[23] José Luis Nieva

11 Edorta Barrutabeña and Asisko Urmeneta, *Gartxot. Konkista aitzineko konkista* (Donostia: Elkar), 54.
12 Arturo Campión, *Discursos políticos y literarios* (Bilbao: La Gran Enciclopedia Vasca, 1976). In this introduction all references to this work will be taken from this edition.
13 Arturo Campión, *Obras completas* (Pamplona: Mintzoa, 1983–1985).
14 Vicente Huici Urmeneta, "Ideología y política en Arturo Campión," *Príncipe de Viana* 42, no. 163 (1981), 641–90; "Arturo Campión. Aproximación a un vasco desconocido," *Muga* 9 (1980), 56–65; and "Vida y obra de Arturo Campión," *Bidebarrieta* 4 (1991), 109–16.
15 José Javier Granja Pascual, "Divergencias lingüísticas y literarias entre Arturo Campión y Sabino Arana," *Fontes Linguae Vasconum* 16, no. 43 (1984), 155–82; "Arturo Campión y la Sociedad de Estudios Vascos," *Oihenart. Cuadernos de lengua y literatura* 5 (1985), 75–93; "La Gramática de Arturo Campión y Luis Luciano Bonaparte," *Euskera* (1985), 31–49; and "Arturo Campión y la historia," *Príncipe de Viana*, Anejo 10 (1988), 169–82.
16 José de Cruchaga y Purroy, "Arturo Campión. Prólogo," in Arturo Campión, *Obras completes*, vol. 1 (Pamplona: Mintzoa, 1983), 19–83.
17 Ricardo Cierbide Martinena, "Posicionamiento de Arturo Campión ante el tema lingüístico y la pérdida de los Fueros en el País Vasco en 1876," *Fontes Linguae Vasconum* 15, nos. 41–42 (1983), 5–16.
18 José Ignacio Tellechea Idígoras, "Cartas inéditas de Arturo Campión a Serapio Múgica (1899-1921)," *Anuario del Seminario de Filología Vasca Julio de Urquijo* 18, no. 1 (1984), 3–38.
19 Koldo Mitxelena, "Campionen 'Gramatica' eta beste," *Euskera* 30 (1985), 63–70.
20 Elías Amézaga, "Ficha bio-bibliográfica de Arturo Campión," *Letras de Deusto* 19, no. 44 (1989), 29–38.
21 Jose Mari Satrustegi, "Arturo Campionen itzala," *Euskera* 39, no. 2 (1994), 407–16.
22 Enrique Miralles, "'Don García Almorabid', de Arturo Campión, y la novela histórica de fin de siglo," in *Del romanticismo al realismo: Actas del I Coloquio de la Sociedad de Literatura Española del siglo XIX*, ed. Luis Felipe Díaz Larios and Enrique Miralles (Barcelona: Universitat de Barcelona, 1998), 317–30.
23 Santiago Cunchillos y Manterola, "Prólogo," in Arturo Campión, *Blancos y negros. Guerra en la paz* (San Sebastián: Ttarttalo, 1998), 11–18.

Zardoya;[24] Carlos Mata Induráin;[25] Gregorio Monreal Zia;[26] Juan Cruz Alli Aranguren;[27] Joxemiel Bidador;[28] Iñaki Iriarte López;[29] and Emilio Majuelo.[30] Arturo Campión was, moreover, the focus of a doctoral dissertation by José Javier López Antón, who analyzed his work and carried out a thorough analysis of Campión's personal archive, housed in the Royal and General Archive of Navarre. López Antón addresses the Navarrese polymath in other works as well.[31]

Outside the academic world, in 2011, one of Campión's most celebrated short stories, *El bardo de Itzaltzu*, inspired the illustrator Asisko Urmeneta to make the animated movie *Garxot*, which narrates an epic twelfth-century tale set in the Navarrese Pyrenees. Shot in Basque and directed by Urmeneta and Juanjo Elordi, it involved multiple collaborators and music by Benito Lertxundi. The justification for the movie and attention it drew to Campión and his work was captured in the book *Gartxot. Konkista aitzineko konkista* (Gartxot: The Conquest before the Conquest) by Edorta Barrutabeña and Asisko Urmeneta.[32]

24 José Luis Nieva Zardoya, *La idea euskara de Navarra, 1864–1902* (Bilbao: Fundación Sabino Arana; Euskara Kultur Elkargoa, 1999).
25 Carlos Mata Induráin, "'Chocarán el puchero y la olla': conflictos sociales e ideológicos en 'Blancos y Negros', de Arturo Campión," in *Grupos sociales en la historia de Navarra. Relaciones y derechos. Actas del V Congreso de Historia de Navarra*, vol. 2, ed. Carmen Erro and Iñigo Mugueta (Pamplona: Eunate; Sociedad de Estudios Históricos de Navarra, 2002), 165–78.
26 Gregorio Monreal Zia, "Una historia de la Revista Internacional de los Estudios Vascos (1907–2000)," *Revista Internacional de los Estudios Vascos* 46, no. 1 (2001), 11–46.
27 Juan Cruz Alli Aranguren, "Arturo Campión y Jayme-Bon, escritor y político (1854–1937)," *Notitia Vasconiae* 1 (2002), 469–548.
28 Joxemiel Bidador, "El euskara y la literatura en lengua vasca en la obra de Arturo Campión," *Fontes Linguae Vasconum* 38, no. 102 (2006), 299–320.
29 Iñaki Iriarte López, "La importancia de llamarse Unax: Arana, Campión y los signos externos del vasco," *Historia y Política* 15 (2006), 45–64.
30 Emilio Majuelo Gil, "Arturo Campión (1854–1937): historialaria kontzientzia kolektiboaren sortzaile," *Gerónimo de Uztariz* 26–27 (2010–2011), 46–61; and *La idea de historia en Arturo Campión* (Donostia: Eusko Ikaskuntza, 2011).
31 José Javier López Antón, *Arturo Campión entre la historia y la cultura* (Pamplona: Gobierno de Navarra, 1998). See also by the same author: "De la identidad vasco-americana a la tesis vasco-caucásica: El enfoque de Arturo Campión sobre el origen mítico de la lengua vasca," *Fontes Linguae Vasconum* 27, no. 70 (1995), 467–86 and "La actitud lingüística en Campión. Catolicismo, tradición y foralidad," in *El euskera en tiempo de los* éuskaros, ed. Roldán Jimeno Aranguren (Pamplona: Gobierno de Navarra; Ateneo Navarro, 2000), 63–104.
32 Barrutabeña and Urmeneta, *Gartxot. Konkista aitzineko konkista*.

Campión's memory has been honored by naming streets after him in Antsoain (Navarre), Donostia-San Sebastián and Irun (Gipuzkoa), and Bilbao and Sestao (Bizkaia). In 2017 the Navarrese government awarded him the Gold Medal of Navarre posthumously, a distinction he shared with his fellow *Euskaros*, Hermilio de Olóriz and Julio Altadill. In the agreement to concede the award, the Navarrese government highlighted the fact that the distinction granted to the three personalities was due to:

> their contribution to the history, culture, and identity of Navarre, to their defense of the historic rights of the ancient Kingdom of Navarre, and, above all and especially, for their decisive work when it came to defining for Navarre a permanent symbol of its identity that it lacked until that time: the flag of Navarre as it is known today, whose design was approved by the foral provincial government in 1910.[33]

A Short Biographical Sketch

Born in Pamplona-Iruñea on May 7, 1854, he was the son of Jacinto Campión—a highly cultured Pamplona-Iruñea liberal who became president of the Orfeón Pamplonés musical band—and Amalia Jaimebón e Inarra.

Educated at the Instituto de Pamplona, while an adolescent he wrote his first literary texts and press articles. In his early youth, influenced by his father, he participated in the Navarrese federal republican movement. He wrote for the progressive newspapers *La Menestra* and *La Montaña*, and was a member of the liberal republican militia at the Battle of Orokieta (Oroquieta) against the Carlists in 1872. With the fall of the First Republic in January 1874, he abandoned republicanism.

Although he began to study law in Oñati (Gipuzkoa), he completed his undergraduate degree at the University of Madrid

---

33 Foral Decree 97/2017, October 31, by which the Gold Medal of Navarre is conceded posthumously to Mr. Arturo Campión, Mr. Hermilio de Olóriz, and Mr. Julio Altadill for their contribution to history, culture, and identity in designing the flag of Navarre.

in 1876, the year in which the Carlist War ended and the Basque fueros were abolished. Some newspapers of the era, such as *El Imparcial*, equated Carlism with the fueros, and believed that foral ideas were behind Carlism, thereby justifying the abolition of the fueros. The fervent young Navarrese writer endeavored to argue against these theories. In his position defending the fueros, Campión, alongside other Basque writers—including his good friend Juan Iturralde y Suit—founded in Madrid the newspaper *La Paz*. Campión was an assiduous collaborator in the publication until its closure on August 22, 1878. Those collaborations were a prelude to what would later be his intellectual preoccupations, as exemplified in his articles "The fueros and the liberal idea" (May 19, 1876) and "On the preservation of the Basque language" (October 25, 1876).

In his Madrid years he also wrote his first book, *Consideraciones acerca de la cuestión foral y los carlistas en Nabarra* (Considerations on the foral question and the Carlists in Navarre), dated February 7, 1876,[34] a few days before the Carlist War came to an end. From a liberal position, he argued that Navarrese liberals had defended self-government, so that Navarre could not be a victim of the attitudes and wars of the Carlists against the liberal system. He tried to demonstrate that the fueros were in line with and compatible with liberal principles and counter to Carlist postulates.

On his return to Pamplona-Iruñea, we know little of his career as a practicing lawyer. His significant inheritance could have allowed him to not dedicate himself fully to the legal profession, investing his efforts instead in managing his assets and in developing his vast intellectual work.

Campión himself intervened decisively in founding the Asociación Euskara (Basque Association) when he suggested the creation of just such an association in his article "The Basque language" in the aforementioned Madrid newspaper *La Paz*,[35] a proposal that was carried out by Iturralde y Suit.

---

34 Arturo Campión, *Consideraciones acerca de la cuestión foral y los carlistas en Navarra* (Madrid: Imprenta de Gregorio Juste, 1876).
35 Arturo Campión, "El euskara," *La Paz* (Madrid), April 9, 13, and 24, 1877.

The Asociación Euskara was founded on November 13, 1877, and it was strongly influenced by the growing foralism following the abolition of the Basque fueros. It was an open talent initiative in which there was a place for any Navarrese, whether a resident or displaced, who sympathized with its objectives. One of its first acts was to send out invitations to significant personalities in Araba, Gipuzkoa, and Bizkaia, urging them to support the Navarrese project with the creation of similar collectives. The Asociación Euskara thus became the emerging epicenter of the important nineteenth-century Basque cultural renaissance. Its publication, the *Revista Euskara*, counted on contributions by Campión, marked by the ideas of foral reintegration and the defense of the Basque language.

One of the most admirable episodes of Campión's intellectual career took place during those years when, on being rebuked for not speaking Basque, he set out to learn it, declaring himself a fervent supporter of Louis Lucien Bonaparte. His superb intelligence allowed him to learn the language in a surprisingly short period of time, to the extent that, in December 1877, at the age of twenty-six, he wrote the Basque-language ballad *Orreaga*. He published it in the Gipuzkoan, Bizkaian, Lapurdian, and Zuberoan dialects, and in eighteen linguistic varieties from Navarre, with the aim of carrying out a comparative linguistic exercise. Published initially in 1878, the ballad was reprinted two years later in the first volume of the *Revista Euskara*, preceded by an introduction and followed by grammatical and lexical observations.[36]

During his youth he made friends with the great Basque intellectuals, like the scientist Antoine d'Abbadie, the man of letters Miguel de Unamuno, the historian Jean de Jaurgain, and the foreign Basque experts of that time, at the forefront of whom was the linguist Louis Lucien Bonaparte. In Navarre he was surrounded by his colleagues at the Asociación Euskara, such as Juan Iturralde y Suit, Nicasio Landa, Esteban Obanos, Florencio

36 Arturo Campión, *Orreaga/Roncesvalles. Balada en dialecto guipuzcoano acompañado de versiones a los dialectos bizkaíno, labortano y suletino, y de diez y ocho variedades dialectales de la región bascongada de Navarra desde Olazagutia hasta Roncal* (Pamplona: J. Lorda, 1880).

Ansoleaga, Estanislao de Aranzadi, Hermilio de Olóriz, Salvador Echaide, Aniceto Lagarde, Antero Irazoqui, Fermín Iñarra, Serafín Olave, among others.

Arturo Campión continued to write historical and linguistic studies, literature, and political discourses for the rest of his life. He disseminated his political thought, his literary creation, and his historical erudition through books and specialized journals, although he was also a habitual contributor to the press of the time as a collaborating polemicist in newspapers and journals such as *Lau Buru, La ilustración Navarra, El Arga, El Aralar, Irurac bat, El Eco de Navarra, La Avalancha, Hermes, El Noticiero bilbaíno, El vasco, Euskal Erría*, among others. His writings uncovered for Basques of the late nineteenth and early twentieth century a hidden history—that of a homeland stripped of its identity—as well as the value and symbolism of a language that was disappearing and a political doctrine that passed from traditionalism toward Basque nationalism. He taught how to love the Basque Country through Navarre, making the slogan *"Euskalerriaren alde"* ("in favor of the Basque Country") his own.

His research led him to preside over different bodies such as Euskal Esnalea, Euskal Erria, the Institute of Historical Studies, and the Commission for Historic and Artistic Monuments in Navarre. His work was also recognized outside the Basque Country, and he was honored by being appointed a corresponding member of the Academies of History, Moral and Political Sciences, and the Castilian Language.

Campión had, moreover, a prominent political dimension. It was marked by a constant search for a political creed that was more adapted to his ideals: the staunch defense of God and the fueros. He had the virtue of being an independent politician, so that he never came to be affiliated with any political party. His political position was marked by his experience of losing the Basque fueros in 1876. Campión considered himself above all a Catholic foralist, the two principal pillars on which he forged his identity and grounded his doctrine.

As already noted, he abandoned the republicanism of his early youth; but he always defended federalism, a formula he considered compatible with the historically respected foral rule of law. Influenced by Iturralde y Suit, he favored foralist federalism as a consistent option in the recovery and respect for the fueros through decentralization. As he advocated in a speech given at the Traditionalist Circle of Pamplona-Iruñea on May 29, 1892, and which is reproduced in this book in full: "Let us suppose that Spanish liberalism, perched on the central government, instead of espousing unitary solutions, would have espoused federal solutions: foral forms and bodies would have fitted perfectly within the national constitution."[37]

Campión's defense of foralism was located within a modern federalism, which sought to obtain for Navarre and the Basque Country as a whole as much decision-making power as possible. In this sense, Emilio Majuelo considers Campión not a pragmatic regionalist but instead an early Basque nationalist, prior even to Sabino Arana, with whom he later held major differences. Despite the fact that Campión never favored the independence of the Basque Country, his thought reflected an early nationalism. Foralism was based on pragmatism, grounded on a historicism that understood prior agreements between the Basque territories and the monarchy.[38]

On the basis of those ideological postulates, during the period of the Restoration, Campión was a foralist linked to Ramón Nocedal's ultraconservatism. He was a councilmember in the Pamplona-Iruñea City Hall in 1881. With the split between ultraconservatives and Carlists in the period 1888–1889, he opted to stay within the ultraconservative fold, based on the conviction that a Basque regional party could be created. From this political position he criticized Carlism, which he considered Spanish on account of its aim to exchange one Spanish king for another and for defending the cause of the fueros without any

---

37 Campión, "Discurso en el Círculo Regional Tradicionalista de Pamplona, el 29 de mayo de 1892." in *Discursos políticos*, 62.
38 Majuelo, *La idea de historia*.

pro-sovereignty conviction. Thus, in another of the political and literary speeches published in this volume, the "Lecture on the Origins and Development of Navarrese Regionalism," he would not hesitate to argue that "they punished us harshly because in a moment of generous hallucination we forgot that we were Basques and Navarrese, in order to remember only that we were Spanish."[39] However, his perception of ultraconservatism changed as the ultraconservatives increasingly moved away from a regionalist perspective, in order to accentuate their centralism. For the time being, he continued to be an ultraconservative, based on the conviction that "in the long run, ultraconservatism would favor the formation of a distinctly Basque party."[40]

His most brilliant political activities were marked by his election to the Spanish parliament on April 11, 1891, as an ultraconservative candidate within the Navarrese Catholic Coalition under the slogan "God and the Old Laws." One moment that stood out was his bold and energetic intervention before the tax minister, Germán Gamazo, on the occasion of a parliamentary debate on the budget proposals. Article 17 of these proposals sought to bring the quota of Navarre's fiscal contribution to the state up to the same level as the other provinces, by which Navarrese foral singularity, achieved with the Consensual Law of 1841 and upheld in the Tejada-Valdosera Agreement of 1877, would disappear.[41] In a celebrated speech given in the Spanish parliament, he defended the fact that:

We Navarrese representatives are here fulfilling the traditional mission of our race, which both in ancient and modern, and even in contemporary, history is expressed by the verb "resist." We are here writing a new chapter of that history without parallel that shows Basques defending their territory, their house, their home, their customs, their

---

39 Campión, "Conferencia acerca del desarrollo del regionalismo nabarro, dada en la Lliga de Catalunya la noche del 3 de junio de 1891," in *Discursos políticos*, 34.
40 Múgica, *Los titanes de la cultura vasca*, 174.
41 Campión, "Discurso en el Congreso de los Diputados el día 22 de julio de 1893," in *Discursos políticos*.

language, their beliefs, against the brutal ambition of Celts, Romans, Goths, Franks, Arabs, and achieving the miracle of preserving unscathed, throughout many centuries, their minute nationality, despite [all of them].

His parliamentary experience also led him to confront Ramón Nocedal himself. Both were engaged in a long controversy that lasted several years on the interpretation of the pontifical doctrine of political action, with articles appearing in different journals of the time, and which Campión summarized in his book *La batalla chica del Sr. Nocedal* (Mr. Nocedal's little battle).[42] Another reflection of this was the speech given in Congress on January 14, 1895 that is reproduced in this book.[43]

Increasingly alienated from official ultraconservatism, in 1901 Campión gave a talk at the Basque Center in Bilbao titled "The Basque Personality in History, Law, and Literature"—a text also included in *Discursos políticos y literarios*[44]—and, on that basis, he came into very close contact with Basque nationalist ideas. After Sabino Arana died in 1903, he came to preside over a meeting of the Euskaltzaleen Biltzarra (Association of Bascophiles) in Irun, Gipuzkoa, in 1904, although it was not until 1905 that one could fully consider Campión as ideologically linked to Basque nationalism. The turning point was marked by his important lecture, "Nationalism, Foralism, and Separatism," given at the Basque Center in Donostia-San Sebastián.[45]

Campión saw in Basque nationalism a possible consolidation of his political ideals, but the pro-independence posture sustained by Luis Arana distanced him from that breakaway position. The two currents within the Basque Nationalist Party (Partido Nacionalista Vasco, PNV)—pro-independence and pro-autonomy—managed

---

42 Arturo Campión, *La batalla chica del Sr. Nocedal* (Pamplona: Imprenta y Librería de José Erice, 1893).
43 Campión, "Discurso en el Congreso de los Diputados el día 14 de enero de 1895," in *Discursos políticos*.
44 Campión, "La personalidad éuskara en la Historia, el Derecho y la Literatura. Conferencia leída en el 'Centro Basko' de Bilbao el día 27 de abril de 1901," in *Discursos políticos*.
45 Campión, "Nacionalismo, fuerismo y separatismo. Conferencia dada en el Centro Vasco de San Sebastián la noche del 7 de enero de 1906," in *Discursos políticos*.

to come together thanks to the idea of full foral reinstatement, reflected in a 1906 program-manifesto. No Basque nationalist could oppose foral reinstatement, although some may have understood it, as Sabino Arana did, as a move toward independence; while others, like Campión, viewed it as integration within Spain while preserving autonomy.[46]

Not being a member of the party, Campión remained outside the internal debates of the PNV, but he made clear his differences with pro-independence positions, advocating "unionist nationalism," that is, a Basque nationalism within a federal Spain, as he called for in another talk in *Discursos políticos y literarios*:

With what aim should nationalism direct its propaganda? To ensuring that that juridical separation descends from the abstract sphere of principles to the concrete world of deeds, taking shape in reality, and leading to a secessionist movement such as in Spanish America or that of Cuba? Or on the contrary, should efforts be aimed at reestablishing the broken unity, to covering the cracks through which anti-Spanish separatism may seep, and to renovating what were in their day the old and venerable pacts with the Spanish Monarchy? I do not know whether secessionist nationalism exists; but I declare with the greatest possible solemnity that mine is unionist.[47]

This seed sprouted in the subsequent political party, Basque Nationalist Communion (Comunión Nacionalista Vasca, CNV, 1916–1930), led by Engracio de Aranzadi Echeverría or "Kizkitza," the principal inspiration behind a conservative, pragmatic, and Catholic nationalism that was against any pro-independence proposals.

---

46 Ludger Mees, "La Restauración y la Dictadura de Primo de Rivera," in *Los nacionalistas. Historia del nacionalismo vasco, 1876–1960*, ed. Carmen Gómez, Javier Fernández, and Santiago de Pablo (Vitoria-Gasteiz: Fundación Sancho el Sabio, 1995), 82.

47 Campión, "Nacionalismo, fuerismo y separatismo," in *Discursos políticos*, 275–76.

Campión, then, without being active in any political party, disseminated his ideology through speeches and talks—such as those published here—as well as newspaper articles, short writings, and, of course, in a somewhat indirect way, in his literary and historiographical work.

Having become an undeniably key figure for Basque nationalism, he contributed his knowledge of and close relationship with the Catalan world to the new pro-autonomy movement in the period 1915–1920; uniting the four southern Basque territories in one single cultural and university body was one of hsis objectives. Following the model of the Institute of Catalan Studies, which incorporated Catalan scientific and cultural figures, the Basque provincial councils encouraged the creation of Eusko Ikaskuntza, the Society of Basque Studies, at the Congress of Oñati in 1918. Campión was appointed honorary president of this institution.[48] And he collaborated actively in numerous initiatives such as the publication of his work on the historical evolution of Basque local government.[49]

One outcome of the Congress of Oñati in 1918 was the creation of Euskaltzaindia, the Academy of the Basque Language, in which from the outset Campión was appointed a full member[50] as part of the appointment of four other members: Resurrección María de Azkue, Luis Eleizalde, and Julio de Urquijo. A year later, Campión, alongside Pierre Broussain, was commissioned to draw up the *Informe a la Academia de la Lengua Vasca sobre la unificación del euskera* (Report to the Academy of the Basque Language on the standardization of Basque), the most important task for Euskaltzaindia since it would create the foundation for establishing a standard form of Basque.[51]

48 Estornés, *La construcción de una nacionalidad vasca.*
49 Arturo Campión, *El municipio vasco en la Historia. Asamblea de Administración Municipal Vasca* (San Sebastián: Sociedad de Estudios Vascos, 1920), 3–36.
50 Satrustegi, "Arturo Campionen itzala," 407–16.
51 Arturo Campión and Pierre Broussain, *Informe de los señores académicos A. Campión y P. Broussain a la Academia de la Lengua Vasca sobre unificación del euskera* (Bilbao: Imprenta de Ave María, 1920).

During those years he combined his work in research and administration in cultural institutions with politics, when he was elected a senator for Bizkaia during the 1918–1919 legislature. Those elections, in which Basque nationalism triumphed, led Campión to proclaim that,

> We won because nationalist ideas are founded on the reason of truth . . . The Basque people, an ethnic extension of a particular race, arrived late but arrived at the finish line, at the feeling of its national unity, broken and scattered for several centuries among different nationalities . . . The Spanish Basque is not French, is not Spanish, but is Basque. Thus the Basque is not Spanish or French, but Basque. Here you have, dear compatriots, the intimate essence of nationalism. The Basque was made Spanish and French by the political constitutions that men write; but he was made Basque by the constitution written by God in the book of nature . . . Looking at the pure ideology of eternal law and justice, it is undeniable that Basques and Spaniards are separate.[52]

After leaving the Senate, he threw himself into research and publishing, and divided his time between Donostia-San Sebastián and Pamplona-Iruñea. Although he was never a political party man, he participated in acts of great symbolism such as the speech given on the occasion of the inauguration of the batzoki, the PNV center, in Errenteria in 1920.[53] Having become a symbol for Basque nationalism during the Second Republic, he was involved in controversy during the final year of his life, coinciding with the time of the civil war.[54] On September 13, 1936 Donostia-San Sebastián fell to the rebel side. Campión resided there at that moment. The following day he dictated to his nephew and heir, Arturo Ferrer, a short text in which he wrote: "I have the pleasure

---

52 Quoted with a commentary on by Barrutabeña and Urmeneta, *Gartxot*, 52.
53 Arturo Campión, *Discurso que pronunció con motivo de la inauguración del nuevo Batzoki en Rentería, 25 septiembre 1920* (San Sebastián: Tipografía Baroja, 1920).
54 Roldán Jimeno Aranguren, *Miguel Javier Urmeneta (1915–1988). Segunda República, Franquismo y Transición* (Pamplona: Pamiela, 2015), 80–82.

to state that this city of red tyranny has been liberated, I want to express at the same time my most energetic protest at the unspeakable behavior of Basque nationalism, my unwavering adherence to the National Council of Burgos."

Ferrer handed in the text to the military authorities in Pamplona-Iruñea on September 15, the same day it was published in the *Diario de Navarra* newspaper. Today we know the tragic circumstances in which Campión was obliged to sign that declaration, with the city occupied, shut away on account of ill health in his house, called Emilia Enea, bewildered and frightened by the events, and with his two nephews and heirs at risk of losing their lives. The national side used that note to launch a media campaign against republicanism and Basque nationalism.

Campión died in Donostia-San Sebastián on August 18, 1937. From Catalonia, the conservative Catalanist politician Francesc Cambó, who also supported the rebel side, paid tribute to him by reflecting on the intellectual, political, and human dimension of the deceased:[55]

> Artur Campión, the Navarrese-Basque who so appreciated his land and worked so hard for it, has died!
>
> I imagine the horrible tragedy that this man must have experienced during the last months of his life: for him Navarre—his Navarre—incorporated the Basque people and was the purest of this, its most solid base. He hated Carlists and Liberals because, for a cause alien to the Basque people, they had divided the race, provoking two criminal fights between brothers. Poor Campión: he had the immense misfortune to see the third; the worst one; the most stupid one.

---

55 Francesc Cambó, "Homenatge a Artur Campión, 25 de agosto de 1937," in *Meditacións. Dietari (1936–1940)* (Barcelona: Editorial Alpha, 1982), 173. Original in Catalan. Reprinted in López Antón, *Arturo Campión entre la historia y la cultura*, 211–12.

He was a Basque nationalist, more nationalist and of a
better quality than all the others who say they are . . .

He dedicated a long life—he died at the age of
eighty-four!—to his homeland. He was, in my opinion, the
first person of value of his race in modern times. Researcher,
philologist, historian, working alone, without help, he
carried out the task that in Catalonia it took the whole
life of dozens of patriotic intellectuals.

**The Political and Literary Speeches Compiled in the Current
Publication**

By the end of the nineteenth century, Arturo Campión had
accumulated an abundant written oeuvre in the form of books, short
stories, newspaper articles, specialized journal articles, speeches,
lectures, and so on. At one point he decided to gather together
his Basque-themed writings that had appeared in newspapers and
journals. That is how the *Euskariana* series started, with the first
volume appearing in 1896: numbers 1, 2, and 6 included short
stories;[56] numbers 4, 5, 7, 9, and 11 were collections of his historical
works;[57] and numbers 8, 10, and 12 concern the extensive work,
Los orígenes del pueblo euskaldun. Iberos, keltas y baskos (The origins
of the Basque-speaking people: Iberians, Celts, and Basques).[58]

56 Arturo Campión, *Euskariana. Parte primera. Historia a través de la leyenda* (Bilbao:
Imprenta de la Biblioteca Bascongada de Fermín Herrán, 1896); *Euskariana.
Parte segunda. Fantasía y realidad* (Bilbao: Imprenta de la Biblioteca Bascongada
de Fermín Herrán, 1897); and *Euskariana. Sexta serie. Fantasía y realidad. Volumen
segundo* (Pamplona: Imprenta y Librería de J. García, 1918).
57 Arturo Campión, *Euskariana. Cuarta serie. Algo de Historia. Volumen segundo*
(Pamplona: Imprenta de Erice y García, 1904); *Euskariana. Quinta serie. Algo
de historia. Volumen tercero* (Pamplona: Imprenta y Librería de J. García, 1915);
Euskariana. Séptima serie. Algo de Historia. Volumen cuarto (Pamplona: Imprenta y
Librería de J. García, 1923); *Euskariana. Novena serie. Nabarra en su vida histórica*
(Pamplona: Imprenta y Librería de J. García, 1929); and *Euskariana. Undécima serie.
Algo de Historia. Volumen quinto. Gacetilla de Historia de Nabarra. Mosaico Histórico*
(Pamplona: Imprenta y Librería de Jesús García, 1934).
58 Arturo Campión, *Euskariana. Octava serie. Orígenes del pueblo euskaldún. Iberos,
keltas y baskos. Primera parte* (Pamplona: Imprenta y Librería de J. García, 1928);
*Euskariana. Décima serie. Orígenes del pueblo euskaldún. Testimonios de la Geografía
y de la Historia clásicas. Tercera Parte. Testionios de la Lingüística. Primer volumen*
(Pamplona: Imprenta y Librería de Jesús García, 1931); and *Euskariana. Duodécima
serie. Orígenes del pueblo euskaldún. Iberos, keltas y baskos. Tercera parte. Testimonos de*

Campión could have compiled his speeches and lectures given between 1891 and 1906 in another *Euskariana* volume. We do not know why he did not do so. Perhaps he thought that the nature of the literary and political speeches and lectures would break the essence of that series. Whatever it was, in 1907 he compiled these short texts that he had given in different forums during the previous fifteen years under the title *Discursos políticos y literarios.*[59] The year of publication is especially interesting in Campión's political evolution because, as noted, this was when he became affiliated morally and ideologically with Basque nationalism.

In its final part, the work includes a section titled "Notas y comentarios" (Notes and Commentaries) by Campión himself, in which he contextualizes each text, makes different observations about their content, and even responds to some critical reactions to those speeches and lectures. These observations conclude with their author pointing out that, "the subject of these speeches was often common to several of them in certain passages, hence the inevitable repetitions that extend to the same material form of thoughts when I thought I had guessed right in expressing them." To be sure, some ideas and scholarly data are repeated in some of the texts, but, as a whole, they are perfectly complementary and offer a magnificent synthesis of Campión's doctrine.

The fourteen speeches and lectures reproduced in the present work are the following (numbered according to the chapters in the original work):

1.   "Speech of Thanks Read at the Floral Games held in Barcelona on May 17, 1891." In the original this appears in both a Catalan version, read out at those games by the Catalanist lawyer Narcís Verdaguer i Callís, and a Spanish version. The English-language version in the present publication has been translated from the latter. The speech expresses Campión's enthusiasm for Catalonia, and offers very succinct data about the history and culture of that country.

Lingüística. Segundo volumen (Pamplona: Imprenta y Librería de Jesús García, 1936).
59   Campión, *Discursos políticos.*

2.   "Lecture on the Development of Navarrese Regionalism, Given at the Catalan League on the Evening of June 3, 1891." Here, Campión covers the main elements of what was at the time termed "Navarrese regionalism," a concept through which he describes the historical, political, and cultural singularities of Navarrese difference. In the face of criticism from Bizkaian Basque nationalism for using the term "regionalism," Campión recalls that when he used in that lecture and other works of that era, "the term nationalism had not acclimatized in Spain. Mr. Arana Goiri imported it into the Basque Country, thereby providing a good service to the cause of protest, refining the terminology and clarifying the situation, which was somewhat unsettled due to the errors that the term *foralism* had been adapted."

3.   "Speech at the Traditionalist Regional Circle of Pamplona on May 29, 1892." A speech focusing on the Catholic meaning of foralist demands. As well as reiterating the concept of "regionalism" from the previous lecture, he calls for the lost Navarrese liberties and the reestablishment of Navarrese legislative power.

4.   "Speech in the Congress of Deputies on May 24, 1893." This is an especially symbolic speech since, as Campión himself states in the end notes, he was the first representative in Congress after 1876 to protest against the anti-foralst attacks on the part of the central government, as well as being the first representative to defend "regionalism" free of any party political ideals.

5.   "Speech in the Congress of Deputies on July 22, 1893." This is a celebrated defense of Navarrese law in the face of the homogenizing ambitions of the aforementioned minister, Germán Gamazo.

6.   "Speech in the Congress of Deputies on January 14, 1895." This text is framed within the already mentioned long polemic Campión maintained with Nocedal on the interpretation of pontifical doctrine about political activity. Specifically, Campión's intervention in Congress centers on the welcome among Spaniards for the politico-religious ideas of Pope Leo XIII. It is a speech that, as the author himself points out in his notes to the book, "is a tribute of submission and respect for the authority of the bishops and the pope. Absolute submission and respect, without distinction, evasion, or fudging." It is a speech that, as he also states in the notes in 1907, "indicates the most painful phase of my political life, whose resumption has been made impossible."

7.   "The Basque Personality in History, Law, and Literature: Lecture Given at the Basque Center of Bilbao on April 27, 1901." This is an enthusiastic adhesion to the cause of the Basque race and homeland through the historical, legal, linguistic, anthropological, and literary features that Campión considered most significant.

8.   "Speech at the Basque Festival of Azpeitia on September 30, 1901." This is a reflection on the loss of Basque and the importance of its recovery.

9.   "Speech at the Basque Festival of Oñati on September 29, 1902." This is a call to restore the Basque foral system.

10.   "Speech at the Basque Festival of Irun on September 27, 1903." He goes over the causes that led to the disappearance of Basque and that continue to be, at that time, the main threats to this language.

11.   "Address in Basque to the Bascophile Association in Irun on September 29, 1904." A short text written in Basque demanding support for the Basque language and culture.

12.   "Lecture in the Basque Center of Donostia-San Sebastián on May 29, 1904."These are reflections on the Basque homeland and state.

13.   "Nationalism, Foralism, and Separatism."This is a lecture given at the Basque Center of Donostia-San Sebastián in the evening of January 7, 1906. It is, as has been noted, a profound reflection on those three concepts and one with which he adheres publicly to Basque nationalism.

14.   "The Tree of Gernika: Speech at the Solemn Evening Event held in Donostia-San Sebastián on July 11, 1906, on the Occasion of the Basque Festival and Organized by the Council of the Floral Games."These are personal evocations and disquisitions on the symbolic transcendence of the tree of Gernika and the importance of Bizkaian foral institutions.

Arturo Campión's Contribution to Historical Studies

Arturo Campión was, first of all, a historian who demonstrated a deep knowledge of the history of Navarre, both for the extraordinary use he made of the historiography existing up to that time, and for the first-hand research carried out in the Archive of Navarre, during those years directed by his good friend Hermilio de Olóriz. His zeal in recording data was reflected in an equally rigorous methodology. There are dozens of texts in which Campión analyzed different aspects of the history of his homeland. Two works stand out especially: the first, "El Genio de Navarra," was published between 1884 and 1888, and remained unfinished.[60] It is, perhaps, the work in which he summarizes the key points of his intellectual

60   Arturo Campión, "El Genio de Navarra," in *Euskariana. Cuarta serie. Algo de Historia. Volumen segundo* (Pamplona: Imprenta de Erice y García, 1904), 1–245.

ambitions. The second, "Nabarra en su vida histórica" ("Navarre in its Historical Life," 1914), was conceived within the book *Geografía del País Vasco-Navarro* (Geography of Navarrese-Basque Country), although it later appeared as a book in its own right in 1929.[61] This work brought together all the knowledge he accumulated throughout his life. Here, Campión attempted to give a voice to a historical subject, Navarre. He traces a line across the historical life of this ancient kingdom, beginning with the Vascones as predecessors and ancestors of the current Navarrese, up to the conquest of the kingdom by Ferdinand the Catholic in the years 1512–1522. Here he attempts to give a conclusive response to the canonical interpretation established by Spanish authors in the most controversial chapters of history such as those relating to the Visigoths and the Castilian conquest of Navarre.

His vision of the history of the Basque people is also reflected in his *Discursos políticos y literarios*, in which he states what some constants in his work are: "the fractions of the Basque people, historically organized in states, were truly nations... The four Basque nations retained their own internal sovereignty... the four Basque states remained, after their incorporation into Castile, independent nations like before."[62]

As Emilio Majuelo observes,[63] Campión was an active part of the Basque and Spanish intellectual environment of his time, although it was the influence he received from European authors that is most noteworthy for understanding his work. He professed great admiration for late nineteenth-century French and German historiography, which he accessed through his perfect knowledge of the French language and, to a lesser extent, of German. He made use of new French historical works by authors like Jules Michelet, Edgar Quinet, Odysse Barot, and, most especially, Hippolyte Adolphe Taine. The discovery of German historiography led him to try to learn the German language, which he did not master. Campión, moreover, was strongly influenced by authors

61 Campión, *Euskariana. Novena serie. Nabarra en su vida histórica.*
62 Campión, "Nacionalismo, fuerismo y separatismo," in *Discursos políticos*, 250.
63 Majuelo, *La idea de historia.*

with whom he had a close relationship at different times in his life, most notably by his Navarrese *Euskaro* colleagues and other contemporary Basque writers, both from Hegoalde and Iparralde. It is worth noting the close relationship he had with the famous Galician writer and journalist based in Madrid, Emilia Pardo Bazán, with whom he maintained an intense epistolary relationship that showed mutual admiration.

In Campión's historiographical perception, the influence of German authors such as Johann G. Herder and Wilhelm von Humboldt, from whom he adopted the vindication of the study of states and peoples as historical subjects, was of particular importance. From the influence of German historiographical historicism and Hegelian idealism, Campión established a methodology to study history in which the Basque people became a historical subject. Campión thought of history from a present moment in order to then analyze the past by observing the course of his people by means of different historical stages. He took on the patriotic responsibility of facilitating the understanding of history through the discovery of the people's conscience and as an indispensable creator of national history. The search for this national history led Campión to incorporate into history elements such as climate and food, intermingling them with customs or housing to end up establishing the fact that these physical agents became historical agents and, therefore, they were indispensable for establishing the history of the Basque people.

His rigor was demonstrated in the importance he gave to documented evidence, since he considered that only through research could historical truth be restored. He applied a critical method to the documents, from which he extracted data that would be submitted to historical and philological analysis, in a conscientious work of document critique.

When he studied the history of the Basque homeland, Campión, did not focus solely on institutional history, but also covered, through a multidisciplinary perspective, the study of the language, society, and culture of the Basque people. For such an ambitious objective, the Navarrese writer opted to use the auxiliary sciences of history such as philology, linguistics, genealogy, anthropology, and archaeology.

Our author was cautious when dealing with the prehistoric eras, which were so unknown at that time. Fleeing from the fashions of the moment, he was very tempted to speak of race as a differentiating factor of the Basque people. As one would expect from an author of his time, he opted to characterize a potential "Basque race" in some of his works but it was something that ultimately he abandoned, abandoning physical assumptions and focusing on history as the differentiating factor, as explained in one of the texts in his *Discursos políticos y literarios* and included in the present work:

> If the Basque race, a *substratum* of the Basque people, and the Basque people, an amplification of the Basque race, organized states and formed nations, and they are perfectly within their rights to restore them, it is not because their skull, nose, jaws, and faces are like this or that, nor because their eyes, hair, and skin display this or that coloration, nor because their size reaches a certain height, but because Basques brought into play their natural qualities, and practiced the heroic art of making them worth something, and they loved independence, and they did not fear death.[64]

Arturo Campión's Contribution to Literature

Arturo Campión excelled in a special way as a writer, supplying publishers with numerous narrative works that were very successful at the time, and which made him a well-known writer in the Basque Country. He wrote three historical novels and about thirty short stories.

The first of his novels was *Don García Almorabid*, published in 1885.[65] It is a story of dramatic love set amid the tragic events of the

---

64 Campión, "Nacionalismo, fuerismo y separatismo," in *Discursos políticos*, 234.
65 Arturo Campión, *Don García Almorabid. Crónica del siglo XIII* (Tolosa: Casa Editorial de Eusebio López, 1889).

thirteenth-century Navarrería war that ravaged this neighborhood of Pamplona-Iruñea. Campión's erudition is captured, in addition to the exquisite historical setting of the work, in the explanation of the institutions of the Kingdom of Navarre and in the explanatory notes regarding the meaning of the words in Basque that it incorporates into the text.

His novel, *Blancos y negros: Guerra en la paz* (Whites and Blacks: War in Peace), published in 1899, caused more controversy in the Basque Country of that time.[66] Written in a highly realist way, it describes the existing political division between Carlists and Liberals in Urgain, a fictional town in the Burunda Valley. Unamuno synthesized its content by pointing out that "the author's tendencies and feelings, his ardent regionalism, his hatred of centralizing Jacobinism and Spanish Unitarianism, the son, as he says, of the War of Independence; his deeply rooted Catholic sentiments, hostile to the internecine struggle between Carlists, *mestizos*, and ultraconservatives, are tendencies and feelings that are discovered at every step in the work."[67]

His last novel, *La Bella Easo* (The beautiful Easo), published in 1909 in two volumes,[68] was Campión's favorite, since in his own words he sought to represent "what I want it to be and what I do not want it to be, what I love and what I hate: this work is my whole thought." The story contrast the austere selfless life of the inhabitants of a farm with that of the frivolous Jayápolis, a cheerful, charming, and elegant city, that becomes a reflection of Donostia-San Sebastián of that time, in which the socialist doctrine is disseminated and working-class struggles abound.

Campión's shorter texts, in the form of narrations, short stories, and legends, are in general based on historical topics or related to contemporary political questions. They are full of descriptions replete with tenderness and passion, reflecting a

66   Arturo Campión, *Blancos y negros. Guerra en la paz* (Pamplona: Imprenta de Erice y García, 1899).
67   María Mercedes Landa Sopeña, "La literatura vasca en la obra de Unamuno," *Bulletin hispanique* 95, no. 2 (1993), 603–21.
68   Arturo Campión, *La Bella Easo*, 2 vols. (Pamplona: Imprenta y Librería de J. García, 1909).

literature committed to the Basque language, the defense of the fueros, and the historical identity of Navarre. Written generally in Castilian and to a lesser extent in Basque, they are short, easy to read stories. The descriptions are highlighted by an obsessive concern for the reliability of the historical data provided and the realistic description of the landscape. The Basque characters are archetypes of the idiosyncrasies of the country and reflect the political and cultural problems of their time.

Some of his most famous stories are *Gastón de Belzunce (leyenda histórica)* (1879), *Agintza. La promesa* (1879), *El coronel Villalba (tradición nabarra)* (1879), *Los hermanos Gamio* (1880), *Una noche en Zugarramurdi. Fantasía clásico-romántica* (1881), *La visión de don Carlos, Príncipe de Viana* (1882), *Okendoren eriotza. La muerte de Oquendo* (1883), *Pedro Mari* (1895), *La cieguita del puente (Historia vulgar)* (1896), *Roedores del mar* (1916), *El bardo de Itzaltzu* (1917), and *El tamborilero de Erraondo* (1917). The latter touched on the theme of the Basque diaspora. It addresses the heartrending realization of the disappearance of the Basque language and its consequences in central Navarre through the eyes of a sheepherder who emigrated to Argentina. The consequence of the frustration experienced by this Basque taborer (player of a small drum or tabor) on returning from the Pampa and confronting the reality of a Spanish-speaking populace is an escape back to the Latin American refuge of this old man, who does not recognize his people devoid of their language.[69]

Arturo Campión's Contribution to Basque Linguistics

For Campión, Basque identity was based on its fueros, but also on the Basque language. "For us, in fact, Basque is something much more than an instrument of scientific research; it is the language of our parents and adoring it leads us to the natural feeling of love toward native things," he wrote in 1884.[70] Likewise, in his

69   Arturo Campión, "El último tamborilero de Erraondo," in *Euskariana. Sexta serie. Fantasía y realidad. Volumen segundo* (Pamplona: Imprenta y Librería de J. García, 1918), 145–57.
70   Arturo Campión, *Gramática de los cuatro dialectos literarios de la lengua euskara*

speech at the Basque Festival of Oñati in 1902—included in *Discursos políticos y literarios*—he points out that the only note of any worth in the Basque Country was "the exaltation of their race, the veneration of their language, the love of their fueros, with the eternal hope and irrevocable decision to recover them."[71]

His concern with the crisis of the Basque language was reflected in his activity in various bodies from the Euskara Association of Navarra to Eusko Ikaskuntza and Euskaltzaindia, in his scientific study of the language, in the publication of literary texts in Basque, and in some translations.

The most outstanding of his contributions to the Basque language were his studies of grammar. The aforementioned ballad *Orreaga* was followed by the book *Ensayo acerca de las leyes fonéticas de la lengua vasca* (Essay on the phonetical rules of the Basque language), in 1883.[72] This was preceded by several articles on Basque grammar that appeared from 1881 onward in the journal *Revista Euskara*. These were eventually compiled into a book, giving rise to his essential *Gramática de los cuatro dialectos literarios de la lengua euskera* (Grammar of the four literary dialects of the Basque language).[73] A work of 795 pages, plus an extra 74 including appendices, it is dedicated "to His Highness Louis Lucien Bonaparte," to which he adds the slogan "Euskal-Erriaren alde." The quality, rigor, and complexity of this voluminous work of almost 900 pages stand out; it is a work of great merit for having been completed by someone who learned the language as an adult. It was a seminal work, because until then it had not been possible to analyze the Basque language with such scientific precision, far surpassing the previous grammars of Larramendi and Lardizabal.

Campion understood that languages developed historically and that they could not be studied in isolated fashion. They were a fundamental part of a people's culture, so the evolution or decline

---

(Tolosa: Establecimiento tipográfico de Eusebio López, 1884), 13–14.
71 Campión "Discurso en las fiestas éuskaras de Oñate el día 29 de septiembre de 1902," in *Discursos políticos*.
72 Arturo Campión, *Ensayo acerca de las leyes fonéticas de la lengua euskara* (San Sebastián: Imprenta de Hijos de J. R. Baroja, 1883).
73 Campión, *Gramática de los cuatro dialectos literarios*.

of a language directly marked the evolution or decline of the people who spoke it. For this reason, the linguistic issue was not just a scientific objective, but it also became a political, educational, and identity issue. Arturo Campión received the Basque-Iberian influences of authors such as Fita, Hübner, Schuchard, and, above all, Wilhelm von Humboldt, for whom he professed great admiration.

By Way of a Summary

The political and literary speeches contained in this book are a very significant sample of the Arturo Campión's thought. The ideology of the Basque polymath evolved over time, although it always sought a pragmatic political formula that respected the historical rights of the Basque people. The alternatives he found along the way made him move from foralist liberalism to ultraconservatism, ending up at pragmatic Basque nationalism. The importance of this book, as already pointed out, is that its texts cover the period between 1891 and 1906. Although he participated in ultraconservatism from a foralist and federalist position, Campión was already developing his own unique doctrine that contributed so much to the doctrinal development of Basque nationalism. He ended up supporting this ideology in 1906 through his celebrated speech titled "Nationalism, Foralism, and Separatism," which is included, as one would expect, in his *Discursos políticos y literarios*. Here, he states that:

> I do not belong, gentlemen, to the number of those that adjust their political conduct to that maxim that is like a symptom of the spirits that are idealists, not because they pursue an ideal goal (which those of this kind love all the noble spirits), but because they do not take charge of reality, and therefore rather than idealists, they are visionaries.
>
> The maxim to which I allude is: those closest to us are those farthest away from us, and therefore they are those whom we must combat with the greatest might. This maxim is absurd. Save for the doctrinal integrity of nationalism,

so that there is no place therein for deleterious principles that may weaken or distract it from its single objective, nationalism must possess a mobile scale of sympathies in order to apply it to the political forces that contact it, according to the degree of political and social *euskarismo* they may contain.[74]

Let us go, then, via Arturo Campión, to better understand the history of the Basque Country through someone who witnessed the dramatic dismantling of the fueros and the rapid loss of the Basque language, the two pillars of the Basque political and cultural personality. Because, as my own father states as regards Campión, "his Navarrese soul having been wounded, he put his intelligence and knowledge to the service of this cause."[75]

Bibliography

Alli Aranguren, Juan Cruz. "Arturo Campión y Jayme-Bon, escritor y político (1854–1937)." *Notitia Vasconiae* 1 (2002): 469–548.

Altadill, Julio. "El espíritu de Campión. Su labor anímica." *Euskalerriaren Alde* 20 (1930): 247–57.

Amézaga, Elías. "Ficha bio-bibliográfica de Arturo Campión." *Letras de Deusto* 19, no. 44 (1989): 29–38.

Arocena, Fausto. "Los seis grandes." *Boletín de la Sociedad Vascongada de Amigos del País* 14 (1958): 455–57.

Barrutabeña, Edorta, and Asisko Urmeneta. *Gartxot. Konkista aitzineko konkista.* Donostia: Elkar, 2011.

Bidador, Joxemiel. "El euskara y la literatura en lengua vasca en la obra de Arturo Campión." *Fontes Linguae Vasconum* 38, no.102 (2006): 299–320.

---

74 Campión, "Nacionalismo, fuerismo y separatismo," in *Discursos políticos*, 256–57.
75 José María Jimeno Jurío. "Arturo Campión Jaimebón," in *Navarra en época moderna y contemporánea* (Pamplona: Pamiel; Udalbide; Euskara Kultur Elkargoa, 2007), 388.

Campión, Arturo. *Consideraciones acerca de la cuestión foral y los carlistas en Navarra*. Madrid: Imprenta de Gregorio Juste, 1876.

———. *Orreaga (Roncesvalles). Balada en dialecto guipuzcoano acompañado de versiones a los dialectos bizkaíno, labortano y suletino, y de diez y ocho variedades dialectales de la región bascongada de Navarra desde Olazagutia hasta Roncal*. Pamplona: J. Lorda, 1880.

———. *Ensayo acerca de las leyes fonéticas de la lengua euskara*. San Sebastián: Imprenta de Hijos de J. R. Baroja, 1883.

———. *Gramática de los cuatro dialectos literarios de la lengua euskara*. Tolosa: Establecimiento tipográfico de Eusebio López, 1884.

———. *Don García Almorabid. Crónica del siglo XIII*. Tolosa: Casa Editorial de Eusebio López, 1889.

———. *La batalla chica del Sr. Nocedal*. Pamplona: Imprenta y Librería de José Erice, 1893.

———. *Euskariana. Parte primera. Historia a través de la leyenda*. Bilbao: Imprenta de la Biblioteca Bascongada de Fermín Herrán, 1896.

———. *Euskariana. Parte segunda. Fantasía y realidad*. Bilbao: Imprenta de la Biblioteca Bascongada de Fermín Herrán, 1897.

———. *Blancos y negros. Guerra en la paz*. Pamplona: Imprenta de Erice y García, 1899.

———. *Euskariana. Cuarta serie. Algo de Historia. Volumen Segundo*. Pamplona: Imprenta de Erice y García, 1904.

———. *La Bella Easo*. 2 volumes. Pamplona: Imprenta y Librería de J. García, 1909.

———. *Discursos políticos y literarios*. Pamplona: Imprenta y Librería de Erice y García, 1907; reprint, Bilbao: La Gran Enciclopedia Vasca, 1976.

————. *Euskariana. Quinta serie. Algo de historia. Volumen tercero.* Pamplona: Imprenta y Librería de J. García, 1915.

————. *Euskariana. Sexta serie. Fantasía y realidad. Volumen segundo.* Pamplona: Imprenta y Librería de J. García, 1918.

————. *El municipio vasco en la Historia. Asamblea de Administración Municipal Vasca.* San Sebastián: Sociedad de Estudios Vascos, 1920.

————. *Euskariana. Séptima serie. Algo de Historia. Volumen cuarto.* Pamplona: Imprenta y Librería de J. García, 1923.

————. *Euskariana. Octava serie. Orígenes del pueblo euskaldún. Iberos, keltas y baskos. Primera parte.* Pamplona: Imprenta y Librería de J. García, 1928.

————. *Euskariana. Novena serie. Nabarra en su vida histórica.* Pamplona: Imprenta y Librería de J. García, 1929.

————. *Euskariana. Décima serie. Orígenes del pueblo euskaldún. Testimonios de la Geografía y de la Historia clásicas. Tercera Parte. Testionios de la Lingüística (primer volumen).* Pamplona: Imprenta y Librería de Jesús García, 1931.

————. *Euskariana. Undécima serie. Algo de Historia. Volumen quinto. Gacetilla de Historia de Nabarra. Mosaico Histórico.* Pamplona: Imprenta y Librería de Jesús García, 1934.

————. *Euskariana. Duodécima serie. Orígenes del pueblo euskaldún. Iberos, keltas y baskos. Tercera parte. Testimonos de Lingüística. Segundo volumen.* Pamplona: Imprenta y Librería de Jesús García, 1936.

————. "El P. José de Moret." *Príncipe de Viana* 1, no. 1 (1940): 34–37.

————. *El Genio de Nabarra.* Buenos Aires: Ekin, 1942.

————. *Obras completas.* 15 volumes. Pamplona: Mintzoa, 1983–1985.

Campión, Arturo, and Pierre Broussain. *Informe de los señores académicos A. Campión y P. Broussain a la Academia de la*

Lengua Vasca sobre unificación del euskera. Bilbao: Imprenta de Ave María, 1920.

Cierbide Martinena, Ricardo. "Posicionamiento de Arturo Campión ante el tema lingüístico y la pérdida de los Fueros en el País Vasco en 1876." *Fontes Linguae Vasconum* 15, nos. 41–42 (1983): 5–16.

Clavería, Carlos. "Un recuerdo a Don Arturo Campión." *Vida Vasca* 32 (1955): 167.

Corella, José María. *Historia de la Literatura Navarra.* Pamplona: Ediciones Pregón, 1973.

Cruchaga y Purroy, José de. "Arturo Campión. Prólogo." In Arturo Campión, *Obras completas.* Volume 1. Pamplona: Mintzoa, 1983.

Cunchillos y Manterola, Santiago. "Prólogo." In Arturo Campión, *Blancos y negros. Guerra en la paz.* San Sebastián: Ttarttalo, 1998.

Estornés Zubizarreta, Idoia. *La construcción de una nacionalidad vasca. El autonomismo de Eusko Ikaskuntza.* Donostia: Eusko Ikaskuntza, 1990.

Garriga, Gabino. "En el centenario del nacimiento de don Arturo Campión." *Boletín del Instituto Americano de Estudios Vascos* 5 (1954): 85–89.

Granja Pascual, José Javier. "Divergencias lingüísticas y literarias entre Arturo Campión y Sabino Arana." *Fontes Linguae Vasconum* 16, no. 43 (1984): 155–82.

———. "Arturo Campión y la Sociedad de Estudios Vascos." *Oihenart. Cuadernos de lengua y literatura* 5 (1985): 75–93.

———. "La Gramática de Arturo Campión y Luis Luciano Bonaparte." *Euskera* 30, no. 1 (1985): 31–49.

———. "Arturo Campión y la historia." *Príncipe de Viana.* Anejo 10 (1988): 169–82.

Huici Urmeneta, Vicente. "Ideología y política en Arturo Campión." *Príncipe de Viana* 42, no.163 (1981), 641–90.

———. "Arturo Campión. Aproximación a un vasco desconocido." *Muga* 9 (1980): 56–65.

———. "Vida y obra de Arturo Campión." *Bidebarrieta* 4 (1991): 109–16.

Iriarte López, Iñaki. "La importancia de llamarse Unax: Arana, Campión y los signos externos del vasco." *Historia y Política* 15 (2006): 45–64.

Irujo, Andrés María de. "La editorial vasca Ekin de Buenos Aires." In *VIII Congreso de Estudios Vascos (8. 1954. Baiona, Uztaritz)*. Donostia: Eusko Ikaskuntza, 2003.

Jimeno Aranguren, Roldán. "Las revistas jurídicas navarras (1940–1977)." In *Los juristas y el 'régimen'. Revistas jurídicas bajo el franquismo*, edited by Federico Fernández-Crehuet and Sebastián Martín. Granada: Comares, 2014.

———. *Miguel Javier Urmeneta (1915–1988). Segunda República, Franquismo y Transición*. Pamplona: Pamiela, 2015.

Jimeno Jurío, José María. "Arturo Campión Jaimebón." In *Navarra en época moderna y contemporánea*. Pamplona: Pamiela; Udalbide; Euskara Kultur Elkargoa, 2007.

Landa Sopeña, María Mercedes. "La literatura vasca en la obra de Unamuno." *Bulletin hispanique* 95, no. 2 (1993): 603–21.

López Antón, José Javier. "De la identidad vasco-americana a la tesis vasco-caucásica: El enfoque de Arturo Campión sobre el origen mítico de la lengua vasca." *Fontes Linguae Vasconum* 27, no. 70 (1995): 467–86.

———. *Arturo Campión entre la historia y la cultura*. Pamplona: Gobierno de Navarra, 1998.

———. "La actitud lingüística en Campión. Catolicismo, tradición y foralidad." In *El euskera en tiempo de los éuskaros*, edited by Roldán Jimeno Aranguren. Pamplona: Gobierno de Navarra; Ateneo Navarro, 2000.

Majuelo Gil, Emilio. "Arturo Campión (1854–1937): historialaria kontzientzia kolektiboaren sortzaile." *Gerónimo de Uztariz* 26–27 (2010–2011): 46–61.

———. *La idea de historia en Arturo Campión*. Donostia: Eusko Ikaskuntza, 2011.

Mata Induráin, Carlos. "'Chocarán el puchero y la olla': conflictos sociales e ideológicos en 'Blancos y Negros', de Arturo Campión." In *Grupos sociales en la historia de Navarra. Relaciones y derechos. Actas del V Congreso de Historia de Navarra*. Volume 2, edited by Carmen Erro and Iñigo Mugueta. Pamplona: Eunate; Sociedad de Estudios Históricos de Navarra, 2002.

Mees, Ludger. *La Restauración y la Dictadura de Primo de Rivera. Los nacionalistas. Historia del nacionalismo vasco, 1876–1960*. Vitoria-Gasteiz: Fundación Sancho el Sabio, 1995.

Miralles, Enrique. "'Don García Almorabid', de Arturo Campión, y la novela histórica de fin de siglo." In *Del romanticismo al realismo: Actas del I Coloquio de la Sociedad de Literatura Española del siglo XIX*, edited by Luis Felipe Díaz Larios and Enrique Miralles. Barcelona: Universitat de Barcelona, 1998.

Mitxelena, Koldo. "Campionen 'Gramatica' eta beste." *Euskera* 30 (1985): 63–70.

Monreal Zia, Gregorio. "Una historia de la Revista Internacional de los Estudios Vascos (1907–2000)." *Revista Internacional de los Estudios Vascos* 46, no. 1 (2001): 11–46.

Múgica, Gregorio. *Los titanes de la cultura vasca*. San Sebastián: Auñamendi, 1962.

Nieva Zardoya, José Luis. *La idea euskara de Navarra, 1864–1902*. Bilbao: Fundación Sabino Arana; Euskara Kultur Elkargoa, 1999.

Payne, Stanley G. "Navarra y el nacionalismo vasco en perspectiva histórica." *Príncipe de Viana* 45, no. 171 (1984): 101–16.

Satrustegi, Jose Mari. "Arturo Campionen itzala." *Euskera* 39, no. 2 (1994): 407–16.

Tellechea Idígoras, José Ignacio. "Cartas inéditas de Arturo Campión a Serapio Múgica (1899–1921)." *Anuario del Seminario de Filología Vasca Julio de Urquijo* 18, no. 1 (1984): 3–38.

Zalba, José. "El maestro en su taller. Cómo trabaja Campión." *Euskalerriaren Alde* 20 (1930): 258–62.

Chapter 1

Speech of Thanks
Read at the Floral Games of Barcelona
on May 17, 1891

Gentlemen:

The love I feel for the Navarrese land, my homeland, and even to the whole Basque land, is so vivid and pure that, it is solely with extreme repugnance and in order to satisfy powerful motives requesting of my will, I usually decide to leave its confines; looking like the ground on which I tread and the air I breathe in other regions, thorny and vaporous in traumatic exile. What is more, hand on heart and in all Basque truth, I state and declare, gentlemen, that my eyes alone are widened by the fertile orchard of Lleida and discover the lofty heights of the heroic Manresa mountain ranges, from the deepest insides of my being ascends a surge of tender thanks and fervid enthusiasm that it appears that they are insinuating that I do not find myself outside my homeland, and they place in my trembling lips the words of Don Pedro the Ceremonious, "I salute you, oh Catalonia! Land populated by loyalty."

And how would it be possible for the noble affection of gratitude to not flutter around in my soul? So long as I live the reminiscence of those days of tribulation that witnessed the sweet yearned for peace converted into the cruelest and abhorrent scourge of war will never be erased from my memory, when across all parts of Spain the barbarous cry of Brennus resumed viciously, and bayonets dripping the blood of brothers were driven into the oak of Gernika, and the spurs of fortunate generals, who were not illustrious for immortal deeds, slashed into the holy book of our fueros! That was the disgraceful moment of revolutionary settlement; four Spanish provinces charged with the blame for everyone, like the scapegoat in Leviticus with the sins of Israel.

The unhappy Basque Country lay bleeding, lifeless, its eyes looking up to heaven, thinking, on hearing the hoarse rants of hatred and envy, that piety had now fled the world! But it went to find refuge in Catalonia, whose magnanimous arms picked up the Basque Country from the bloody ground, held her withered head, cleaned her atrocious wounds and cured them with sedative balms; she wrapped her body, broken by the efforts of combat and pain, in the tunic of the Good Samaritan, and extending her mouth to the ears of the persecuted victim, whispered in a voice more loving than the cooing of turtle doves: "Sister, my sister!" And she said more, still, as if this were not much; she raised her giant body, and intensifying in her chest the indomitable spirit of the defenders of foral legality, the austere and adamantine spirit of Fivaller, of Claris, and of Casanova, she faced up to the winners and said to them: "Cease! The work of force is unjust! Do not kill law, proclaiming yourselves unworthy of the victory." Sublime depreciation that passed like a breath of resurrection over the tombs of the dead heroes around the banner of Saint Eulalia! And I, who have not forgotten either the anguish or the relief, with the vividness of fondness from the first day, exclaim: "Blessed be you, Catalonia, land of justice and compassion."

There is nothing greater than love, gentlemen, and when I say I love Catalonia it appears that I am saying it all. But I would be maiming the reality of my feelings, I would be imposing a harsh servitude on myself, like the miser who hides his treasures, if I were to attempt to stifle any manifestation of my enthusiasm for the grandeurs and the glories of this illustrious Catalan nation, an enthusiasm that inflames my blood, captivates my intelligence, and dazzles my eyes.

Where is there any people who have received from the open hand of Providence any richer, numerous, and contrasting gifts? Tell them of the wooded Pyrenees, the energy, the tenacity, and the resistance befitting of the mountain races; take them to the celestial sea that bathes its gentle hospitable coasts with the aromas of Mediterranean civilizations, and make them an easy route by which their vessels may traverse the dual odyssey of commerce and war; nature, now frowning in the mountains, now beaming on the plains, sometimes bathing hillsides in the shade of the forests, sometimes raising snowy peaks over bleak valleys, sometimes embroidering golden sands together with silver fringes, sometimes converting the land into small baskets of exotic flowers, shakes its artistic imagination with all the contrasts, tints it with all the colors, embalms it with all the perfumes, undoubtedly so that its creations may highlight and cultivate all styles and genres, from the placid golden idyll of the sun, to the legendary drama glimpsed by the glare of the light that the mists absorb.

The corralling of the autochthonous or primitive race in specific mountain districts, its mixing with invaders in others, the constant infiltration of foreign influences through the broad routes of the sea and the western plains, and the influx of nature continually acting on the ethnic elements are the causes that explain the admirable development of Catalan civilization and the truly protean genius of Catalonia. What diverse aptitudes! What different tendencies! What countless examples of human intelligence and character! The heroic temple of the Christian martyr, in the pious and peaceful Fructuosus of Tarragona; the renunciation of profane science for the sake of sacred science and the burning love for humanity, in the glorious Dominican Raymond of Penyafort; the topical satire of Juvenal, concentrated in the *quartettos* of Beltrán de Born, the only poet in the world who has sung about the horrors of his own wars; the jovial Boccaccian narration in Pedro Juan de Martorell; Brother Ramón Martí, through whom Hebrew-Christian philology was raised to the category of science; a Raimundo Lull, philosopher, poet, mystic, utopian, theosophist, visionary, magnificent summary of all his wisdom and the dream of the Middle Ages, fused with the heat of personal genius, procerus intelligence and imagination, bathed by the soft light of platonic ideas; Brother Nicolás Aymerich, champion of positive reason and religious purity, of a rough impassioned nature, the personification of holy Catholic intransigence against all lines of errors; a Roger de Lluria, who sealed with his bloody rods even the fish in the Mediterranean; a Raimundo Sabunde, a giant on whose forehead reverberated the last flashes of medieval mysticism and the dawn rays of Cartesian pyschologism, a golden ring that in which the names of Suso and Tauler were set; an Arnaldo de Vilanova, a distinguished doctor, profound philosopher, an encyclopedic spirit in whom the sciences of observation went hand in hand with the arts of foretelling, who combined in one single man the wise man and the pessimist, the surveyor and the alchemist, the laboratory experimenter and the apocalyptic oracle, the *eternal Gospel* and the prosaic canons of the reasoned lay spirit; a Don Juan Margarit, creator of historical and geographical research on primitive Spain, a diplomat, politician, and illustrious soldier, the savior in Girona from the cruel Henríquez and from the perfidious Fernando, leader of the Royalist party, whose bloody hands laid the first blocks of stone in the Castilian-Aragonese union, destined with time to transform into an evil sepulcher of regional liberties; a Casanova, whose soul rose to heaven asking for justice and demanding revenge, pushed by the flames that were engulfing Barcelona, less infamous than the fire in which the Castilian tormentor made ash of the Catalan standards and the *grammallas* of the *concelleres*. And in the modern era, the gigantic people of engineers, manufacturers, and industrialists that attached to the crest of the old Catalan paladin the reddish plume of smoke from the factories, and mounted among the diamonds of the county crown the dazzling stars of electric light.

On the one hand, the idealist side, the philosophers, the mystics, the poets, the painters: Father José del Espíritu Santo, Amat, Gallisá, Bisbe y Vidal, Vallcendrera, Abad, Balmes, the Marquis of Avilés, Comella, Ribot y Fontseré, Verdaguer, Guimerá, Calvet, Fortuny; the other on the realist side, the politicians, the historians, legal advisers, doctors, naturalists: Montaner, Desclot, Pujadas, Dorca, Fontanellas, Hisern, Guimbernat, Bolós . . . both centers that, in a measured rhythm, direct and attract the fast-flowing currents of Catalan history. Legislators drew up the *Llibre de los Usatges*, that of the *Consulado del Mar*, and they debated sensibly and seriously in the honorable and free Parliament, leaving for posterity everlasting monuments of wisdom and prudence;

here, the merchants speak of their profits in the *Lonjas*; there, troubadours' lutes around the *amador de toda gentileza* ring out, and the songs of sirens at the Parthenopean court of Alfonso V humble; another day, a handful of epic adventures make the treacherous Byzantine and inhumane Turk tremble. This history stores examples of all these heroisms and magnanimities: the art of adding kingdoms without taking away liberties is demonstrated by the conquerors of Mallorca, Sicily, Naples, and Sardinia, who knew how to counter the possessive unifying monarchy of Castile with a federative monarchy, a solar focus that shed rays of justice over the radiant chorus of related peoples. Anyone looking for the archetype of a chivalrous popular king, a protector of the privileges of his nation, a guardian of the rights of his vassals, a promoter of the authentic elements of his people, has it there in the flesh in the person of the most excellent Don Jaime, greeted prophetically by the Archbishop of Tarragona with the words: "*Ecce filius meus dilectus, in quo mihi bene complacuit.*" creator of the Parliament, organizer of the Municipalities, defender of indigenous rights, whose conqueror's crown was woven by the oaks of Mallorca and the palm leaves of Valencia; terror of the Moors on account of his lance, an illustrious figure of letters on account of his *Llibre de la sabiesa* and his *Crónica*; so heroic that "win or die" was his emblem, and so generous that he gifted kingdoms to Castile. Whoever hesitates in choosing between loyalty and fortune evokes the Spartan shadow of Dalmau de Rocaberti, he who lit the Peralada fire, an inextinguishable light of patriotism. Peoples who fight for their independence turn their eyes to Girona, the sublime city of cities; and those for whom the dreadful moment of extermination is near should learn to put a heavy price on their lives in the bastion of San Pedro and to preserve their rights by spitting in the face of the winners the immortal protest of Barcelona: "You should know, too—said the *concelleres*—that slavery, being guaranteed and forced, as an obligation of their position, they explain, declare, and protest in the face of those present and testify for posterity that they have carried out the last exhortations and efforts, protesting against all the ills, ruins, and devastations that may occur unexpectedly in our common Homeland, as well as the elimination of all its honors and privileges..." Canons rolled along streets without any stones in vain; bombs exploded, gunfire boomed, homes were destroyed, fire raged, the Bourbon soldiers blasphemed and howled, all in vain; that loud hubbub, that outburst and clamor of the end of the world, did not manage to exterminate the echo of the city proclamation that still resounded, vibrated, and boomed in the virile heart of Catalans.

Excuse me, gentlemen, if I have to come to recall in the peaceful festival of beautiful letters scenes of blood and devastation that, for the good of all, would have been much better had they never taken place. But desirous to demonstrate to you my feelings, it was completely impossible for me to hide the fact that, in the same way as your joys, I am also affected by your grievances and your sorrows hurt me. This love and admiration for Catalonia are the only things I can argue in the severe court of my own trial in order to not feel totally enveloped by confusion on account of the lofty and unmerited honor that I have received from you. How else would I have dared to take a seat in the illustrious Council of your Floral Games, such celebrated cultured and patriotic solemnity, worthy of in its spirit and also in the details of the execution of this rich, noble, and excellent city of Barcelona, "a pleasant coincidence of firm friendships and in a unique place and beauty," of patronizing it? No longer personal merits, exclusively visible for your courtesy and benevolence; but what hurts me most is not the undeserved representation of a great literary tradition that is given to me to show off; which there in Navarre, although there is no shortage of notable writers, is that their works fall under the jurisdiction of Castilian literature; and, even if the greatest of the Basque-language prose writers should be Navarrese, in my inexcusable arrogance, I would want to put him the shoulder to shoulder with your universal writers of deserved renown.

The energetic, concise, flexible, rich, and harmonious Catalan language displays itself to all adorned with jewels chiseled by the most exquisite art. While the other neo-Latin languages lie entombed and stifled by the ties of brutality, yours soared with an eagle's wings through the purest sky of Provence. Rhyme, that inestimable skill in modern poetry, adorns Provençal literature above all else. Emperors, kings and princes, many of them foreigners, cultivated it, and in their proud breasts they took inspiration from Dante and Petrarch. Its social action is so powerful that it equates commoners with nobles: History preserves the name of a lady, Matilde de Montagnac, who spurned four princes for a simple troubadour: the terrible Beltran de Born, who "did not rest in peace even in his tomb." The strings of *Faith, Homeland,* and *Love* vibrated. Troubadours enjoyed political influence: Beltran Carbonell, Boniface de Castellane, Guillermo Figuera, Arnaldo de Moncut, [and] Ramon de Miraval gathered around the House of Tolosa when, from the North, a new irruption of barbarians was released (moved more by national passion than by jealous love) that preyed on the civilization of the Middle Ages, awkwardly stained by the Albi heretics, and dragged the hero of Las Navas to his death in the nefarious fields of Muret; Marcabru intoned the Marseillaise of the Middle Ages, and with a new *albada* that would accompany the trills of the nightingale, and next to the *serena* crowned with stars, as the snake hissed a relentless *quartetto*; closing this wonderful cycle that enclosed within a golden arch, strewn with precious stones, Provence, Catalonia, and Valencia, the sublime eroticism of Ausiàs March.

The Catalan language, the language in which Vidal de Besalu, Cavestany, Guillermo de Bergada, Jordi de Sant Jordi sang; the one that ran with a nervous, sober, polished, and luminous style through the pages of Muntaner, Desclot, Eximenis, and Bernardo Metge; which the rapid genius of Raimundo Lull made resound in Tunisia and Sicily, in Paris and Moscow, like a dethroned queen dragged along by the dust of the roads, after the catastrophe of 1714, plebeian rough poets. Even with all that, the ineffable goodness of God was decreed to renew for her the miracle of Lazarus. And Catalan literature, evoked in Aribau's *Oda a la Patria* and attracted by the penetrating eloquent notes of *Gayter del Llobregat*, shook off the bronze dream, adhered to the royal crown, and freed itself from the shady branches of Ter, of Francoli, of Segre, of Besós, flocks of melodious nightingales that haunted the world. Today this literature is a splendid constellation that reigns supremely in the sky over Spain, because, as the distinguished Santander writer Pereda says, it possesses the *only* Spanish epic poet and the *only* contemporary dramatist in whose tragedies the weighty inspiration of Shakespeare shines. I would like to quote all the names of the poets, the dramatists, the novelists, the storytellers, the writers of the Catalan Renaissance; but I do not have the breath to undertake this homicidal enumeration. Believe me, gentlemen: if those names do not jump from my pen, I keep them in my heart.

My old and glorious land does not resemble in any way this literary movement, nor should you intend to honor in my person the merits of a literature. You have dispensed me the unforgettable and deeply grateful benefit of choosing me among all my contemporaries, to personify your sympathies to Navarre. The two Pyrenean peoples shake hands at this moment; in joining them, they recognize one another and say: "we have been linked before." Your kings have also been ours; people of your race also settled our towns and cities; dialects of your language also echoed in the courts of our monarchs and served to draw up innumerable documents in our archives, and supplied the words for our troubadours Guillermo de Tudela, Juan de Viana, and Diego de Valtierra. Unconquered Navarrese warriors irrigated the fields of Mallorca with their blood, fighting under the *señera* of Don Jaime. One Corbarán de Lehet was a general for your almogavars, and the corrupt paleologist heard the Basque *irrintz* with the same terror as the *desperta ferro*! We were also taken by the crazy epic of your expeditions, and we made the legendary exploits of Roger de Flor flourish in the Orient. Our tears and yours, blended and mixed together there on the tomb of Don Carlos, like the waters of the Catalan and Navarrese rivers flowing into the Ebro, which brings kisses from Navarre to Catalonia.

May God make my stay among you a prelude to and an omen for an unbreakable fraternity! And if at any moment the hungry lions should take out their anger on your sandbanks, may the chains of our coat of arms trap them!

I have spoken.

Chapter 2

Lecture on the Origin and Development of Navarrese Regionalism given at The Lliga de Catalunya on the Evening of June 3, 1891

Gentlemen:

I come to fulfill the commitment that, some nights ago, I incurred with you to address regionalism in Navarre. My original intention was to explain succinctly the origin and development of that literary-poetic movement by means of an oral discourse; but as I have to allude to, at the very least, events in which I have taken part actively, I do not want my enemies, who also have regionalism in my land, to be able to assume or suspect that, taking advantage of your unfamiliarity with those events, I have painted things to you in my own way. Words may fly, writing remains: my observations and judgments will remain written, and such conduct, on the present occasion, seems to me more befitting of Catalan seriousness and Navarrese integrity.

I must speak about regionalism, on the occasion of informing you about a great Navarrese poet, a friend from childhood, a brother in soul, Hermilio de Olóriz. In my land, too, as in yours, political demands were announced and preceded by the golden buglers of poetry! Priceless gift of Providence, that which you and we have received from her! To possess poets whose powerful voice must awake the vibrant trumpet with cries capable of awakening the dead: those who do not feel love for their homeland are dead.

Father Isla, in a certain famous book that he wrote to mock Navarre, said—and it is the only serious proposition printed in his work—that what the Navarrese most revered and loved in the world, after the blessed Jesus, were their fueros and freedoms.

Had the caustic priest written twenty-five or thirty years later, that phrase, as regards what he says about the fueros and freedoms, would never have emanated from his pen; by that time the love and reverence of my countrymen was following, already, other paths.

The first and gravest spoliation that the Navarrese regional spirit experienced was due to the War of Independence. A few years earlier, despite the fact that the philosophical spirit originating in the French Revolution, with its theories about abstract man, his natural rights, and national sovereignty, was permeating the upper echelons of society, there still existed, alive and present in all consciences, the concept that Navarre was *a kingdom in itself, different in jurisdiction and laws from the rest*, and joined in a federative way to Castile through the personal bond of the monarch, under solemn pacts and contracts of incorporation that guaranteed the sanctity of the swearing an oath on behalf of the Castilian monarchs: the Pamplona Parliament in the year 1794, in the middle of war with the French Republic, had to authorize the inhabitants of the kingdom, whose battalions were incorporated into the Spanish army, that if they so wished, whenever an action should commence within Navarrese territory, they could leave it to conclude it: this fact depicts better than any other how everyone then believed Navarre to be a nation united to another nation.

But the War of Independence altered profoundly such a mental and emotional state: Navarre was invaded by the Napoleonic army like the other territories in Spain; the provincial government [*Diputación*] of the kingdom, encircled by foreign bayonets, had enough spirit to declare war on the tyrant; bands were organized, then battalions were organized that fought just as much in Navarre as in Aragon and Castile; in fact, it ruined the foral structure, since the central and other regional revolutionary authorities, whether revolutionary or spontaneous, ruled directly, although intermittently, and nobody questioned whether a measure or disposition went against the fueros, but only if it were or seemed patriotic; the natives of the Kingdom of Navarre mixed with those of other kingdoms, and that great conflagration, with the community of interests, risks, and aspirations, resulted in a predominance of the *national* tendency over the *local* tendency, orienting the public spirit toward central bodies, persuading it that there was bigger business than Navarrese business and that it was not even possible to consider and resolve this separately from the generals.

The deplorable civil conflicts that the enthronement of liberalism brought with it increased the support for and strength of that current. Navarre was represented in the Cadiz Parliament by representatives in whose name the country did not intervene, by virtue of the scandalous prerogatives that, as regards this matter, were attributed to the regent; those representatives, although with little vigor or strength, adopted the same attitude that their predecessors in the pseudo Baiona Parliament had done: defend the constitutional *status quo* of Navarre. Yet the Cadiz Parliament did not take into account a *pro formula* opposition, nor would it even have stopped, either, in the face of better established reasons and more energetic gestures: the light wind of the Geneva theories filled the vacuous brains of those good gentlemen who ordered Spaniards to be "fair and munificent," and the sinister group of demagogues that communicated the movement to the deluded, to the cowards, and the imbeciles was unable to respect historical and traditional rights, in the same way that the French constituents, years before, started to curdle those of the Lower Navarre, identical, in a everything, to ours. The Cadiz Parliament inaugurated an unending series of parliamentary lies, extolling in the preamble of its paper Constitution the fueros and laws of Navarre, and abolishing them within it body: in the end, gentlemen, a feat wholly worthy of a randomly gathered group of legislators who entered the Revolution through the door of perjury.

The work in Cadiz was the object of universal loathing in Navarre; when Ferdinand VII returned from France, the Elío brothers, both generals, presented the monarch with a statement signed by the provincial body, demanding the reestablishment of the fueros. The king restored them, and the old laws remained in force until the shameful pronouncement by Riego in Cabezas de San Juan. During those years an important event for Navarre took place: General Espoz y Mina, a heroic soldier but an uncouth, cruel, envious, and vindictive man, whose mausoleum disfigures the noble Gothic cloister in the cathedral of Pamplona, constructed there providentially, without any doubt, so that the infamy of the idol and the blindness of political passions was clear to everyone's eyes; General Espoz y Mina, I repeat, on account of not having been appointed viceroy, declared himself openly liberal, and a fanatical liberal. His example swept along many of his brothers in arms and people who adored in him a hero of independence. From that day on there was a nucleus of Spanish-style liberals in Navarre, that is, unitary centralists, and the more so the less numerous and loved they were; a tyrannical minority that needed help from outside Iberia in order to impose on its fellow citizens the triumph of some ideas by these abominations.

The second constitutional period exacerbated the aversion of Navarre to liberalism; another Spanish party was formed, the Royalist Party, although with touches, hints, and dashes of regionalism; on hearing Riego's name, people felt imprisoned by a kind of epileptic fury; there had to be a prohibition, by royal decree, of acclaims and cheers for the general; even so, conflict was not avoided, among which it is worth recording that of Saint Joseph's day in the year 1822 in Pamplona, on which civilians and the urban militia attacked the *Imperial Alejandro* regiment, in a highly exalted revolutionary way, attacking it mercilessly with knives even inside San Cernin's church. The unrest grew steadily, stirred up by news regarding the French attitude; in the end, the country rose up and the uprising was formidable; even the most peaceful valleys in the Pyrenees, and others that today enjoy the deserved renown of being liberal, rose up with their priests at the forefront; only the Baztan defended, with arms that were neither foreign nor mercenary, the constitutional regime. The cry of the rebels was "Religion, King, and Fueros." Just as the entrance of the hundred thousand sons of Saint Louis was launched above the Ebro against the liberal troops with whom they had sustained a brilliant and obstinate fight, the first care of the *Governing Council* was to reestablish the provincial government of the kingdom and reassign it with its faculties and powers. Yet despite such a commendable spirit, they demonstrated during the campaign symptoms that showed how deep the intoxication caused by the general ideas was going. The Junta of Navarre was dependent on the Urgel Regency, to the improbable point that by orders of the latter, despite the displeasure of the volunteers and the distress of the country, in severe violation of the fueros and laws, the Navarrese division under the orders of Baron Eroles came to Catalonia, and later, in March of 1823 and by order of General-in-Chief Don Carlos O'Donnell, it withdrew to the French border leaving defenseless its homeland, whose fertile lands in the Ribera were destroyed barbarically in a redskins' invasion practiced by the infamous *Chapalangarra* [Joaquín Romualdo de Pablo y Antón]. Now it was clear, the royal cause, rather than the cause of the fueros, demanded this strategic movement: here is the first of the atrocious but deserved punishments that have befallen Navarre for having betrayed the flags, eternally legitimate and eternally preferential, of its national autonomy!

Ferdinand VII reestablished the fueros again; but the wicked and ungrateful monarch, a centerpiece unworthy of the love of millions of Spaniards, did not adhere to respecting them; he called, it is true, parliaments in 1828 and 1829, but his anti-foral acts were so many, so important, and recurring that, in 1831, the council of the kingdom had to tell him, in a respectful but austere and firm representation, that "his most loyal Navarrese saw themselves, practically, stripped of the liberties that the king had pledged allegiance to." Ferdinand VII died, and the vast majority of the country, seeing in Don Carlos a representative of traditional ideas, went over to his side; foral law, however, favored Doña Isabel II, and this unhappy lady was proclaimed Queen of Navarre, under the name of Isabel I, by the council of the kingdom, made up, in the main, of royalists. Zumalacárregui, in an incredible proclamation that spread throughout the land all the principles of the political and civil constitution of the kingdom, raged against the representatives the death penalty and confiscation of their goods. And that august corporation, the ultimate representative of foral legitimacy, scorned by unitary liberals and odious of the Carlist royalists, had to give way, as soon as possible, to a revolutionary council.

The legitimate council had requested, unsuccessfully, of the prime ministers of the governing kingdom, a meeting of parliament as a means of pacifying the country and settling, legally, the dynastic dispute. But the Liberals, who used to hide behind the fueros as regards the succession of Don Ferdinand VII, in the other points they dispensed with them; and even worse were the Navarrese liberals, as the city council of Pamplona demonstrated, proceeding, against the express orders of the provincial council, to appoint lawyers who had the brand-new constitutional code of Mr. Martinez de la Rosa.

While the civil war lasted, the representative of new ideas and of old ideas fought in Navarre. The Carlists said that the restoration of the fueros would come as a consequence of the ruin of the liberal system, but they behaved as if the fueros did not exist. The liberals, in turn, totally forgot about them: what is more, in the year 1837, the central powers having demonstrated the wish to obtain an end to the war by means of foral reintegration, the provincial council of Navarre asked the Spanish parliament—a shameful an ignominious request!—that the fueros should not be reestablished. Besides this tendency, befitting of the fanatical or progressive liberals, another tendency had been taking shape, moderately foralist, which yearned for their partial reintegration, and this tendency triumphed as a result of the Bergara Agreement, with a result of that the famous Consensual Law of August 18, 1841. By virtue of this law, Navarre, in return for draft military service, with the faculty of covering it with men or money, at its discretion; the abolition of viceroyal authority and its privative parliaments and courts of law; the admission of laws of examination and judicial organization and civil codes to be elaborated taking into account the institutions of foral countries, obtained positive advantages: full provincial and municipal autonomy, exemption from the stamped paper tax, the payment of a fixed and invariable contribution, the maintenance of a territorial court and captaincy general in Pamplona, the pleasure and enjoyment of common mountains and pastures in the Andia and Urbasa mountain ranges and in Las Bardenas, as well as other less substantial benefits. Navarre, for its part, has fulfilled and more all the obligations imposed on it by the law of '41: not so the Spanish state, which has violated and ignored countless times that convened in its articles, making good of the infamous bad faith of the Carthaginians. Navarre lived quietly for many years in the numbing shadow of this deadly law, which flatters certain prosaic feelings of material well-being, slowly sliding down the inclined plane of assimilation: even with all that, there were two occasions on which the flame hidden by the mountain of ash burned; one, when a Minister Narváez sought to impose the rural guard; the other, when Mr. Montero Ríos abolished the Court of Pamplona. From the banks of the Ebro to the high Pyrenees, the alarm was sounded; and those governments, so arrogant with the weak and the neglected, retreated saying: "the indomitable Basque people that we had thought dead already are asleep: we should not awaken them."

II

Yet the antimonarchical, antisocial, and antireligious excesses of the September Revolution were responsible for awaking them. This was a strange period, because there were a relatively small number of anti-foral attacks and, in any case, incapable of producing an armed movement. Catholic fervor, monarchical conviction, and the traditionalist spirit ran high, but love for the fueros remained at the limits of a moderate temperament, for all that, in the accumulation of prosperity and fortunes that many fantasized the supposed traditional Spanish monarchy would bring with it, some vague sentiment and confused hope for complete foral restoration palpitated. The Carlist uprising in the North was an eminently national reaction, provoked by revolutionary policies; something similar to the retching of a stomach that has ingested poisonous substances and battles to expel them. The Navarrese youth dashed to enlist in the ranks of Don Carlos, because in that country there was an unconscious custom of being Carlist, just as they inherited physiognomic features and family habits; that youth fought, in its opinion, to restore religion to Spain, to enthrone the legitimate king of Spain, to defend the fundamentals of moral and social order in Spain; they did not endeavor for the good of Navarre, but insofar as it formed part of the entirety of Spain. There was never in the nation a less selfish uprising or one with such general aims: as if it were sinning earnestly on account of quixotic generosity and sacrificing its own wellbeing for the sake of others' wellbeing. And here, gentlemen, an event took place that describes and defines ultra-Iberian politics: those centralizing parties that spend their lives preaching against supposed regional exclusivisms, those that make patriotism consist of giving up one's own typical features, a renouncement that they term bombastically becoming more and more Spanish, those that denigrate regional aspirations with the moniker parochial politics, punished us severely because in a moment of generous hallucination we forgot we were Basques and Navarrese, to remember exclusively that we were Spanish. And thing is that patriotism in the hands of the typical parties is the club that beats the homeland.

At the end of the second civil war, under the patronage of the foral provincial councils, the newspaper *La Paz* was founded in Madrid, edited by the late extremely eloquent Bizkaian orator Don Miguel Loredo. Most Basque-Navarrese writers, publicists, and patricians figured on the list of the newspaper's collaborators, as well as a group of young people that, on the occasion of the consequences of war, began to pick up their pens. The politics of *La Paz* consisted of two fundamental dogmas: the juridical defense of the rights of the Basque-Navarrese Country, and the demonstration that these institutions were democratic and free, emphasizing the absurdity that the parties that were bragging about having defeated absolutism should abolish them. Later, when their restoration was considered, the dogma of the Basque-Navarrese union was added, that is, the common and combined action of the four Basque provinces and the sacrifice of individual political ideas that divided them, as a gift to the foral idea that matched their wishes. Fines and trials that embittered Loredo's life and aggravated his physical ailments fell on *La Paz*, the favored target of the servile mistrust of prosecutors in the Cánovas mold. I published a short work in that newspaper titled "El euskera" [the Basque language], in which I mused on the excellence of the Basque language, which shortly before I had started to study, and the importance of literature as a factor in the national consciousness of peoples; I dedicated it to a very esteemed friend whose conversations, in part, had suggested doing so to me, to Don Juan Iturralde y Suit, a man of singular and multiple artistic qualities, a poet although he writes in prose, a publicist, a scholar, an archeologist, a painter, and an illustrator that creates whatever he wants to in diverse fields, although, unfortunately, he usually wants to on few occasions; to whom, to an extremely obvious intelligence, one might add an exquisite moral rectitude, a very good natured heart, and pious love for Navarre. The short work was well received by the regional press, and Mr. Iturralde, whom one always finds leading the way for all the aspirations raised in the Basque-Navarrese Country, came up with the formation of the Asociación Euskara de Navarra [Basque Association of Navarre]. Thirteen of us congregated at his home, at his request, founded this distinguished society that, according to its statutes, proposed the cultivation of literature, the knowledge of history, the maintenance of traditions, and the promotion of the moral and material interests of the Basque-Navarrese Country. In order to best achieve its aims, it had an organ in the press, the *Revista Euskara*, which was published in monthly notebooks. The Association named as honorary members several people that had distinguished themselves in the defense or study of things related to the country, from Pi y Margall to Pidal, from Mañé y Flaquer, to Prince Louis Lucien Bonaparte, not a prince, but king of the Bascophiles. It established relations with the distinguished protector of Basque letters in the French Basque Country, Monsieur d'Abbadie, and organized the first Basque-language poetry competition in Spain, which was held in the place of Elizondo, capital of the picturesque Baztan Valley. This competition revealed the greatest poet that has ever sung in the Basque language, Felipe de Arrese y Beitia, who planted an elegiac willow on the tomb of our liberties, whose funeral was intoned by all the voices of Pyrenean nature in his verses. And thanks to the Asociación Euskara, the Basque-Navarrese Pyrenean plain, covered in oaks, beeches, and hollies, adorned its scrubland with Grecian laurel.

The Basque festivals were not purely literary; there were prizes for written composition and one for the sharp ad-libbing of the improvisers or *bertsolaris*, the ability of *pelota* players, the agility of women who took part in a race carrying jugs of water on their heads, the ongoing spectacle of the male and female sickle and scythe grass reapers, the merit of the stockbreeders who presented the best examples of the bovine, mule, equine, and porcine races, and even the iron lungs of the farmhand *irrintzilaris* or shrill screamers. A form was sought in which all social classes and all authentic interests could come together in this regenerative movement, which had its golden age, however much, as regards political passions, repressed but not crushed, twisted the knife to stick it into the Asociacón Euskara. The boost had been given to the other three provinces: newspapers and journals of an exclusive regional nature were created; patriotic societies and committees for floral games were founded; poetry competitions were started that were often backed by the provincial councils and city councils of the capitals and most important towns; hundreds of distinguished men organized themselves; historical, juridical, and linguistic works were published; other writings by the precursors of the movement that, for lack of favorable circumstances, still remained unpublished, were published; inspired composers set the admirable songs of the country to majestic rhapsodies, and nor was there a complete lack of painters that evoked with their brushes dramatic scenes in national history, nor witty writers who brought to theater stages representations of the people's customs full of *native flavor*. And one can only admire in this flourishing the fact that, its creators being men born in different provinces, some of them citizens of the French Republic, others subjects of the king of Spain, all originating in diverse political factions, some using the Castilian language, others the Basque language, the words of passion running through their minds were one and the same, and although the languages may have differed, the speech matched: they all sang about and celebrated the glories of the past, the hopes for the future, the innate virtues of the race, the healthy customs that illustrated it; the family, the small homeland; the homeland, the big family, the holy love for the fueros that no one will uproot from our grief-stricken chests; experiencing and developing art at the heart of pro-Basque activism, like men under a rib vault.

III

There is no space here in this untidy sketch, written in haste without books or documents to hand, to enter into the minutiae and details of our regional-literary movement. I must focus on one specific figure, and I must start by saying, without offending anyone and without denying any merit, that just as among our prose writers in the Castilian language Villoslada is to be applauded, so Hermilio de Olóriz, who stands out among all the poets in the same language for the importance of his work, even though it is still not very ample, in "Amaya" has written the idealistic poem of the Basques, and especially the Navarrese.

Hermilio de Olóriz does not have a history: his books and poetry are his public life. He was visited in his early youth by the muse that used to come and sit in front of the students; yet the misfortunes of his country placed in his hands the bards' harp and in his lips the heroic horn. He has written a Navarrese collection of ballads that contains three poems: "Roncesvalles," "Olast," and "Pamplona;" a dramatic essay titled "En manos del extranjero" [In the foreigner's hands]; another poem called "Roncesvalles;" an ode to "Las Navas de Tolosa;" two more poems titled "Calahorra" and "Alesbes;" several free verses, among which I recall "El Naufragio" [The shipwreck] and "A Castilla" [To Castile]; a translation in verse of the celebrated and apocryphal, yet haughty, "Aztobiskar kantua" [Song of Atzobizkar]; another of the "Arbol de Guernika" [Tree of Gernika]; two prose books; *Fundamento y defensa de Los*

Fueros [Bases and defense of the fueros], *Compendia de la historia de Nabarra* [Compendium of the history of Navarre]. He has been honored at the floral games for his ode to "Las Navas" and his poems "Roncesvalles" and "Calahorra." Now he is busy with—may God forgive him and reward him at the same time!—the patriotic, but prosaic and tiresome task of creating a *Diccionario de hombres notables de Nabarra* [Dictionary of prominent men of Navarre]. Every now and then he cultivates poetry and writes compositions like that which I am going to have the honor of reading to you.

Olóriz is the poet of heroism; his love for his homeland is formed out of the molds of Tyrtaeus. The spirit of his poetry is sometimes romantic, but its form is always classical. The flow of his feelings and ideas is not broad, but is instead profound. His vehemence erupts in lavish images, in apostrophes of passion, condensed, like the charge of a projectile, in a tight style, of marble purity; he describes with vividness, color and majesty, always demonstrating the salient features of the events described. His poetry "to Castile!"—which has not ever been prudent to publish, but which was the obligatory conclusion to patriotic meetings and banquets—is the most virile and passionate of all, although in artistic importance it is very inferior to any of them, just as his improvised strophes were never refined or embellished; the expression of outraged patriotism reached a peak of fury, truly awful at times. I could have chosen other more exuberant poetry than that which I am going to read to you; but this, besides being *unpublished*, which would provide me with the opportunity to offer the Lliga de Catalunya a literary first, contains certain elegiac notes entirely new in the lira of Olóriz. It was inspired by the ruins of the Olite Palace, constructed by King Carlos the Noble, a wonderful masterpiece of medieval civil architecture. During the War of Independence, General Mina, justifying himself on supposed strategic reasons, set fire to it; today greed surrounds this work of barbarism. Olóriz sees in these ruins a personification of crestfallen Navarre, and in its memory he turns to the remembrance of past glories; a battle with the Romans, the Christian preaching of Saint Fermin, the rout of Roncesvalles,

Sancho Abarca's expedition through the Pyrenees, covered in snow and swept away by avalanches, to set Pamplona free from the Moorish siege, and the melancholic figure of the Prince of Viana. I have it here (*Mr. Campión reads out the poetry of Olóriz*).

IV

The political movement began somewhat later than the literary one, and once initiated, both followed separate currents that, often, blended into one another. When the Asociación Euskara de Navarra was constituted, the provinces of the North were subjected to a state of siege, from whose ominous dominion the Martínez Campos administration freed them; it was, therefore, impossible to think then about political activity, nor was anything else considered other than bringing together lovers of the country, and nourishing and augmenting the foralist spirit. But as Asociación was dominated by younger, impatient, and rash elements, and on the other hand there were many members that could not understand, due to a lack of sufficient culture, the social reach of the literary renaissance to which that was boosting, and were asking constantly for something *practical* to be done, they declared themselves to be willing to leave in the opposite case, entering resolutely onto the path of political struggle.

The Asociación, as such, never took part in that; a daily newspaper titled *El Arga* was founded, whose slogan, to match the Bizkaian political movement led by the distinguished Sagarmínaga, was: "Basque-Navarrese Union." But as the editors, collaborators, and protectors of *El Arga* were the same people who were at the head of the Asociación, people baptized those in favor of the new political ideas with the name *Euskaros*, and in establishing an inconvenient identification between these and the Asociación, in the end this led to the separation of many that had to make do with writing verses, making music, and giving awards to fat cows.

The struggle began during the elections for foral and provincial representatives: foralists presented as a candidate for the district of Pamplona a very respectable gentleman, the son of a distinguished Navarrese family, who held the post, if I remember correctly, of president of the Asociación Euskara; but look gentlemen, at how the success of such great and just causes rests on such light circumstances: the foralist candidate, a very rich property owner who spent part of the year in the Baztan Valley, on account of specific local questions that occurred some time ago, and which the Pamplona committee ignored, was not sympathetic to certain important figures in the valley; they resolved to cause relentless trouble for him, and in order to defeat him more easily, they opposed him with a candidate who was a son of the Baztan, a clearly intelligent and energetic man who carried the liberal flag. The elections were extremely close; triumph depended on a few votes, and a skilled falsification got rid of the foralist candidate. These elections infuriated many spirits; bitter communiqués and leaflets were written, and various criminal lawsuits were initiated. Shortly thereafter the winner was appointed Governor of Navarre by the Sagasta administration, and from that official post he was able, even more than before, to hurt the *Euskaro* party. Nevertheless, the former managed to win an almost completely triumphal list of candidates (except four) in the first municipal elections held in Pamplona, against the monarchist-liberal-republican coalition that the governor led directly, and from then on the municipal administration of the capital remained his, and even in elections for provincial representatives he obtained victories. Yet on the other hand, the Baztan figure managed to distance most of the liberal (and I use this word in its inappropriate sense of supportive of the constitutional regime and the legitimacy of the Isabel branch) elements from foralism, with only those liberals that were convinced of the impossibility of serving two masters at the same time, and between parties and country that had opted for country, remaining with foralism. Had the foralists chosen another person as their first candidate (and bear in mind, gentlemen, that no one would have surpassed him in patriotism, integrity, self-sacrifice, and intelligence), he would have been elected without a fight and perhaps never or, at most, later, at a time of greater strength for the party, this split would have been verified.

What were the ideas that the foralist party supported? And on saying party I am making use of a comfortable term, because in reality there was never a coordinated aggrupation in Navarre, with an immutable program and supreme authorities that governed disciplinarily over their affiliates. The system adopted was that of spontaneous committee; these elected the candidates, and their presentation by the foralist newspaper spread the significance that they now had to display unfailingly before the public. The designation of people was done with a far-reaching spirit, without any kind of intransigence, seeking assistants, attracting good intentions, combining elements that would represent the driving social forces, based on the assumption, which was always correct, that those among them that shared wholly the ideas of the initiators would set the dominant tone for those selected: in this way, many people that were mere sympathizers ended up embracing foralism steadfastly.

Foralism consisted of three or four fundamental ideas: the Basque-Navarrese union, the separation from ultra-Iberian parties, the defense of the 1841 law as the provisional *status quo*, subject to denouncing the central government for failing to fulfill it, only the bravery of the foralist currents would legitimize the claim for more complete autonomy; and meanwhile, cultivating and favoring the maintenance and development of all the typical authentic features of the Navarrese people. That ideal union, as regards the union of individuals I mean—not of the Basque provinces, for this is irrevocable—was to be sure a magnanimous ideal, but so difficult to achieve that there was therein something, perhaps, utopian. Excellent as a formative procedure, it was not as valid when it came to making dynamic forces static, making wishes take shape around a fixed nucleus; to some extent, it consecrated officially the *dualism* it sought to destroy. For this reason, a new position in foralism responded to the segregation of liberal elements; the newspaper *El Arga* was replaced by *Lau-Buru*, whose slogan was "God and the Fueros;" the Catholic and pro-autonomy tone was accentuated, understanding the pact of 1841 to be broken; null, formally speaking, on account of the Parliament of Navarre, the only power with which the king was authorized to alter the constitution of the kingdom, not having taken part in its formation, it left the opportunity of the circumstances to raise the prospect, around the central government, of our demands. This was a time when foralism was at its strongest: the Liberal party, reduced to the hesitant and weak defense of the law of '41, its own exclusive work, was impotent in struggling against this sum of traditionalist forces; the most prudent and enlightened part of Carlism supported with all its soul this policy, understanding that it condensed what was viable from its old creed; the intransigent element, without any organization, without any leaders, weighed down by the disappointments of the war, consumed itself with sterile lamentations.

The contemporary resurrection of Carlism has been something forced in Navarre; years ago, the Basque provinces had Carlist councils, Carlist newspapers, Carlist provincial councils and city councils, without the movement spreading to Navarre; Carlism was asleep in the shade of an olive picker who would have ended up killing it. Don Carlos and his principal advisors were deeply concerned about this apathy, and sought to remedy it by creating something that had never existed in Navarre, a Carlist newspaper. That was, gentlemen, a moment of heartbreaking anguish. Taking into account the political precedents in Navarre, one feared that Carlism would be broken like a flood that overpowers and possesses everything in its wake; we believed the struggle to be useless, that our work, on account of not having being able to avoid the reconstruction of all the old parties, had failed; we decided that our presence in the political arena would increase the cohesion of our enemies, and we resolved to concentrate on the peaceful literary propaganda of the Asociación Euskara, closing the *Lau-Bauru* and leaving everything in the hands of God. And the adorable Providence, gentlemen, which finds good in the bad and which after the arid winter brings a lush spring; Providence, gentlemen, indicating perhaps that our designs pleased it, allowed for the newspaper created to revive Navarrese Carlism to become the sword that struck at the heart of Spanish Carlism, and made the men who were most distant from us at that moment to become those that pitched their tents alongside our camps. In the chaos of ideas, swarm of passions, and clash of interests, one single idea shone purely, immaculately, and serenely, the polar star of our tempestuous horizons: the impeccable lag of regionalism!

Today, gentlemen, foralism constitutes in Navarre a compact nucleus, hardened in a hundred battles, which looks with hope to the future; more important for the quality and personal influence of its followers than its number. Its ideas are those of *Lau-Buru*: God and the fueros, the Catholic thesis, and foral affirmation. It marches on to attack the omnipotent centralizing modern state, a monster aborted by rationalism, grounding itself in religion, rights, and justice. No movement can prosper in Navarre if Catholic sap does not circulate through its trunk: God is, gentlemen, the most important figure in the Basque Country, and we would be renouncing in a cowardly way the most august and fertile of our traditions if we were to renounce Christ and, like Judas, sell it for thirty pieces of silver. Foralism has found in the regionalist doctrine the formula that divests it of a certain local exclusivism, that was thrown justly in its face, and that constituted the greatest danger to its efforts failing. We are not alone in Spain and those that think and feel alike must necessarily understand and ally with one another. I say that Navarrese foralism looks with hope to the future. And why not, if it already seems like a new day is dawning? The monarchical Liberal party is just a name, a hothouse flower that wilts and dies as soon as it leaves its official source of heat; republicanism does not attract followers outside certain social classes in Pamplona; Carlism split irrevocably; yet still, all these parties, thanks to the propaganda of recent years, have been saturated with regionalism and they are sowing our flag out of a fragment of the bloody tattered rag at their disposal. And the thing is, gentlemen, that in Spain nothing remains to be taught in regard to the matter of political systems: different parties have come and gone, and in the arches of triumph with which peoples celebrated their apotheosis, now only cypress branches of disillusion grow.

It is the moment for Catalonia, instructed by our reversals and well educated by our errors, to think about political action. Just as we Navarrese put the clock forward, it seems to me—oh Catalans!—that you are falling behind too much. I see huge heavy rainclouds over your spirit and your efforts; but as yet no vengeful ray of lightning of so much injustice has been released from them. Do not wait for the moment of catastrophes, because it will catch you off-guard. Do not imitate the conduct of that fashionable soul walking around dressed in leather waiting for the latest *dandy*. No one improvises the action of political forces: one must captivate spirits, win over positions, acquire influences; in politics, the axiom *beati possidentes* is also true. Above all, do not compromise the work with lavish intransigencies and idealistic yearnings; remember that ideas sparkle in the sky, but that interests fight on the ground. Do not imagine that you will be, from the first day on, the irresistible catapult that in one fail swoop destroys the fortress; instead, aspire to be the wedge that slowly dislodges fibers and ends up splitting and cutting open the haughty tree: once the cut has been made, the castle will be yours. In politics no one wins, for all that right may be on their side, just as the magnitude of one's yearnings should be reduced to the limits of the possible.

I who speak to you, dedicated to contributing to the patriotic and most noble rapport between Navarrese traditionalism and foralism, did not refuse to appear on a traditionalist list of candidates during the last municipal elections in Pamplona, save always for the integrity of principles, and maintaining the community of certain essential dogmas. What a strange coincidence, a revealing sign of the times! Other friends of mine of well-known *Lau-Buru* leanings, in coetaneous fashion, were on the list presented by Pamplona Carlism.

Now, gentlemen, goodbye! My spirit remains with you; and among the many wonders I have seen in this land, I will tell my fellow countrymen that what I most admire and revere for its burning patriotism, elevation of ideas, purity of intentions, and cordiality of affects, is the Lliga de Catalunya!

I have spoken.

Chapter 3

Speech at the Traditionalist Regional Circle of Pamplona on May 29, 1892

Gentlemen:

Invited by the governing council of this Catholic center to give a lecture in its meeting rooms, it seemed to me that my profound gratitude did not sit well with a refusal; and despite my infrequent experience of this kind of work and my repugnance at speaking in public, born out of the paucity of my abilities, I resolved to overcome all the reasons that were telling me to resist taking on such a weighty task. Here I am gentlemen and my friends, willing to respond to your gift with my good intentions and wishes: wishes and intentions, unfortunately, and not effective acts, must be the result of my efforts to attract your attention and express concepts to your ears whose form may not be entirely unworthy of the sublimity of the thoughts I would like to communicate to you.

I come, gentlemen, to continue among you my most modest work, to resume among you the task that has absorbed all of my faculties for almost sixteen years; a work and a task that can be summarized in the following briefest of forms: Catholics are becoming more and more foralist, and foralists increasingly Catholic. I am among you and I appreciate not having moved outside of my home; since although relatively important differences separate those that think like you and those that think like me, I contend, without any fear of being mistaken, that such importance is secondary, that it does not touch on anything substantial. You constitute a national party, and we would like to constitute a local party, linked to other local parties by the common bond of regionalist aspiration; you believe that the ancient Spanish kingdoms must be resuscitated, and we, without opposing any reason *in theory* to the contrary, indeed being sympathetic to the idea, believe that in this day and age there are no *particularist* sentiments if not in a few regions of Spain, so that only here will foral restoration make sense and be practical, with the rest receiving a broadly decentralizing system, whose juridical foundation will be rooted in the state, while in Navarre, the Basque provinces, Catalonia, and perhaps Galicia—the regions I alluded to previously—the restored regime mjst be constructed on their own particular historical personality.

Yet this diversity of criteria should not hinder you and us from finding, in the case of two passers-by, that we are walking on the same path, although not all the way: you, for example, continue on to Gallur, which is Aragonese land; we exit in Olite, where the ruins of the palace belonging to our excessively forgotten monarchs is: or put another way, we find ourselves in the case of two neighbors, intimate friends, separated by a wall, in the circumstance that the wall, instead of being under lock and key, is made of chipboard and canvas, and what is more is mounted on a sliding frame; thus the neighbors move among the rooms continuously, families get together, they share pleasures and sorrows, and they find themselves disposed to communicating their plans, debating their projects, and even, if it suits, confiding in one another. Let us speak, then, but do so out loud so that everyone may hear us and understand where our mutual sympathies lay, from what point they depart, and at what point they meet and bind together like an unbreakable bundle.

I hope that the topic chosen will be to your liking because it will match, correctly, your sentiments as Catholics and Navarrese: *the Catholic sense of foralist demands*; here is the topic that I aim to develop in its principle aspects, although with the necessary brevity so as not to abuse your generosity.

This foralist claim, insofar as Navarre is concerned, as the body of a Catholic demand, which is who represents the soul of an immortal soul and exhilarating spirit, is an episode in our perennial history and a feature of our millennial physiognomy. On countless occasions I have delved into what the historical mission of the Navarrese people is, and I have tried to understand what their predominant essential features are, [and] I have found them in the word "resist." I always conceived of it seated in the blessed shade of the tree of tradition, listening, like the elderly woman by the Catalan sculptor, to the legends and the stories of the centenarian crow; I always observed it changing gradually, coming out of the shadows of the past into the splendor of the future in imperceptible degrees of crepuscular light. And this wandering mission painted in my eyes the image of a cliffy coastline gently cracking, opening up, collapsing, eventually unfolding to become gulfs and bays, yielding better to the silent and incessant action of deep waters, and not to the clamorous rage of waves.

The Vascones, a tribe of the noble Basque race, had little time to enjoy peacefully the plot of land that Providence pointed had out for them for the future in the dispersion of the human family. Soon the Celt launched against them his barbaric hordes, and following stubborn and bloody battles, they had to concede extensive and fertile plains and transform the Ebro into a defensive moat; without even maintaining on its right bank anything other than a strip of land, a relic of their abundant patrimonial heritage, outlining then the boundaries of Navarre with such a vigorous sketch that multiple historical events did not manage to erase them, and they survived all the cataclysms that temporarily shook their borders and boundary markers.

And in the same way that they resisted the Celts, they resisted the Romans tenaciously, and the Goths, and the Arabs, and the Franks of Charlemagne and Louis the Pious, engendering Sanchos and Garcías who recovered the territories unjustly held by the invaders. And being only a handful, but a handful of heroes, surrounded by strong and totally unscrupulous neighbors, achieved the outstanding miracle of preserving unscathed their tiny nationality, despite France, despite Aragón, despite Castile; and they received such bountiful and generous inspiration to be able to go with Don García Sánchez to Alhandega, with Don García the Tremulous to Caltañazor, with Don Sancho the Strong to Las

Navas, with Theobald I to Antioch, with Theobald II to Carthage, with Phillip the Noble to Algeciras, with Charles II to Normandy and Paris, with the prince Royal Duke of Durazzo to Athens and Morea; producing throughout the world the amazement that stems from greatness out of the modest, until that ill-fated day arrived, for which never enough tears have been shed, a day when the Pyrenean mists thickened and blackened into funereal reflections, that day on which Navarre, due to the fratricidal passions of its children, fell exhausted at the feet of Ferdinand the Catholic!

Gentlemen: This people, blessed with an inconceivable power of resistance; this people, who withdrew from the dissolving influence of the great Roman civilization their ethnic personality, as demonstrated by the language, wonderfully beautiful, which still resounds in our valleys, with the fact that the rest of the people in Spain lost their language and accepted Latin, the father of the modern peninsular languages; this people, whose political and civil institutions were always inspired by the desire to perpetuate the past, a desire demonstrated by the freedom to make a will and donations *propter nupcias*, ingeniously combined so that the *natal home* continued to exist, and the surname was perpetuated, and there is abundant evidence of truly *stable* families that served as a perpetual nucleus of condensation throughout these evolutions in history; this people so tied to their way of remaining pure that they raised custom, although against the law, to the category of principal source of their rights; this people, at a special point, present an astonishing exception that should fill us with pride and gratitude. They had their primitive religion: there, on full-moon nights, the worshipped the *nameless god* with symbolic dances and rites and heathen ceremonies, saturated in naturalism. Well, this tenacious, stubborn, brave people, so tied to their opinion, and it would seem, constantly getting angry with all the movements and transformations; this people that resisted all change, precisely in matters that touch the very depths of both individuals and society, where the sensibility is most vivid, and the will to retain most energetic, and the repugnance toward variation most unshakable, when it came to religion, they showed themselves to be more docile, malleable, flexible. The light of the Gospel shone and, his eyes dazzled, the fierce indomitable Basque fell to his knees and, raising his forehead, received the rejuvenating waters of the Baptism. The Vascones, gentlemen, in contrast to all the other peoples of the land, did not make martyrs out of the preachers of the eternal truth: they accepted their teachings submissively, and on that memorable day of their conversion they signed a perpetual pact with the redeeming cross and planted it on the highest peaks of their mountains, and swore to defend it and die for it; a promise they fulfilled yesterday and continue to fulfill today against the unfurled flags of Hell.

The puritan mystic Carlyle, using very broad terms, has said: "our era is characterized by the struggle between belief and non-belief." We will clarify the terms and translate them into Castilian: our era is characterized by the struggle between Catholicism and Rationalism, between *new* law and ancient law, between the Church and the Revolution. This and nothing else is the truth: and this struggle, veiled or manifest, is at the heart of all pending questions. The Church has always had enemies; errors and heresies have always been raised against it; yet these errors and heresies were, to put it one way, merely theological, although they did influence the political system in society just as they influenced the private conduct of the individual: it was never possible to remove even a single stone from the dogmatic edifice without the apparently tiny crack of evil erupting, threatening to flood the world. But error and heresy of an essentially political nature, which looked directly at the governance and system of the state, taking material form in a system that did nothing but apply to the customs and actions of life the principles adopted by the *naturalists*, are modern errors and heresies, children of our time. That system, within the Catholic school, has a technical name all of its own, a name that will prevail against those that attempt to distort it making use of insubstantial distinctions that sound like so many hidden loopholes, and against which, through ignorance or malice, just and honest ways of thinking are applied; that system takes the name of liberty, an inestimable benefit of God, and is termed *Liberalism*. Do you know what, in sum, *Liberalism* is, gentlemen? A system thought up to de-Catholicize nations, contracting principally when it is peaceful to make liberty error, as is happening in now in Spain, and going too far in persecuting truth when it is ferocious, as is happening in now in France, a nation from which we should not avert our eyes because it marks out in advance the path and stages through which, probably, we have to tread, because as Donoso indicated, the French people have climbed the main mast of the Revolution and since then they have been making gestures at all the earth's peoples.

The first explosion of Liberalism in Spain produced, likewise, its first attack on the foral system. Scarcely born, Liberalism killed the fueros: the birth of one and death of the others were almost coetaneous events. Those representatives at the Cadiz Parliament, nursed at the unchaste breasts of the French Revolution, their vacuous minds satiated with the theories of the *Social Pact*, resolved to draw up a *Constitution*.

There is nothing there, gentlemen! Glance through the work of half dozen fashionable authors, borrow a few abstract principles from them, debate them pedantically with citations from Greek and Roman history, take out a couple of dozen sheets of paper, open a bottle of ink, and distribute the aforementioned principles systematically into titles and articles, without forgetting to order that Spaniards be just and fair; and then to believe that this *handbook* of rights and obligations, and that *form* with the national powers, is a true constitution, that is, the mandatory regulation of social life, a reflection of men's convictions surrounding this marvelous and complex universe, a condensation of their moral beliefs and physical necessities, the effect of the convergence of perennially active, mysterious, and profoundly germinative historical forces, like seeds scattered in a furrow, the solid product of time, reason, and experience, is among the most absurdly ridiculous things one can imagine; it is a mistake to think of a doll, supplied with ingenuous resources, as a person. Because the difficult thing, gentlemen, is not *writing down on paper* a constitution, or one hundred constitutions, but creating at the same time men with whom it may be comfortable and exist. That is how the public life of nations subject to similar experiences of a political laboratory oscillated always between coups d'état and revolutions; periods of violent crises cut by other periods of material peace, in which the arbitrary nature of the governments never ceased to be felt.

That is how, at the end of the day, the legislators in Cadiz presented their new constitution, and which, on presenting it, in a celebrated preface or prologue, they said: ". . . the meeting of Aragón and Castile was followed, very shortly thereafter, by a loss of liberty, and the yoke was aggravated in such a way that lately we had lost, it is painful to say, even an idea of our dignity; if one exempts the happy Basque provinces and Kingdom of Navarre, which, presenting at each step in their venerable fueros a dreadful protest and complaint against the usurpations of the government, and an overpowering reprimand for the rest of Spain on account of their dishonorable suffering, roused unremittingly the fears of the court, etc."

Of the Navarrese the distinguished Father Isla said that, "after consecrated Jesus, what they love most deeply are their fueros and liberties." Consider, gentlemen, the pleasure that the words of the constitutional commission would have caused in Navarre, all the more so since Phillip IV, the degenerate monarchy had been emphasizing its plan to abolish the regional institutions and replace all the other powers in Spain. Now our fueros were strong and safe! Now the central government, instead of sabotaging them cunningly, presented them before the eyes of Spaniards as a sign of glory and made of them the archetype of restored liberties! Now the compassionate hands of the Cadiz legislators, moved by filial veneration, were going to heal the wounds that the fueros received from the overbearing and arrogant kings! The golden age that optimistic progressivism established in Spain was going to yield its richest and most exquisite fruits on Navarrese land.

This flattering picture, believe it, without any doubt, gentlemen, which was a reality… but no, do not believe it, you have not even believed it for one moment, because you know Liberalism, of which Donoso said that its task is to proclaim existences that it annuls, and annul the existences that it proclaims. And as, truly, this is one of its tasks, showing itself to be more absolute than monarchs due to its abominations, and even more of an enemy of homeland traditions than the Frenchified Baiona Parliament, at the same time that it was exhorting and extolling the fueros in the preamble to the Constitution, abolished and eradicated them calmly in the text, fabricating with the stone ruins new temples of horrendous idolatry of the so-called *constitutional unity*. That parliament was sketched perfectly out of this kind of physiognomy: it came into parliamentary life via the door of perjury, and entered into political life via that of lies.

Navarre never accepted the work of the Cadiz Parliament that, in one single stroke, hurt its pure religious beliefs and offended its secular rights. Our grandparents' mood would be revealed broadly in the following paragraphs by the representation that, in the name of the Kingdom of Navarre and as its commissioners, Lieutenant General Don Javier de Elío and his brother Don Joaquín placed in the hands of Don Ferdinand VII on May 20, 1814:

> H. M., whom divine Providence destined for the throne of the Spains to fulfill their happiness and be the protector of the Holy Religion of our fathers, you know full well the value of the oath that, by the example of your august predecessors and as a consequence of the said Constitution (that of Navarre), in the capacity as prince heir to the throne you deigned to offer . . . and Navarre would think it were offending the delicate conscience of H. M. if to this testimony falling from heaven and to the other similar one that the Provincial Council of Navarre, surrounded by risks, created in the face of the Spains and its enemies in the Cathedral of the City of Tutera [Tudela] in September 1808, proclaiming him the legitimate sovereign, were added other outstanding titles of the many one could recall in order to accredit the justice of this respectable request; since it is a fact that a demarcated Catholic prince, as

is H. M., for a model of the righteous in the pageantry of the future, is merely the imperious voice of Religion falling from heaven pronounced from the Throne of God Himself, that which is exclusively decisive in every matter, without consideration of human reflections, and to whose empire yield the specious titles with which politics, in the interest of violence, extortions, and artifices, could present as voluntary the acceptance of a new Constitution that always detested the kingdom, and did not even, in fact, manage to be carried out but its legitimate representatives, which are the Three Estates, congregating, which should make in effect the Parliament, in which, together with the sovereign (which is and will always be H. M.), only reside the faculties to alter, add, or clarify the precious treasure of its fundamental institutions.

If time, sir, were allowed to throw a veil over this farce or acceptance, made between tumult and force, one of the most brilliant merits that the kingdom could incur, as a gift to H. M., and the just cause of the Nation, would appear. Far from having subscribed to the said new Constitution, it has always given the external appearance of express disapproval, distancing itself from the system that most of the provinces observed, from congratulating the Parliament for establishing it, the abolition of the Inquisition, the decree of February 2, and other reforms, and asking openly for the same Parliament to convoke that of Navarre, to resolve its own particular things, by means of a substitute representative, during the first moments in which most of the Kingdom was free of enemy oppression, as it would result from its laws, and having the glory of being, perhaps, the only one that by these same principles did not want to fix the tombstone of the Constitution in the square of its capital, in order to avoid in the future that which brought about that burden; and of assuring H. M. that even the insignificant passive tolerance in its publication was premeditated work for the good of H. M. and the entire Nation, with the aim of avoiding the ill-fated results of a civil war, which was inevitable with the Parliament and the provinces that had sworn it . . . capable of having hindered the course of the victories and triumphs of the allied armies (Archivo de la Diputación. Sección de legislación y contrafueros. Legajo 22. Carpeta 33).

It concluded by asking for the repossession of the fueros and liberties of the kingdom that Don Ferdinand VII, a morally undeserving object of such ardent and loyal love that Spaniards professed toward him, reestablished in effect, although in fact he mutilated and infringed them on repeated occasions, because he loved the royal absolutism that many of his predecessors managed to implant too much. The Old Regime also often strayed from the straight path and the monarchs overstepped the mark of their legitimate faculties, so that it is not befitting, to the detriment of modern license, to rehabilitate or attenuate their attacks on the honest Christian liberty of peoples.

Excuse me, gentlemen, this long citation, which seems to me very interesting because it reveals to us the formative period of the dominant public spirit in Navarre, a spirit that is the driving force of the tenacious and most vigorous resistance to the Revolution, opposed by this ancient kingdom. The second constitutional era, initiated by Riego's uprising, found the meager Navarrese liberal element swelled through the personal influence of General Espoz y Mina on his old comrades in arms and his enthusiastic friends; but also the traditionalist spirit more alive, energetic, and awake. The name of the decrepit revolutionary hero generated little more than execration. Hearing him cheer on Riego and ignite disturbances and confrontations was one and the same thing. This hatred was revealed clearly on Saint Joseph's Day in the year 1822 in Pamplona, when the fine temple of the Pamplona youth once again demonstrated its credentials. The Imperial Alejandro regiment, noted for its revolutionary passions, having been challenged seriously by the civilian population, sent a certain furious statement to Congress, completely worthy of the perversity of its ideas and its cowardice, describing the city as a "revolutionary flashpoint," "disobedient and despicable," calling for it to be "outlawed" and that, "if considered necessary, that such a town should disappear from the peninsular map." The youth, acclaiming religion, the fueros, and the king, threw themselves into the fray and constituted the real division of Navarre.

As one can see, once the great struggle between ancient and modern Spain began, Navarre steadfastly took a position among the ranks of the former, remaining loyal to its incontrovertible tradition of *resisting*. It fought, shedding blood from its veins and spending the gold in its chests without limits or measure. It was brave and generous, innocent, trusting, and loyal, inaccessible to self-interest, disillusion, ingratitude. In the face of such deeds, I salute it as one salutes heroes and martyrs, and I kiss the land irrigated by such very noble blood, shed—Oh, who could not ignore it! —in the shadow of newfangled flags. Navarre, gentlemen, made a mistake ideologically in identifying the cause, to some extent eternal, it was defending with a cause deprived of foral qualifications, with the cause of a gentleman "who can die." And when, despite so much sacrifice, and despite not having lacked favorable situations and convenient occasions, Navarre was defeated, those of you who fought for the banner of Don Carlos are authorized to repeat those memorable words that one of his favorites today, Mr. Llauder, expressed on March 21, 1876:

> More than time itself, H. M. will not want to achieve his mission without using the means that the experience of the past and good sense demand, just as a building cannot be built without the materials that are required for it, or with others that are not indispensable to finish it. The facts have shown, moreover, that it would be useless to try; for no matter how much plotting, no matter how serious the crises of Spain were, how much money was raised, no matter how many armies were formed, H. M.

would never reign *because God would turn against us*, as he already did, and because Spain would not call on H. M. to see in him its salvation.

Yet taking all things into consideration carefully, it is of no use repeating these words: for the ties that bound you to Don Carlos have been broken forever.

The resistance movement against constitutionalism corresponds to another, to some extent parallel, movement against foralism. History records the dates of 1820, 1834, 1837, 1841, 1844, 1847, and 1876, as testament to the rage of liberal parties against the Basque-Navarrese fueros. In mid-1841, the usurping provincial council, behind the back of foral legality, arranged with a progressive government a certain modification of the fueros that is the downward slope by which Navarre, wounded by paralysis, is slipping toward constitutional unity. The concessions and renunciations that Navarre did then led to the state. The same thing did not happen with the recognition of foral rights by the government; that recognition has been subject to perpetual revision and the iniquitous trial of bad faith and force.

In this dealing between Liberalism and the fueros, it has been common to confuse concepts that should be differentiated carefully, because confusion usually serves as a parapet behind which some totally erroneous conclusions are defended. If within the fueros we were to distinguish between form and spirit, the foral bodies and the legislation that those bodies produced and contained, we would see that the fueros are not incompatible *per se*, throughout their range, with Liberalism. What are the fueros? The particular rights of a country, autonomous constitutions of independent ancient nationalities that they preserved and retained on joining together with a larger nationality. Moreover, as these nationalities were Catholic, of course their legislation was Catholic as well. This, and no other, is the specific point at which, essentially, the fueros and Liberalism are incompatible, to the same extent and proportion that the Catholic spirit and the naturalist spirit, which inform them respectively, are opposed to one another.

Let us assume that Spanish liberalism, perched on central government, instead of sponsoring *unitary* solutions, had sponsored *federal* solutions: foral forms and bodies would have fit perfectly well within the national constitution. The conflict would have erupted in another way, being more obvious; because as these bodies, assuming the Catholic spirit burning within them, would have had to detest and reject the modern liberties of conscience, teaching, publishing, association, etc., Liberalism would have had to try and safeguard their exercise by means of a federal constitution, restricting, on this point, *the legislative power* of the state or provinces. This is the procedure that most of the modern federal constitutions adopted, and that which the school of Mr. Pi y Margall extolls. Because thinking that Liberalism must acknowledge fully autonomous powers wherever its dominance is not assured, even if just in a wretched corner of the national territory, reflects the delusions of a sick person: for such cases of danger it reserves the supreme resource of suppressing liberty, that liberty it invokes so hypocritically all the time.

Meditating, as I do, on a liberalism that would respect foral bodies is meditating within pure *theory*, when it comes to looking at Spain. The liberalism we know in our homeland, *historic* Spanish liberalism, that from the Cadiz Parliament and Argüelles, to Mr. Cánovas del Castillo and the Restoration Parliament, without neglecting to take into account the liberal republicanism that was babbled about in the dense wild oratory of Mr. Castelar, which is based on the sibylline tripod of the Salmerón's arcana, and which is acclaimed and settled in the *officious* revolutionary thought of Mr. Ruiz Zorrilla, is a liberalism that is an enemy of the foral form and spirit, a liberalism that broke the extremely beautiful glass and spilled the even more beautiful liquor that it contained. And of course! Is there by chance anyone who does not know what the *trademark* is of Spanish liberalism? The world has never witnessed such complete intellectual sterility as that of the liberal parties of Spain; they have copied everything, they have imitated everything, they have translated everything; they never invented anything, not even a *cursed party*, gentlemen, which, at first sight, seems like a very pure and national thing. There are varieties within the specific unity of liberalism: there is, for example, Anglo-Saxon Protestant liberalism, and French philosophical revolutionary liberalism. Well, it is the latter that crossed the Pyrenees, although there was never a lack in our parliaments of half a dozen "English-style" liberals that used to enhance the debates, saying things that no one had given any thought to after applauding them. Ultra-Pyrenean liberalism, for perfectly well-known reasons, which are the "classical" spirit, distinctive of the French temper, and the disastrous policies of the conceited absolute monarchy, which abolished several institutions that had served as a brake and a limit on it, has taken on, since then, a markedly unitary and centralizing character, supportive of the omnipotence of the state; liberalism that, after inventing all that about the *one and indivisible Republic*, and guillotining the melodious Girondins, who were guilty of federalism, produced, logically, the Caesarian empire of Napoleon I. Had Anglo-Saxon liberalism taken root in Spain, one would assume that the foral bodies would have persisted. Unquestionably, gentlemen, that liberalism possesses a high degree of "historical meaning" of which Latin liberalism lacks any trace whatsoever, and what is more it is repulsed by any extension of state responsibilities or functions elsewhere. It is better, equally, to take into account that this liberalism showed itself to be easily respectful of historical and local institutions where they were informed by the Protestant spirit; yet it barely perceived in them the aroma of Catholicism, respect was more awkward, and it repudiated its traditions and mutilated its programs. An example of what I am talking about is Ireland. With all that, the impossibility of any other convenient solution, the very utility of England, the legal precedents and imperatives of justice, deftly gauged by Gladstone's generous talent, would achieve, make no mistake, gentlemen, sooner or later, uprooting its prey to the British leopard.

Whoever seeks to understand at root the true ideas and sincere sentiments of Spanish liberalism with regard to the fueros, should go over the debate in Congress in the year 1876 on abolishing those of the Basque provinces and modifying again those of Navarre.

I will ignore the sophisms, the historical lies, the truncations of privileges, resulting from the commission regarding the works of the falsifier Llorente; I will disregard the repugnant allegation of force made by Mr. Cánovas del Castillo, and I will go in search of the political thought of the school in a certain speech by the fusionist Mr. Navarro y Rodrigo:

> The government must have been inspired by that most noble and broad criterion of homeland that has inspired the policies of the great and true statesmen, the policies of Cisneros and Richelieu, which were *based on the most* ... by the policies of our contemporary men of state, by Bismarck and Cavour, who did not turn to *disregarding trivialities* in order to create the astonishing unity of Germany and Italy ... Measures of a *general character*, measures whose benefits extended to everyone, this is what is important: *it does not matter if some get hurt.* No, Cisneros and Richelieu did not take into account the interests that could cause harm when creating their glorious and grand nationalities, the complaints of the small kingdoms and the small principalities, which had to blend into the great melting pot of German unity, did not stop Bismarck in the work he carried out before the eyes of modern Europe ... *Particularisms have had their day, they are no longer in fashion. Everywhere there is a move toward unity and to strengthening the action of central power...*

This is how, in 1876, the representatives of the old progressivism expressed themselves, in perplexed Frenchified language! What strange people! Their clocks stopped in 1812, and they have not worked out how to get them ticking again since! You are definitely out of fashion! Time is sweeping you aside and dissolving you, stunning you first of all with the proposal of awful social problems that your paper constitutions or your declarations of rights or your national sovereignty never envisaged! The hordes of people incited by you hold out their hands, not to buy national goods, but to put them in the pockets of your well-behaved and peaceful *bourgeoisie*, showing that the Revolution, even though a chaotic thing, a disorganized movement, an epileptic fit, has its own tremendous and inescapable logic!

Let us return now, gentlemen, to look at another victim that is infinitely higher and more august than the fueros, at the sacrosanct religion (which also began to suffer under the Cadiz Parliament). Let us sketch out, if our tears allow, the picture that represents simple religious tolerance in the Constitution, stretched out by a sectarian spirit through to a broad freedom of worship; we see professorships in institutes and universities, sustained by the money of Catholic contributors, occupied by men of perverse ideas who darken, perhaps forever, the intelligence and the heart of the young; let us parry like the stupid practice of duels; condemned by the Church, by the Code, and still more by the most rudimentary common sense, it finds scandalous observers including ministers of the Crown and, on the part of the authorities, all the complicity and tolerance it needs in order to execute on a daily basis its often *simulated* deeds and flamboyant *simulations*; let us list all the revealing symptoms and signals that the "liberties of perdition," as His Holiness Leo XIII has termed them, have come to us at a time of their greatest splendor and vigor: a notoriously influential freemasonry in politics, in which it occupies the highest posts, publishing newspapers, disseminating its errors, rubbing shoulders with legal and honest associations, taking delight publicly in congresses and banquets in which it carries out that miracle of making what is dreadful appear ridiculous; a certain section of the printed press slandering systematically religious people, ridiculing spiritual ceremonies, attacking Catholic dogmas, mocking Christian morals, propagating crude superstitions, false religions, and materialist, pantheist, positivist, and skeptical systems, whose succession and rapid movement, although incapable of producing a defined tendency in Spanish thought, turns out the lights of faith in many intelligences; meetings, talks, and gatherings in which the fundamental truths of the moral, social, and juridical order are rejected and fought against; where not long after blasphemy and impiety, the defense of theft and murder reverberates; where the future punishment of modern society is indoctrinated, that is, the atheist, socialist, communist, collectivist, and anarchist proletariat, capable of dying fanatically besides an oil can and of seeking social regeneration in the cowardly and vile dynamite firecracker, without governments knowing anything else to do except punish, with senile intermittence, such shameless and brutal attacks on the monarchy, because those attacks are still left to run free soon after being carried out with composure: the pornographic mire extending everywhere and affecting the most chaste homes with its foul material of a corrupt society . . .

But, what else, gentlemen? The Spanish Episcopate meeting in the always heroic city of Zaragoza, on the occasion of holding the Second Catholic Congress, raised to the throne a kind of memorial of grievances and demonstration of Catholic aspirations as regards a law of public education that fulfills the promises recorded in the current Constitution and the Concordat, in establishing in Alcalá de Henares a general seminary of higher ecclesiastical studies and the handing over of a church university to convert it into a free autonomous university, in the sanctification of public holidays, in the frequent invasions of ministerial legislation in Concordat matters, in the forgetting of certain rulings in the Concordat; in the execution of article 23 of the Concordat, which saves from expropriation rectors' homes in every parish and their vegetable gardens; in the failure to fulfill article 37, which establishes the reserve fund with which the reverend bishops must attend to sick clergy, to rundown churches, and many other needs not foreseen within general attention; in the lack of specific rulings that impede the abuse and scandal on the part of some idiots that, overcome with passion, feign to apostatize religion with no other motive than acquiring a union prohibited by ecclesiastical laws and sometimes even by natural law; in the awarding of the necessary authority so that conscripts may contract marriage on the day they are sent to the heart of their family with indefinite license; in the protection that religious service prepared in seminaries deserves.

Never mind that these aspirations were so reasonable in themselves that not even the most forewarned could brand them exaggerated; never mind that they were adapted to basic law and fit within the prevailing legal body; never mind that they were preceded by the most solemn and clear adhesion to the governing dynasty, an act that, perhaps, was the initial point in the most important political evolution of the century, that is, the recognition of the current forms of government and the principles that symbolize them by the Catholic people; never mind that political prudence and love for the constitutional monarchy and the Alphonsine dynasty, so often indiscreetly and excessively careful, advised favoring that evolution, the government ignored these aspirations, and although it seemed willing to fulfill, in part, the sanctification of the festivals, it was perhaps moved to do so more by the connections the point presented with the social question than religious zeal.

Our political life, gentlemen, is that of *legal hypothesis*. One must be under no illusions; *legal* hypothesis, sooner or later, will bring *social* hypothesis: for this, precisely, tireless astute revolution has been invented. There are, in Spain, cities, districts, and, I would even dare to say, regions in which this hypothesis has already consummated traces, although it may seem diluted and dissolved within the great copy of healthy and incorrupt elements. If Spain, considered as a *whole*, belongs to the *Catholic thesis*, degenerate and corrupt members of it drowned in the abyss of error and evil. It was only a few days ago, even, that the illustrious Catholic orator Mr. Nocedal said in Congress: "Defense would have been easier at the beginning; perhaps soon, if this continues, it will be late. But today there are still elements and forces, if they sit there (on the *blue bench*), that are not fervent Catholics now, but true men of state in order to contain the most extreme ones of the revolution and restore what was lost." Consider seriously these words and, persuaded of the things that invariably must entail, if followed thus, from this path: first, the tolerance of error; then, its comparison to truth, and, finally, the seigneury of error that, representative of government and raised to the courts, will put shackles and gags on the truth.

Navarre will be among the last of the peoples to give in. Here, thanks to God, Catholicism is the continent of all life, individual, familiar, and social. Christ reigns over the home and over the public square. Observe how the most extreme opinions, transplanted in Navarre, are toned down, lose their salient angles, and sharp thorns: this blessed territory only tolerates, for the moment, the frailer yields of the revolution. Total infection, were it to occur, will come late; the danger, with all that, exists, and he who does not see it is blind.

One remedy alone has been discovered. One must struggle without fainting to preserve what makes up our pure, original, Navarrese physiognomy: the customs inherited, the laws regulating our patriarchal family, the remains of our administrative autonomy that remove us from the direct influence of the modern state, to the exasperating influence of governments that, elsewhere, have managed to make many consciences with suggestions of self-interest capitulate and succumb. But this is little, gentlemen, with being much; one must with all obstinacy, resolve, and the valor of our invincible race undertake claims to the ancient liberties and achieve, after this ill-fated parenthesis, an opening of the doors of the *Precious* to prepare a clear way for Navarrese legislators. The Catalans meeting in the immortal Manresa registered, a short while ago, on the flag of their aspirations, the meeting of the Catalan Parliament; the desire for administrative and political reconstitution, "*quals primers vagits,*" in the words of the distinguished propagandist from Sabadell, "*acaban de dexarse oir al general alegria desde la vehina ciutat de Manresa, que ora com en temps de la Reconquesta está destinada á esser tal volta nostra Covadonga.*" Since the Revolution triumphed eradicating the regional institutions, let us beat it, in turn, by restoring them, a very old and wholly true adage of taking advice from the enemy. And if one day we can only be freed from the *social* hypothesis that has seized Spain by the Navarrese Parliament, from whose hands, as well as other less important benefits, we will receive the Catholic legislation our consciousness demands.

My distinguished friend Don Fidel de Sagarmínaga, the master of the good foralists, in a patriotic book said: "The Basque-Navarrese Country cannot renounce its autonomy. It is very important that this argument remains recorded in everyone's minds. The Basque-Navarrese Country does not favor any political system other than that resulting from the reestablishment of its autonomy..." Yet autonomy, if it must be real and complete, requires the Basque-Navarrese Country to regain its own legislative power. We should pursue, non-stop, foral restoration, which represents a right that no one, legitimately, can hold over us, and let us make of it the instrument for Catholic restoration.

What a beautiful flag, gentlemen! We all fit under its ample folds, as true Catholics and foralists, and do not look too closely at the name it takes, but at the goal it proposes. This policy, practiced with prudence and resolve, will make the future of Navarre match its past, given that the present is so paltry and miserable. Animated by its virtue, we would turn round to see our homeland resembling the glorious Archangel of Aralar, with his sparkling sword in his right hand and Evil enchained, biting the dust, beneath his soles.

Forgive me, gentlemen, for taking up so much of your kind attention; I appreciate it profoundly. On taking our leave, let us gather in a call to aspirations that are common to us all: Navarre, for our Lord Jesus Christ! Navarre, for its Christian freedom!—

I have spoken

Chapter 4

Speech in the Congress of Deputies on May 24, 1893

It is parliamentary custom, honorable representatives, that the voice of all opinions represented in the chamber be heard during the debate on the Speech. In part out of respect for this custom, I decided to take up your attention so soon, when I had barely taken a seat on these benches. And it is, on the other hand, clear that I am not well-known, nor am I blessed with singularities in my oratory that may excuse or mitigate this haste to extend my words to the chamber in which men of real political importance and regally eloquent orators meet together and congregate.

A novice in parliamentary elections, devoid of the qualities that the Spanish gallery, one of the most distinguished in the world, demands, I must struggle against the obstacles that stem from my personal insignificance, joined to those from which may be aroused the professing of some ideas that, unfortunately, may not gain your sympathy. To a good degree, gentlemen, I would seal my lips now, if the circumstance of being currently the only representative of purely Catholic and foral ideas, without involving any party politics, did not impel me to open them, and if the hope in your benevolent courtesy did not encourage me to do so ... That benevolence, which, as my illustrious friend Mr. Nocedal recalled on a similar occasion, the strong owe the weak, and I, putting to one side all rhetorical artifice, spiritedly reclaim from you!

It is with much pleasure that I take the opportunity with which this broad and tolerant debate affords me, which allows me to ratify before parliament the professing of ideas that I expressed before the electoral body of Navarre, and they are none other than those of obtaining through effort, within the established legality or that from hereon may be established, the greatest splendor of the Church and the restoration of political traditions that made Spain so great.

These ideas place me naturally against the government that occupies these benches, just as it would have against those that preceded it, given that the feature of all of them is to lead the direction of public business toward the left, giving way to the continuation of the insatiable aspirations of the revolution, flooding all the laws with an increasingly radical liberalism, and distancing themselves to the same extent from the aspirations of the hordes that pray and pay, as if they did not represent the important forces within society, and if it were fair and even prudent, and above all worthy of judicious men of state to disregard them continuously, abusing their generosity.

Everywhere, the scarce influence exercised by the Spanish Catholic people in political life weighs us down. This is well demonstrated by the situation of the Church in Spain, which does not correspond at all to the untarnished Catholicism of most Spaniards. The following words by the Honorable Archbishop of Oviedo, in his pastoral letter of March 16, 1890, provoke deep sorrow in one's mind:

> In an eminent and almost exclusively Catholic nation, with a Constitution that does not, to be sure, match the legitimate aspirations of Catholics, but that is less liberal than most styled as such today, and with governments that, as a general rule, maintain good relations with the Sovereign Pontiff and resolve to agree with His Holiness on most s'-called mixed questions, Catholic interests in the higher spheres of governing the state and in co-legislative bodies are more abandoned than in some Protestant countries. Germany has just extended military service to Catholic seminarians; Switzerland and the United States establish pontifical universities; the day of our Lord respected elsewhere, including even prohibiting the circulation of trains; obscene writings are banned; the Catholic faith prospers, and the same authorities surround the true religion with prestige,

while here we see, painfully, that even stipulations agreed on with and promises made to the Holy See in the Concordat are a dead letter in matters of vital interest to the Church...

What can I or anyone add, honorable representatives, that improves on this austere and concise allegation of grievances? On the positive side, the ravages of liberal legislation have extended everywhere. The Catholic congresses and Prelates, like the distinguished Archbishop of Valladolid and his suffragan bishops, complain, in the form of reverent statements, about the harm the Church is suffering: governments systematically neglect them. The penal code, far from protecting, in as many cases and occasions as it should, the rights and prerogatives of our sacrosanct religion, puts it on the same level in the offenses that punish false worship: against this comparison and the deficient penalties they protest, accordingly, for the rights of religious truth and the honor of Catholics.

Freemasonry, despite the repeated condemnations of the Holy See, instead of attracting the punishments of law, obtains its protection: it exhibits its organization and hierarchy everywhere, ridiculous imitations, if they were not so vile, of the true Church, and diffuses its foul doctrines, and as public opinion is not mistaken, it elevates its unhappy sectarians to the highest positions in the nation. Article 2 of the Concordat, among others, is violated scandalously in teaching material; now all errors and heresies, however obvious, have become acceptable in universities, in high schools, in text books, in teaching establishments, without the state getting worked up about those who constantly mock and fight its official religion, maintained with the money of Catholics.

The scarce guarantees that the Constitution included in favor of the Catholic truth a crumbling one after the other, undermined by increasingly liberal interpretations. Now we have the liberal coalition pact, the famous formula of Mr. Montero Ríos and Mr. Alonso Martínez, which threatens all of them. Referring to the rights included in art. 12 of the basic Code, fusionism promised that no laws could veto them, or restrict them, or oppose their possession or exercise for any reason, *including religion*. This is the hostile spirit that encourages the governing party: it has demonstrated so very well, twisting art. 11 of the Constitution so that quite a few apostate concubinator clerics and priests, devotees of the pound sterling, only worthy of punishment and scorn, may, comfortably and ostensibly, offend God.

The courts of justice, their witness stands placed in the shadow of the trial of Pontius Pilate, follow in the steps of and infringe on ecclesiastic immunity, and the governments of His Catholic Majesty, turning a deaf ear to the Pope's shouts, as well as not making any attempt to do anything resulting beneficial, short- or long-term, for the just and necessary freedom of the Pontificate, maintain very cordial, warm relations, like brothers in the European revolution, with the sacrilegious usurpers of Rome: say it, if not, that extraordinary embassy to celebrate the silver wedding anniversaries, or whatever they were, you had sent to Umberto of Savoy.

If one had to address in the detail they deserve each of the points that make up this chapter of charges, one would have to extend this speech beyond the limits of my intentions, which can be summed up in some simple demonstrations that are, to put it one way, like the life faith of a minority whose name has still resounded in Congress debates. Moreover, despite these intentions, I cannot help but focus for a moment, however briefly, in the face of a matter of religious or, more accurately, irreligious policy by the current government, which has hurt the feelings of the Spanish Catholic population more deeply, although I must abstain from its legal aspect on account of running out of orators that preceded me in the use of the word: I am referring to the opening of the Protestant church or chapel.

This issue presents a characteristic feature that imbues it with its own, truly indelible, physiognomy. And the thing is that, not only has Mr. Sagasta's government overlooked the letter and spirit of the Constitution in order to abide by the spirit and letter of the liberal coalition's formula, but it has overlooked it using aggravated procedures that add an adulteration of the constitutional text to the scenario.

In effect, all the archbishops and bishops of Spain unanimously complained about the opening of Protestant churches, and despite that, Mr. Sagasta allowed them to be opened. I want to assume, for a moment, that the prelates were wrong in their interpretation of art. 1, they would have made a juridical mistake in discussing it and explaining it in the way they did. Well, with all that, Mr. Sagasta's government, if it sought to behave in a truly Catholic way, should have lowered its head and accepted humbly, with filial reverence, the Episcopate's criterion, whether it thought it erroneous or not, legally speaking. But it did not do so, and it superimposed its private justice over Church justice, which is a foolproof sign of liberalism. And as the honorable member is afforded so many abilities, he did not permit the opening until after the electoral period, with the goal that the friends of the honorable member were in a comfortable situation to prowl about for Catholic votes.

My dear friend Mr. Nocedal said in one of his marvelous speeches: "I'm Catholic, I'm Spanish, and I'm nothing else..." I repeat the same thing, absolutely the same thing, and in the same scope and sense. I have sketched out the abysses that, in the manner of understanding the religious question, I distance myself from the vast majority of you ... not from your persons, among whom many deserve my admiration for your talent, as well as all my respect, but from your ideas. In the purely political terrain our differences are neither small or light or fleeting, and it suits me more to offer them in bulk, insofar as the government is intent on finishing with the ancient local liberties of Spain. A son of the most noble and ancient Basque race, my love for the Basque-Navarrese fueros is one of the most vivid points of affection in my soul. In this regard, too, I repudiate with all my energy the abuses of liberalism, a continuation of the absolute monarchy of the Bourbons. Those provinces confirmed a perfect right to their foral system, and I protest solemnly against all the laws and decrees that have stripped them of these. This love, although intense, is not exclusivist and extends to all the regions of Spain that have preserved or are recovering the consciousness of their historical personality. Each and every one of them will find me at their side when they call for their lost privilege, inspired by the worship of their Catholic and patriotic traditions, their laws, and their indigenous language. My formula is: for the regions against the central state, without any limitations other than those of truth and justice. I want a Spain united by faith, by the spiritual ties of Catholic civilization, by the intimate sentiment of common nationality, provided with appropriate bodies: not in any way a congregation of anonymous inert provinces, imprisoned in the netting of centralizing unitary systems, obsequiously copied and translated. I wish that in this most beautiful Spanish sky those splendid stars that are called Aragón, Castile, Catalonia, Galicia, Navarre, Valencia, Bizkaia…—an incomparable constellation in world history!—would shine brightly once more.

The liberal parties, which are inspired by cold and pulverizing rationalism, are incapable of bringing about such miracles. The restoration of the religion of the homeland is the prize that God must award the Catholic party, if Catholics listen to the Pope's voice, and form in a tight phalanx. The Catholic faith… Ah, honorable representatives! How sad I am to pronounce such words! I see liberal parties, political parties everywhere… but the Spanish Catholic party nowhere before my eyes. I must not do, at least consciously, from this place anything to oppose the unity of Catholics and being content only with the will of the patient, wise, venerable, thoroughly strong, and meek immortal Pontiff Leo XIII, whose words I listen to on my bended knees and my forehead prostrate on the ground. The formation of a large Catholic party is necessary. Do you know why, honorable representatives? In order to root out liberalism from the laws, as darnel is rooted out from wheat, and to restore the Catholic regional liberties in our homeland.

I have spoken.

Chapter 5

Speech in the Congress of Deputies on July 22, 1893

Honorable representatives:

I find no better launch for my speech than the memory of a certain thought, on account of one of the most illustrious men in this chamber, Mr. Cánovas del Castillo: "with reason or without it, one must be with one's homeland, as one is with a father and a mother." I stand up, gentlemen, to fulfill, inspired by the finest will of my soul, a filial duty: that of defending my native land, and defending it, thanks be to God, with such splendid clear reason, that it could only be obscured, although not hidden, by the deficiency of my own resources and the dearth of my faculties. I beg of you, then, honorable representatives, that if, despite my intentions of not exceeding the limits of moderation, you take my words with bitterness or feelings of anger, forgive them magnanimously, thinking that, before the misfortunes of their mothers, good children think more with the heart than with the head.

We Navarrese representatives are here fulfilling the traditional mission of our race, which both in ancient and modern, and even in contemporary, history is expressed by the verb "resist." We are here writing a new chapter of that history without parallel that shows Basques defending their territory, their house, their home, their customs, their language, their beliefs, against the brutal ambition of Celts, Romans, Goths, Franks, Arabs, and achieving the miracle of preserving unscathed, throughout many centuries, their minute nationality, despite France, despite Aragón, despite Castile, always defeated, in the end, by that fistful of heroes. And bear in mind, gentlemen, how few times the Basques, how few times the Navarrese, were the aggressors. Notwithstanding being blessed with eminent warlike qualities, they barely experienced the passion of conquest, which so dominates other peoples. Yesterday's history is today's history; and in the same way our immortal ancestors defended their home soil against foreign attacks that they did not provoke, we are now defending our rights against those who, to be called enemies, would have to first apostatize the such sweet faith of brothers that unites us all.

That ministry, honorable representatives, is a kind of earthquake; at least, throughout all the regions in the peninsula it produced tremors and movements. Everything shook, moved, and cracked, except high-backed chair of Mr. Gamazo, who remained firmly seated in the well fertilized field of public loans. Indeed, it is admirable how the imperturbability of the president of the council, giving peace to the needle with which Celestina used to sew, conscious that Mr. Gamazo uses and abuses his position as a minister of the Crown, waiting for a more intense seismic phenomenon than the others, should bring down, with the aforementioned high-backed chair, and bury definitively the ministry he occupies. But Machiavellianism, even if from La Rioja, is often passed off as being clever, and it was easy for the great explosion to do away with the ministry, and the arrogant dissident and vindictive leader, on the same level, turned.

Among the various conflicts provoked by the minister for finance, none exceeded in seriousness and importance that regarding Navarre. Article 35 of the draft budget law is very serious because it violates justice openly, in the first instance, imposing tax rates and charges on those from whom they are exempt; and it is most serious moreover because, unnecessarily and in order to achieve a clearly paltry result, which is the relatively small increase in a contribution that will not save the internal revenue service, it poses a capitalist issue for constitutional law, placing a Spanish region in a fix by prohibiting the legislative power of its parliament with the king on certain economic-administrative matters it is responsible for, and prohibiting it so firmly and energetically that they may even have to consider maintaining public order.

The conduct of the minister of finance is more than imprudent, it is imprudence itself; and I cannot find harsh enough words to classify it, especially since it concerns a person of such obvious talent. Real men of state do not provoke conflicts, but instead avoid and prevent them; and even tough reason may help them, something that did not happen with the honorable member and Navarre, they weigh up scrupulously the benefits they may generate and the damages that may result from their projects, and they refrain from formulating them when the latter outweigh the former. And above all, men of state study conscientiously the opportunity and moment for their reforms. This is a study that the honorable member has not carried out, and that would have stopped him from falling into the absurd position of increasing the taxes in a country that finds itself completely ruined. This is a lack of tact and political sense in a big way, and that would have been enough at any other time for the president of the council of ministers to provoke a crisis, to not feel persecuted, as he is at the moment according to malicious tongues, by means of approving the budget, to the total discredit of Mr. Gamazo.

Art. 35 is a new demonstration of the absolutism of the modern state, embodied in the parliament, since royal sanction, through the effect of typical "government by cabinet," befitting of a parliamentary system, is in fact a mere formula, a pure soulless mechanism, and the monarchy tends to be reduced increasingly to a strictly theatrical and decorative institution, "imposing," as Bagehot would say, subordinate to another truly "efficient" institution, which is parliament. Absolute is all power that does not recognize limits or boundaries in the exercise of its faculties; that today modifies the civil rights of people, tomorrow transforms property, and the day after destroys the historic constitutions of people; that places its heavy and brutal hand on all spheres of individual and collective life, without excepting religion. The modern sate, composed exclusively of philosophical elements, the organ of that terrible destructive power that we may term "reasoning reason," is more absolute than the Caesars themselves and the Oriental sovereigns. It constitutes the steep slope down which societies must slip and fall into the despotism that Tocqueville predicted, of which he said that, "it will degrade men without tormenting them."

In effect, art. 35 argues implicitly that the Spanish state does not recognize the existence of rights that limit its law, although they may take on the form of *pacts* or *agreements*. That is to say, honorable representatives, that the Spanish state functions so as to negate and deny that Navarre was an independent kingdom, a perfect nation, a separate nation, later united to other kingdoms and a nation, to another monarchy, as our classic politicians used to say, through the figure of the prince, but distinct in territory, jurisdiction, and laws; and finally, by virtue of the modifications that time brought with it, a province in the Kingdom of Spain, but not a province identical to the rest, but a province blessed with the characteristic physiognomy of its own individuality, in part subject to the immediate sovereignty of the king and parliament, and in part, although modestly, exempt from it.

Against these pretensions of state there is no remedy at our disposal but to deny it jurisdiction and authority in understanding that it alone has that in the economic-administrative matters of Navarre. It is, therefore, a true question of authority by *request*, that which we Navarrese representatives have promoted before the parliament of the nation. Our principal defense rests on demonstrating, as we are doing, that the legal state of Navarre is shielded by a pact whose content and form belong to international private law, and that one of the contracting parties cannot alter it, modify it, or abolish it. In this way, the same nature of things obliges us to address this very serious question of constitutional law. It is necessary for the honorable representatives to understand that Navarre is not reducing the matter to the *ignoble bargaining* over quantities, but is defending a principle, that of the substantial nature of its law, as real and effective within its modest sphere as that of the parliament within its elevated sphere. This question is historical and legal, and it must be addressed and resolved with historical and legal reasoning. But since my dear friends and worthy colleagues have addressed the issue thoroughly, of course they adduced all the historical and legal arguments that were appropriate. I embrace all of those, as well as those concerning the economic aspect of the question, and I reproduce them now, lamenting, honorable representatives, that the nature of the matter does not allow me to avoid tedious repetitions.

I will repeat what I esteem to be invariably necessary for the spirit of my argument, and that as briefly as possible. I will try, in passing, to highlight certain aspects of this matter, which, on account of being omitted previously, will not be, to be sure, of those of major importance. Honorable representatives, the feeling of a duty, as is only fair and as you will comprehend, never more pressing than when selfishness would seek to be able to disregard it, takes precedence over my intense desire to not cause the chamber any bother.

Wednesday, July 21, 1512 (and this is a day triply terrible, because the Basque fueros were abolished on July 21, and on another 21 those of Navarre were being debated) is a day as tragic as it is cowardly for the Navarrese: the sparkling aurei in the crown of Sancho the Great and of García Ramírez were eclipsed among eternal cursed shadows. The troops of the Duke of Alba, breaking through the borders of Araba, penetrated Navarrese territory through the Burunda Valley, whose habitual mists, that day, must have thickened to serve as funerary black ribbons for our history. The traitorous Beaumonts, captained by Don Luis, son of the Count of Lerín, served as the vanguard. The invading troops were going to carry out the threat that King Ferdinand had issued a few days before, in Burgos, to the Field Marshal of Navarre, to "take by force what King Juan did not want to give by his free will." On July 24 Pamplona capitulated by means of an oath by which the Duke would maintain the fueros, privileges, and customs of the people of Pamplona. This capitulation served as a norm and pattern for the successive handing over of cities, towns, and valleys in the kingdom. The occupation of the country was carried out with astonishing speed. By mid-august, only the city of Tutera [Tudela], the castle of Monjardín, the towns of Cáseda and Miranda, and the Aezkoa, Zaraitzu [Salazar], and Erronkari [Roncal] Valleys obeyed the legitimate king. Soon these loyal places would succumb, and by the early days of September, all Navarre was a prisoner of the Catholic King. He began to title himself "The keeper of the crown of Navarre and the kingdom, and of the lordship and command over it;" the papal bull *Pastor ille coelesti* having just been published on August 21, he shamelessly took the title King of Navarre and demanded an oath of loyalty from the Navarrese, beginning with the inhabitants of Pamplona, who gave it as "subjects" and not "vassals," denoting with such a concise phrase and significant distinction that they had resolved to live according to their own laws and customs, and in no way according to whim, to arbitrariness, to the injustice of monarchs and future ministers, among whom they foresaw, without any doubt, Mr. Gamazo.

That is how the end came for the illustrious Navarrese monarchy, the root and stem from which sprouted the most celebrated states in Spain, a matriarchal kingdom that nursed in its breasts the Kingdom of Castile, exchanging roles in the legend of Romulus and Remus, since this time the wolf cub was nurtured with human milk. Ferdinand *the Catholic* was not the "conscious" artifice of the national unity that modern unionists typically portray; it is well proven by his marriage to Germana de Foix, from whom he expected a succession to exceed the kingdoms of Spain. In his invasion of Navarre, he was not guided by any of those illustrious ideals that mitigate or excuse, within certain limits, the crimes of great politicians. He was an ambitious individual who, in a flash, violated the rights of truth and of justice, suffocating in order to do so the voice of blood. Never was there such a complete personification of Machiavelli's *Prince* as that day. And although he became increasingly vain on account of his swift campaign of a month and a half, attributing it to the favor of God, the truth is that he was enthroned among a land shattered by sixty years of civil war, often incited by the country itself, whose population had fallen by two thirds, whose fields were covered with weeds, whose pecuniary resources were exhausted, whose social and political cohesion had been dissolved by a spirit of factionalism that poisoned the whole national body. And if God moved him, it was in the form of a minister of divine frenzied revenge for the horrors of a fight among brothers.

The occupation of Navarre has been classified as a "conquest," and this is the word commonly used. Let us suppose, for one moment, that Navarre was conquered, and let us study, in light of good philosophy, what in such a case Ferdinand *the Catholic*, assuming his root wickedness, could have carried out less illegitimately. Thus we would see what, according to history, he really carried out, and we would know exactly the legal status of Navarre following its annexation to Castile.

The honest end to war is to ensure a beneficial peace. It is the doctrine of Saint Thomas, who follows Saint Augustine. Let us recall a passage in the *Summa*, which pays attention to this: "Those who wage war justly aim at peace . . . Hence Augustine says: 'We do not seek peace in order to be at war, but we go to war that we may have peace. Be peaceful, therefore, in warring, so that you may vanquish those whom you war against, and bring them to the prosperity of peace'" (2nd part of 2nd part, art. 1).

Considered the consequence of a just war, used as a means of assuring peace, as a defense against traps and attacks by a perfidious violent enemy, or rather, in cases of extreme necessity and when there is no other way, conquest, as much as I hate to say so, is legitimate. But that does not give the conqueror limitless rights over the occupied territory. According to Christian law, neither people nor society remains at the mercy of the victor; on the contrary, the latter must respect local and acquired rights, and the freedom and institutions therein; anything otherwise would merit the name of tyrant. One of the most distinguished publicists of the distinguished Society of Jesus, Fr. Ventura, who is inspired by the great theological schools, who has drunk from the pure springs of Suárez, Victoria, and Soto, expresses it clearly:

> The conqueror does nothing but enter into the rights of the dethroned prince; from these rights, resulting from the constitution and the will of the people that fell into

his hands, he receives his new sovereignty. From which it turns out that any new prince who may be ignorant of or infringe the constitution, laws, and liberties of the people he has dominated by force of arms, would erase, *ipso facto*, the titles of his legitimacy, turning into a true usurper (*Ensayo sobre el Poder público* [Essay on Public Power]).

It is clear that the circumstances or conditions that legitimize conquest did not exist in the occupation of Navarre; yet nor is it less true that Ferdinand *the Catholic* remained within the limits of moderation that Christian law prescribes to all conquerors. The occupation of the kingdom was vicious and unjust at root, but the means used to ensure its retention met the demands of law. Let us see how.

On December 17, 1512, Don Ferdinand, now titling himself King of Aragón and Navarre, appointed as viceroy Don Diego Fernández de Córdoba, governor of Donceles, Marquis of Comares, within whose authorization was included the following clause: "We wish and mandate that you, too, before taking use of this occupation, should swear an oath." In effect, the viceroy swore, before the parliament in Pamplona, on "all the fueros, laws, ordinances, procedures customs, freedoms, exemptions, liberties, privileges" of the kingdom, whose political, civil, and social constitution remained wholly intact. In Valladolid, on June 12, 1513, being present the ambassadors of the Kingdom of Navarre, Don Ferdinand ratified the oath given by the governor of Donceles; and in July 1515, the Parliament of Castile being held in Burgos, he incorporated the Navarrese kingdom into that of Castile, but "maintaining the fueros and customs of said kingdom." In the year 1514, that is, due to the unjust occupation of Navarre by the Catholic King, parliament managed to sanction the following ordinance, which today makes up law 2 of article 3 in book 1 of the latest compilation:

Because of the pestering of some, we send on many occasions to this kingdom many documents and our royal commandments, and our viceroys give them in our name, to the great affront of the laws of said kingdom, and in that of its freedom, and against that which before now was provided and we have a jury; therefore, we hereby direct and order that such provisions emanating from us, even if obeyed, are not fulfilled until they are consulted with us.

These royal documents, orders, and provisions may not have been against the fueros, and for this reason the king reserved the faculty to make the corresponding declaration. But as many abuses stemmed from this, in 1561 the Zangoza [Sangüesa] Parliament, looking at the entirety of the foral system, convinced the king to sanction a law that established that royal documents should be "underwritten" by the Royal Council of Navarre before being executed, with a hearing in the royal provincial council, following for that reason a tribunal termed the "underwrite." And later, the parliament even acquired another more solid guarantee: the right to publish or promulgate, by which only the laws that it mandated were obliged to be inserted into printed notebooks.

Navarre, honorable representatives, remained joined to Castile through the common bond of the figure of the prince. It continued to be, despite its incorporation and according to foral terminology, a "kingdom in itself, distinct in territory, jurisdiction, and laws...," and its union was a "principal union." That is how all the kings have acknowledged it as such in their oaths, from Ferdinand the Catholic to Ferdinand VII, inclusive. The kings of Castile first, and the kings of Spain thereafter, came to enjoy the rights that corresponded or belonged to the very kings of Navarre; so that the incorporation, although designated with the name conquest, no longer in accordance with the philosophical principles of Christian law, but in accordance with the texts of positive law stemming from it, was reduced to a mere "usurpation" by the crown, enforced by a prince of a governing house, to the detriment of the legitimate sovereigns. Navarre, therefore, following its incorporation into Castile, remained as much lord and master of its own domestic life, and as exempt from central legislative power, as France or

England. Consider, honorable representatives, that there was never, nor is there, nor will there be any sovereignty in the world capable of modifying or destroying, viably and legitimately, a state of affairs similar to this, if the author of the greatest movements were not the passage of time, in that it has brought with it the consent, either tacit or explicit, of the Navarrese; for as long as such consent is lacking, transformations would be due only to the empire of force; and whatever the force builds, at any opportune time or occasion, the force of the victim has the power to destroy it.

This legal state has lasted, gentlemen, as people say, down to the present. In the years 1828 and 1829 Navarre held general meetings of its parliament in Pamplona. Yet already by that time it had suffered the deadly attacks by two terrible and irreconcilable enemies: monarchical absolutism and its legitimate heir, liberalism, a child of the French Revolution, and a major event had taken place, the War of Independence, which modified profoundly the ideas and feelings of the Navarrese, drawing them from the purely regional into the national sphere.

The miserable royal absolutism, possessing Spain like maggots on a dead body, had decided to finish with the Basque-Navarrese liberties. But as it lacked the spirit and energy to dissect them, it prepared the means to do so cunningly, little by little, as far as those scrawny brains of clerks and insipid men of letters could devise them: making use of the obsequiousness of the Royal Academy of History, the worthlessness of a Llorente, the impertinence of a Zuaznabar, the predatory instincts of a reforming council, the abuses of the royal internal revenue service, it gradually stacked up in "dictionaries," "historical recollections," "critical-historical essays," and "reports," as much data as it thought necessary to destroy our historical-legal state, collected, combined, and expanded on by people who ignored the material or deliberately disfigured it. The idea was to drown us in ink and pierce us with quills, introducing the tricks of curia and scheming stinging feuds into the relations between the state and a most noble Spanish region. Stocked, or, more accurately, armed with weighty tomes replete with deceitful relations and documents, the ministries and offices in Madrid caused obstacles and opposed relying on the exercise of the most unquestionable rights: that arsenal, constructed by falsifiers, has always been open to our enemies.

On September 1, 1756, King Charles IV, as a result of the provincial council of Navarre refusing to comply with certain royal decrees, documents, and orders contrary to the fueros, which had been underwritten without it meeting, ordered that,

> while in a council of ministers there was a thorough examination of the opposing materials, their transcendence, and links to all the points, cases, and facts exposed by the three states of that kingdom, and the origin, causes, and objects of the fueros and exemptions on which they were based to give them the corresponding value for the benefit of their peoples, nothing new was offered in the proper fulfillment of the royal decrees, documents, and orders issued by the secretaries of state and of office, the councils and other courts.

Bloodstained sarcasm honorable representatives! The sentence "nothing new was offered in the proper fulfillment of the royal decrees" meant that the king considered the laws of 1514 and 1561 abolished, those established precisely so that the foral system would not be subject to harm on the part of the monarch's legislative power. In other words, gentlemen, that of nothing new meant introducing the most serious novelty in this matter. Ferdinand VII, with his usual disloyalty, reproduced the royal order of Charles IV on May 14, 1829, despite it being declared null and without any effect in law III of the Pamplona Parliament in the years 1817 and 1818. All the royal documents after May 14 were underwritten without being considered by the provincial council. In this way, the final wall that had held back the advances of monarchical absolutism disappeared. The provincial council of the kingdom was right, then, to tell Ferdinand VII on December 22, 1831, in an austere and spirited representation, "that your loyal Navarrese were in fact deprived of the fueros that the king had sworn an oath to."

Monarchical absolutists had worthy followers of their anti-foral endeavors in the liberals, supporters of the modern constitutional system. Mr. Cánovas del Castillo, with great historical sense, has said in a celebrated prologue:

> As much as I or anyone who belongs to the liberal school flatters him, history cannot nor should not deny that Godoy and his agents and publicists were the true fathers of official liberalism in Spain . . . The Spanish liberal party picked, as in everything, in the Basque question, the traditions of Godoy, of Llorente, of González Arnao.

Now listen, gentlemen, those of you willing to vote against the fueros: your legitimate precursor is, among others of the same kind, that Caballero, a minister of Charles IV, who mutilated and falsified certain laws in the latest compilation, with the aim of providing absolutism with a legal base. There is no small honor in attacking with everything you have!

Anti-foral absolutism was cunning, hypocritical, cowardly. It understood that it was out of synch with the good monarchical tradition and injured the fueros from a sideways angle, in the "details," suppressing their most effective guarantees, seeking in the revision of foral titles a just cause for its excesses and abuses. Anti-foral liberalism was frank, brutal, audacious. It affirmed the sovereignty of the nation, and sacrificed on its altars the historical rights, the solemn pacts, the consuetudinary bases of society and the homeland. The child of political rationalism, it uprooted mercilessly all the institutions that disagreed with the canons of its abstract ideal. Geometric logic substituted history, law, and experience as the sources of legislation. For this reason, the perjured legislators of Cádiz, who believed that constitutions were thought out in cabinets, copied from books, written out on paper, and passed from people to people like a beetroot seed or examples of the bovine race, after pondering up even up in the clouds on the "preliminary discourse" of their artificial constitution about the political institutions of Navarre, abolished them radically. It is true that they began in that "discourse" by declaring the Spaniards, in putting up with absolutism, had lost, through their disgraceful suffering, even the idea of their dignity: thanks, then, to the Cádiz Parliament, Spaniards rose all of a sudden from the degradation of slavery to the barbarity of tyrants.

And now we have face to face, honorable representatives, the new power and the historical institutions. Since the powers that the Cádiz Parliament were attributed to abolish the fueros, successive parliaments have been attributed with them constantly to abolish or modify them in different eras, believe me that this is the most propitious moment to examine the quality of the new sovereignty. The general parliament of Spain, whether it shared sovereignty with the king or exercised it alone, was it more sovereign, more "intensely" sovereign, if the phrase is valid, than kings in the old regime? Formulating the question and obtaining the answer are one and the same. Sovereignty, honorable representatives, is equal to supreme authority, an authority that decides in the final analysis without there being any recourse against it. Power comes from God, considered in his supreme majesty and forces, whether it be the principality of one or of many. But sovereignty is one, always identical to itself, without it varying in essence because the people or corporations therein vary. As a result, if the kings of Spain, while they retained full sovereignty, lacked, as we have seen, the right and faculty to abolish and modify the fueros, nor did the parliaments that later shared with them or have disputed that sovereignty ever possessed the same right and faculty. And what the parliaments have done in the matter is null and vicious at root, and only stems from force.

The alterations that the constitution of Navarre has experienced in the nineteenth century are huge. In some of them one factor, and it made all of them possible, was the transformation in the spirit of the Navarrese as a result of the War of Independence. The kingdom invaded, its provincial council was encouraged to declare war on the tyrant. Militias were armed, then battalions were organized that fought as such both within their own territory and in Aragón and Castile. The foral structure was, in fact, ruined, since central and other regional authorities of a revolutionary or spontaneous formation governed, however intermittently. No one questioned whether a measure or disposition was anti-foral, but whether it was or seemed patriotic. Locals from the Kingdom of Navarre mixed with people from other kingdoms. And that great conflagration, with the community of interests, risks, and aspirations, provoked the predominance of a "national" over a "regional" tendency. In a word: the Navarrese then entered fully into the current of common Spanish life; they persuaded themselves that there existed business of a greater level than Navarrese business, and that it was no longer possible to address or resolve the latter separate from its general counterpart. Two facts demonstrate, on their own, this grand transformation I am referring to. During the war against the French Republic, in the year 1794, the Pamplona Parliament had to authorize the inhabitants of the kingdom, whose battalions were incorporated into the Spanish army, that if they so wished, whenever an action should commence within Navarrese territory, they could leave it to conclude it. That was the extent to which everyone was consumed by the idea that Navarre was a nation united to another nation! A few years later, in the year 1822, the royalist division of Navarre left its homeland vulnerable to the vengeance of constitutionalist troops, and went en masse to Catalonia to fight under the orders of Baron de Eroles by obeying the dispositions of the Regency of Urgel, which would be anything except foral authority.

The Navarrese were affiliated at that time with Spanish political parties. This fact was full of grave consequences. Just as, accordingly, the Cádiz Parliament hurt the Catholic sentiments and the foralist sentiments of the country, so their political was also the object almost unanimously of execration. The Liberal Party was very small, and its formation was due, more than anything else, to the influence or personal prestige of Don Francisco Espoz y Mina, the celebrated guerrilla fighter of the War of Independence; an uncouth, cruel, vindictive, and envious man (*strong rumors*), but, because of his heroic military deeds, he enjoyed, before the eyes of many, the prestige of a demigod. The Navarrese institutions experienced the same ups and downs as political parties. Ferdinand VII having returned from France, the Elío generals achieved, supporting an exhibition of the provincial body, the reestablishment of the fueros, solicited pointlessly from the Cadiz Parliament. Riego's shameful uprising took place and they were once more abolished, only to be reestablished on the fall of the constitutional regime in 1823, and abolished again when the regency of Doña María Cristina handed power over to the liberals in 1834.

You all know perfectly well, honorable representatives, the new phase that foral question wet through at the conclusion of the first civil war. My decent companions and dear friends who preceded me in discussing this have remarked on the extent to which the Bergara Agreement was related to General Espartero's address in Hernani, to the law of October 25, 1839, and to the complementary organic decree of November 16 that same year. Clearly, the afterthought added to the end of art. 1 of the law of October 25, 1839, and which did not figure in the original outline by the government, "without detriment to the constitutional unity of the monarchy," tended to leave alone only the economic and administrative fueros, and it was a battering ram set up to destroy the most essential and valuable part of the Navarrese constitution.

It is clear, likewise, that the interpretation given by the minister of grace and justice on a similar clause, when he said "constitutional unity is saved there being just one constitutional king for all the provinces, the same single legislative power, and one common national representation," could have been composed perfectly with the integral survival of the Navarrese constitution, adopting, or put more clearly, maintaining one of those "composed forms" of the state that political science and political experience know and use; the Navarrese Parliament could, for example, survive and Navarre be represented in the Spanish Parliament, as proposed now by a certain illustrious man of state, one of the few political men in Europe that merits applause and sympathy beyond the borders of his homeland, the venerable Gladstone for Ireland. But these composed forms surpassed the intellectual level of the legislators of the year 1839, devotees of the political geometry of the French revolutionaries. I will, however, put these questions to one side, managing without the duplicity and treachery of art. 1 that appeared or feigned to confirm what, really, it did not confirm, and I ask, honorable representatives, who was the Spanish Parliament in the year 1839 to "confirm" the fueros of Navarre? Could it abolish them fairly? No. Well, if it could not abolish them, nor could it confirm them, and its role was reduced to "recognizing" them. When, where, and how did it acquire that sovereignty over Navarre, which was never possessed legitimately even by the Parliament of the year 1834, nor that of the year 1820, nor that of the year 1812, nor the kings of Spain when they were called Charles I and Phillip II? Examine, honorable representatives, the background of things, and you will discover any reason other than that which encourages all past and present anti-fueros, the reason of force.

In support of what I contend, allow me to read an irrefutable text by the official receiver of the Navarrese Parliament, Dr. Don Angel Sagaseta de Ilurdoz, taken from a pamphlet published in the year 1839:

Settling the true origin and nature of the Kingdom of Navarre, it is necessary to agree that no other kingdom, however extensive, however formidable it may appear, has the right to dictate to it, introduce novelties, confirm or modify its constitutions, hold them to agreement, or vary the permanent provincial council, however defective they may be, they may need timely reforms, or the such prudent lights of the century may reclaim them imperiously: all this will be particular and exclusive to the three states of that kingdom, working by themselves, without being forced, without intervention, without competition from any other kingdom. The small kingdoms do not differ from the large ones in kind or in substance; the large and the small do not constitute in this matter any substantial diversity: although the small kingdom is circumscribed to the terms of an islet, as Horace said of the kingdom of Ulysses, as long as it is independent, in itself it has an intensive, although not extensive, supreme power equal to that of the most populous empire. The small kingdom of Portugal is equal in its rights and independence to the vast Russian Empire.

One consequence of the law of October 25 and the organic decree of November 16, 1835, was the Consensual Law of 1841, whose external history, whose character as an agreement, recognized in a multitude of sovereign dispositions, have been clearly explained by my eloquent colleagues in the provincial council. It is refuted, in vain, that the law of 1841 was drawn up and titled like all laws, and therein there was no record of it having the effect of a pact: things are what they are and not what they are called. Its special character, singularism, was revealed in the period of its formation, and above all during the full independence of the territory in which it was to be applied, from which it could not, legitimately, be divested. The intervention of the Spanish Parliament in the year 1841 served to give a legislative character to a contract or agreement between the provincial council of Navarre, the representative of the Navarrese people, and H. M.'s government, the representative of the parliament of the nation.

The law of 1841, formally speaking, was null because the Navarrese Parliament with the king, the only powers competent to alter, add to, or clarify the precious treasure of its fundamental institutions, did not intervene in it. But the passing of time, which changes everything, and the consent of the Navarrese and their adaptation to the new state of things have legitimized it. Navarre relinquished at that time legislative, executive, and judicial power; it modified its provincial and municipal organization; its best acquitted products and assets were transferred to the state; it was taxed with a fixed annual contribution, instead and in place of a voluntary donation, and it accepted military service under the odious form of conscription. It is impossible, honorable representatives, for anyone to overcome or equal in generosity and open-handedness the noblest Navarrese people!

Navarre, nevertheless, did not give up *everything*. It reserved, within the form of a pact, one *part*; and it is clear that, as regards this part, it retains, maintains, and sustains the full faculties that may be exercised over it.

This is the motive by which the representatives of Navarre, interpreting fully the will of our electorate, opposed the passing of article 37, in which the omnipotent shadow of the state, the violator of the most sacred rights, was reflected. Navarre has fulfilled most loyally, punctually, with proven loyalty, all its commitments. One cannot say the same for the state, which successively has dishonored and violated all the articles of the law of 1841. Today Navarre, feeling an overflow in its magnanimous chest of bitterness for so much injustice suffered, seeks to reclaim in our voice the absolute respect for its consensual law, and the express recognition that this cannot be altered or modified without the agreement of its will. If you do not acknowledge this in that way, honorable representatives, and the state continues disregarding systematically our rights, the time would perhaps have come to repeat the words of O'Connell: "In the unlikely event that parliament should shut its ears to our pleas, we would appeal to the nation; and if it were to retreat into blind preoccupations, we would retreat into our mountains to take council from our energy, our valor, and our desperation."

(Mr. Vice Presdient (La Serna): Mr. Campión, it would be better that, although with the ability you disguise the honorable member so much, you did not expose thoughts of a nature such that they cannot, even disguised, be presented within the national representation.)

Mr. Campión: I was going to say, and I feel that I have been interrupted, that I do not believe that this is ever possible, because our Spanishness and the noble and generous feelings of the chamber should never put us in that case.

(Mr. Vice Presdient (La Serna): Well, if that were not possible, the hypothesis was superfluous, which was already, in the way it was established, somewhat dangerous. The honorable member continues.)

Mr. Campión: Well I think that hypothetically there was no offense or lack of any consideration, since it was to add that we have full confidence in justice and in the feelings of the Congress.

This, thank God, will never be the case because the noble sentiments of the Spanish people beat in your chests. Summarizing the "priceless" goods that Navarre ceded in the year 1841, you will not want to be ungrateful for not respecting the little that remains, similar to the last coins of a splendid treasure: the right to live in peace under the shadow of a law that you yourselves established. And you will respect it, above all, because it is demanded of justice, which so exalts the powerful when they lend it to the weak: It would be a great feat, in the end, gentlemen, to toss the strength of an entire nation against a single province, to be defeated by it in the courts of generosity, reason, and history!

I have spoken.

Mr. Campión: Honorable representatives, I believe that I do not need to intervene further in this debate, if the worthy individual of the commission who has just replied to me has served to give a categorical answer to a question that I am going to have the honor to address to him; and if the honorable member answers it negatively, that answer will be the clearest demonstration that the alarm of all the inhabitants of Navarre in general and the delegation to parliament in particular is justified. I ask Mr. Rosell the following: if the provincial council of Navarre, in virtue of the circumstances in which it finds itself today, cannot agree with H. M.'s government on an increase in its taxation, should H. M.'s government respect this refusal, will it wish to impose on Navarre this increase in contribution by virtue of the powers of the parliament, to which the honorable member has referred?

Tell me Mr. Rosell, yes or no; and if you say yes, Navarre will be calm, because it will see that its law is respected; but if you say no, it will come to recognize that we are right to speak about pacts, about history, about the law of 1841 and about everything we have thought it appropriate to speak about.

(Mr. Rosell: Mr. Campión will understand that I do not have the authority to answer the question he has just addressed to me, and even if I did, I would give from this bench an interpretation that could be considered to be the authentic legal precept that we are debating. The honorable member should read paragraph 2 of the article that we are debating, and draw the consequences. "The government is authorized to agree with the province of Navarre such and such," says the article. You ask, honorable member; if you do not agree, what will happen? Allow me, honorable member, to not answer him, because I do not have the authority to do so, and although I could answer, I think I should not.)

Mr. Campión: As Mr. Rosell has focused mainly on the word "agreement," and the word "agreement" implies the agreement of two wills, from what the honorable member has just stated, I can deduce, in a logical way, that if Navarre refuses to increase the contribution, it will not be bothered by the H. M.'s government.

(Mr. Rosell: Note that this interpretation is that which the honorable member gives the article; but that interpretation is not given by the commission.)

Chapter 6

Speech in the Congress of Deputies on January 14, 1895

Honorable representatives:

Attempting now to unite my voice with that of the distinguished Spanish Episcopate, with that of all the Catholic faithful of Spain, and with that of the illustrious orator who preceded me in speaking, my special and distinguished friend the Marquis of Vadillo, whose benevolent allusion leads me into this debate in order to protest with them, and with the same energy as them, against the scandalous act of the so-called consecration of the apostate and concubinator Cabrera; a consecration that violates not just the eternal rights of truth, but the very text of the Constitution, while at the same time cruelly hurting religious and patriotic sentiments of Spaniards. But this protest of mine, however energetic, and I want no other to surpass it in energy, although all will exceed it in eloquence; this protest of mine will never outstrip the limits of the sphere of activity of the ruling government and existing laws in order to address, not even the thought of, the other highest institutions. For I, honorable representatives, faithful observer of the politico-religious teachings of the great Pontiff Leo XIII, at the same time I protest against certain government acts and the laws they occasion, when they are not authorized to do so, proclaim my respectful subjection to the constituted powers. If possible to condense into one formula my feelings and aspirations, I would say that my motif is: "For the king against the law," insofar as what this entails as unjust or opposed to Church doctrines. Of the two diverse orders of ideas that make up my repudiation of the law and my loyal acceptance of the king I will try, succinctly and with due separation, not as someone who is trying to pronounce a parliamentary oration, here where all kinds of eloquence find a natural home, but as someone who aspires to exercising an act demanded by the circumstances, and above all by my conscience. In order to do so, I reclaim the broadest benevolence of Congress; nevertheless, in return, I promise to be very brief.

Only the truth has rights. This very obvious and evident axiom of yours, which so perfectly speaks to the rational nature of man, whose intelligence and whose will, whenever they assume false opinions and tend toward the malevolent and embrace it, are perverted and corrupted and drift away from their natural dignity, was not taken into account by the authors of the 1876 Constitution, who gave a place in it to the cursed liberties of the new law, and especially to the tolerance of dissident forms of worship, without, in introducing it, including the reasons for achieving in that some important benefit or avoiding some serious detriment, which are those that reconcile its establishment.

This is the reason that His Holiness Pius IX, in a Brief aimed at Cardinal Moreno on May 4, 1876, declared solemnly that, with article 11 of the Constitution, the rights of truth and the Catholic religion were injured, and it infringed on all law, in its most precious and principal part, the Concordat of 1851. Words that are still valid, honorable representatives, because not even the Holy See has rectified or modified them subsequently, nor have their excellencies the bishops ceased to repeat them in all kinds of tones, constantly, since then; and therefore they oblige we Catholics to consider the tolerance of other forms of worship and its consequences as a mere legality, which is based neither on acceptance or approval.

But what art. 11 of the Constitution established then was private tolerance, given to dissidents from the Catholic religion, I mean, to those who are not anti-Christian, for example, Moslems, Jews, etc; tolerance reduced to the enclosure of the church, since public ceremonies or demonstrations not of the state religion are prohibited. This is what one deduces from the very text of the article, from the debate to which it led, and the royal order of October 23, 1876, which, said in parentheses, mixed the good with the bad.

But in time the liberal coalition pact was annulled, the famous formula of Mr. Montero Ríos and Mr. Alonso Martínez was agreed on, by which the Fusionist Party promised and committed to the laws not being able to prohibit, or restrict, or oppose the possession or the exercise of rights and of those termed as such that the Constitution recognizes or awards to Spaniards, for any reason, including religion. And this ill-fated formula aggravated things from the religious point of view.

It is not, to be sure, the Fusionist Party that most stands out for fulfilling the promises, stemming from the spheres of power, it made to the country when it was in the opposition; there still remain, for example, in the region of limbo the prosperity and fortune with which Mr. Sagasta gave a toast in his famous Oviedo speech. But insofar as one looks at the spirit of hostility toward religion, which flutters and palpitates in the recalled formula, fusionism is logical and consistent, unfortunately, and as the days pass, instead of cooling, Mr. Sagasta's "goat-like" loves are inflamed.

In accordance with the formula we had, shortly after Mr. Sagasta rose to power, the opening of the Protestant chapel or church; later we had the stupendous reform of secondary education by Mr. Groizard, infested with naturalism, and the so-called consecration of the apostate Cabrera. There is no doubt; that government and majority tolerate no obstacle in the progressive development of the liberal spirit, and the moral ruins they cause increase every day.

That consecration that the fusionist cabinet has agreed to and protected is a manifest violation of the Constitution of the monarchy. You oppose the idea in vain that such acts, just because they are carried out inside a church, are private; verified liturgical demonstrations and ceremonies within a premises open to the public are public; likewise the establishment of a false hierarchy that shrouds the exercise of jurisdiction, as opposed to another legitimate hierarchy, is public. And you boast about being

Catholics, like you brag about that, logically you have no choice but to humbly lower your head before the unanimous protest of the Spanish Episcopate, master and guide of Catholics, which has blamed you for violating article 11, and we are resolved to repairing the damage caused, obliterating the affront that you have induced gratuitously to the religious and patriotic consciousness of the Spanish people.

The Spanish people, honorable representatives, to be honest, do not understand why or for what reason the tolerance of dissident forms of worship was established; but they understand even less that strange determination to expand the terms of the Constitution, to interpret them broadly, to stretch out simple tolerance to include the freedom of worship. And this is not understood, honorable representatives, because history refutes it; because in their soul the dead generations, "atavism," as they say nowadays, cry out, protesting; because the Spanish people are the eternal crusade; because their purest and most splendid glories, from Covadonga to Otumba, and from las Navas de Tolosa to Lepanto, are victories of the Cross over pagans and infidels; because they gazed at the apogee of their power when the Spanish flag, as big as a firmament, extended across Europe, Asia, and America, and wrapped around the richest empires and most flourishing states, transformed into a hammer of heresy, fighting implacably and tirelessly against Lutherans and Calvinists on the banks of the Rhine, in the cities of Flanders, in the marshy lands of Holland, on the plains of France, on the choppy ocean waves. And the Spanish people do not understand how, without legitimate cause, in a single moment their past is rejected in order to position and raise against the apostolic hierarchy another hierarchy born in the incestuous bed of Henry VIII, another hierarchy whose pope is the King of Great Britain that, from the Rock of Gibraltar, wickedly reduces and eats away at the integrity of our territory.

People that think with imagination and feeling do not understand, as I term it, that yearning to favor, offending the national laws, the diffusion of Protestantism in Spain. And still less do the people, if I may say, understand reflexive persons. Politics usually takes into account, often, many iniquitous or bad things; but it is when these iniquitous and bad things represent important forces that influence events and, by virtue of such force, that they tend to bring about a state. But taking into account a dead body that smells bad; recognizing, to put it one way, the personality of a decrepit, outdated, religion, devoid of any expansive force whose proselytism is reduced to buying unworthy consciences with pounds sterling, is absurd and foolish. Protestantism is incapable of carrying out solid and very extensive conquests, not even with the complicity of bad Catholics. Enlightened Protestants themselves acknowledge and proclaim this, as one can be demonstrated, adducing, among other things, Lord Macaulay's testimony in one of his marvelous *Essays*.

And no other thing can happen. Today, Protestantism, which does not reach the level of philosophy, has already ceased to be a religion. It is a timid attempt in the face of rationalism; a residue, a true *caput mortum* in the face of religiosity. The free examination that gave it life has killed it. Since Hugo Grotius diminished the notion of inspiration in the Bible, and Baruch Spinoza placed it in dispute, free thought and Protestant theology have not raised the barrier that they placed on Orthodox Zion. In this war against holy books, three nations have stood out in the main: England, which invented Christianism without any mysteries, without miracles, rational Christianism, pure deism; France, which in the eighteenth century took the deist errors from the English and, driven by these, employed the arms of mockery, irony, and ridicule against Catholic truths; Germany, which constructed the formidable apparatus of its erudite, solid, and patient exegesis, the mother of infinite errors.

Thus, today there is no rational basis of credibility at the heart of Protestantism, nor any supernatural element. The heavy flagstone has fallen once more over the tomb of Arimathea, and the icy wind of rationalism blew up from the crosses of the celestial body, leaving just dry wood as a symbol of a dead religion.

You are opening the doors into Spain to this set of negations, impieties, and blasphemies. And as a bonus to the importation, without doubt, you award it the violation of the constitutional text? It seems like a lie! A strange phenomenon explained by no one! But I have said it mistakenly, honorable representatives; I am wrong: this fact is explained perfectly. Love for Protestantism is family love; it is the love of children for their parents, because in the end Liberalism is the legitimate descendant of the Reformation.

Undoubtedly, honorable representatives, it must seem paradoxical to many that I am choosing this very moment in which I am directing such serious charges against the governing party, and even against all the liberal parties, to accept publicly the power constituted in whose name and for whose designation these parties govern and are heading toward de-Catholicizing Spain. Well, those that are amazed by this act of mine should know that I have chosen the current occasion of proposals to mark out better and stress the scope and meaning of such an acceptance, in which I begin by recalling that the immortal Leo XIII ordered French Catholics to accept the Republic after its governments had implanted the infamous school legislation that uprooted God from the schools, and subjected seminarians to military service, at precisely the same time at which unworthy ministers, without even having cleaned up the dust that had accumulated when they had crawled at the feet of the Italian cabinet, prohibited bishops from taking part in workers' pilgrimages, and took the holy and patriotic Archbishop of Aix, Monseigneur Gouthe-Soulard, to court, and the vile magistrates who absolved Wilson had him condemned; in other words, when the affronts caused to the Church were more unbearable and numerous. Yet Leo XIII, justly surnamed *lumen in coelo*, dispelled the scandal of the simple and ignorant, and injured fatally the scandal of the hypocritical with certain memorable words that I am going to read to Congress:

> They would have avoided all these regrettable differences [those that came from the opposition to accept the Republic, which showed certain Catholics of what anti-Christian

sentiments the Republic, classified as atheist, Jewish, and Masonic, was possessed] if the difference between constituted power and legislation had been carefully considered. The legislation differs from the political powers and their forms to such an extent that, under the regime whose form is most excellent the legislation can be detestable, and on the contrary, under the regime of more imperfect forms excellent legislation can be found . . . If the importance of the distinction that has just been established is added, its reason is also manifest. Legislation is the work of men who are in possession of power and who actually govern the nation. From which it follows that, in practice, the goodness of the laws depends on the goodness of the rulers rather than on the form of the government itself.

The most sapient Leo XIII went up to here. The most important and luminous distinction recalled is, therefore, honorable representatives, the focus of my acceptance of power constituted in Spain.

Revolutions, civil wars, the vicissitudes of time, in a word, usually bring with them the disappearance of existing governments. Then a *social need* is imposed on governments, that of looking at things themselves, and this social need justifies the establishment of new governments.

"In politics, unlike in any other sphere," says Leo XIII, unexpected modification and changes emerge . . . These changes are far from being always legitimate at root, and it is still difficult for them to be so, and nevertheless the criterion of the common good and public peace imposes the acceptance of new governments, established in fact in substitution of previous governments that in fact are no longer; in this way, the ordinary laws of the transmission of power remain suspended, and it is even the case that, with the passage of time, they are eventually abolished.

"On such occasions," these are also the words of Leo XIII, "the novelty is reduced to the political form adopted by civil powers, as they are transmitted; but in no way does this affect power considered in itself . . . we will say it in other terms: in any hypothesis, civil power, considered as such, is of God, and always from Him, because there is no power that does not come from God." And Leo XIII continues: "Therefore, when new governments are constituted that represent this immutable power, accepting them is not only licit, but it is demanded and even imposed by the need for the social good that gives them life and maintains them." I wanted to repeat these august words, honorable representatives, because they are the key to what I have to add, confining myself to following meekly the teachings of the masters given by God on Israel.

I was one of the pilgrims that was in Rome and heard from the lips of His Holiness the reminder of the duty that concerns Spanish Catholics to subject ourselves respectfully to the constituted powers, and the eulogy of piety and devotion of the illustrious Queen Cristina, for those most expensive gifts to the Holy See, carried out and accentuated with expressive gestures that the elderly and most beloved Pontiff made during the reading of the address. A duty whose fulfillment, as favorable to the good of religion, he has just ratified with phrases of dazzling clarity in his recent and most important letter to his excellency the Archbishop of Tarragona.

Those words of allocution were clear and transparent of him, his not at all abstruse or remote sense, and everyone would have understood them i the same way as long as they did not interject in them and their understanding party passions and interests. But it is true that soon distinctions and subtleties emerged: some interpreted them in their widest sense, others in a more or less restricted sense, although everyone protesting, of course, that theirs came from the heart. What is one to do in such a fix? Who do you follow and believe? In my view, it was the responsibility of Catholics to distance themselves from any "private" judgement and seek the judgment of the Church, whose task it was to clarify of explain the Pope's words, if by chance they required it; in a word, to meditate on the conduct of the Church, which the Pope suggested to French Catholics as an example they should imitate in their civil relations with the Republic, which is the current government of their nation, when he ordered them to accept it. Well, honorable representatives, what did the Church in Spain do? Their excellencies the bishops that were in Rome wrote a collective pastoral in which they demonstrated that they were the first to fulfill the duty of respectful subjection to the constituted powers, just as they had declared in memorable documents. This was a ray of light for submissive Catholics. I, therefore, in so doing rejoice and take pride, make mine, as far as possible, the aforementioned acts of the prelates, go to the messages of Tarragona, Valencia, Seville, and Zaragoza, take from them the words that refer to the vase of respectful subjection, and I repeat them with the same sense and extension that they, offering therefore at this moment, a public and solemn testimony of "loyal submission, respect, high consideration, loyalty, love, fidelity, and unbreakable adhesion" to the eminent H. M. Queen Cristina, who governs on the august principle of which Leo XIII said that, "it grew for the hope of the Kingdom of Spain" (*Muestras de aprobación* [Proof of endorsement]).

This acceptance of civil power in the form in which it currently exists, carried out without further intent and with the perfect loyalty required of Christians, has its natural limits in accordance with its very terms. In the first place, let it be recorded that I agree to it not by virtue of dynastic titles or better laws, nor for any preference toward the current form of government, since all of this belongs fully to the speculative order of ideas, in which each Catholic may have their own as long as they are honest, as I have mine. I respect, accept, and venerate morally and materially H. M. King Alphonse XIII, for the only reason of being such an innocent child representative of that immutable power that comes from God; for the only reason of being the constituted power, which, precisely because it is *constituted* power, is not *abstract* authority nor must it therefore be extracted or separated from the person that currently exercises that sovereign authority.

So that I do not tie the sacred cause of religion to any mortal, transitory, and changeable human cause, to no gentleman who may pass away; I do not declare myself Alphonsine in the typical sense of that word, with which so many are termed who adhere to the royal personage by virtue of their dynastic titles. So that if time, the great transformer of every terrain, despite our perfect loyalty as Catholics and gentlemen, substitutes the current powers for new ones, Catholics could accept them without any diminishing, if then, as now, they were to prescribe their acceptance of the teachings of the Holy See and the demands of the common good of Spain. I do not link, then, two unequally important causes, as Leo XIII did not link them in prescribing the loyal and sincere acceptance of the French Republic; civil power, considered as such power, comes from God and always God: *non est potestas nisi a Deo.*

In second place, when I respect, accept, and venerate the constituted power, I reject and repudiate, more firmly still, liberal legislation, from that which figures in certain articles of the Constitution, to that which the last of the rules may inform; proposing first of all, while it is not repealed, "encouraging by all means that the laws and equity allow for the interests of religion and the homeland," and, together with many Catholics, follow cordially the direction of the Pope, "to resist the attacks of the impious an enemies of civil society." And challenging the liberal parties and emulating Monseigneur Isoard, Bishop of Annecy, when in a similar case he addressed Mr. Jules Ferry, I say to them *mutatis mutandis*: "You are not the monarchy; you are not Spain. We want to follow the sunlight. And if we did not win before, it is perhaps because many Catholics estimated that it was necessary, before applying themselves to combating the form of government, to changing dynasties. But there is only suitable relation between you and us: that of adversary against adversary."

For the same reason that my acceptance of the current constituted power is not involved in accepting liberal legislation, it is perfectly compatible with my regionalist an foralist ideas. On this point I have no reason to nor need to explain any professions of faith: it is enough to affirm that I am what I have always been, to ratify what I demonstrated before Congress in my speeches of May 24 and July 22, 1893, and declare myself a continuator of my own history, not due to modesty or unfamiliarity on your part, honorable gentlemen, less real and effective among those who pay worship to those ideas in Catalonia, Galicia, and the Basque-Navarrese Country. And supposing this compatibility, I must not tire of saying there, in Navarre, to my fellow countrymen:

> Imitate the wise and prudent conduct of your forefathers, who also distinguished between constituted power and legislation, by means of the famous formula *one obeys but one does not fulfill.* See in the constituted powers the common symbol of the nationality to which you are joined by solemn pacts. And if anyone should break or infringe those pacts, it should not be you, so that responsibility, which must be demanded by God and the homeland, should fall fully on the violators.

This policy of accepting the new powers, which is the policy of Leo XIII, the policy of the Church, complies with very high aims. It makes possible, better than any other means, the union of Catholics, divided and bewildered by political passions, cutting at the root the cause of their differences, providing them with neutral ground without humiliating anyone and leaving to the providence of God to lead the destinies of nations, as the Pope said to pilgrims, and leaving to divine providence the judgement of rights, whatever they may be, as His Excellency the Archbishop of Tarragona has just stated, may there be the fullest concord of wills among Catholics in this kingdom, who have at their head a lady that, by virtue of her soul and singular devotion to the Holy See, is worthy of all honor and estimation.

The politics of acceptance fails in the hands of persecutors of the Church the weapon that they have employed constantly since the founding of Christianism, portraying it as an enemy of Caesar, as an enemy of state.

As such, then, Catholics that respect, accept, and venerate the constituted powers will be able to combat strongly bad laws, without anyone being able to accuse them with the appearance of reason that they seek, on the same level, with religious ends, purely political ends, pretexting the former to better achieve the latter.

(Mr. President: If the honorable member would summarize a little on the allusion after the declarations I made, it would be very fitting so that the Honorable Minister of Grace and Justice may be able to answer the interpellation before five o'clock in the afternoon, the time at which we must begin the order of the day.)

Mr. Campión: I am going to finish immediately. The politics, finally, of those that respect, accept, and venerate the new powers by virtue of the criterion of the common or social good, as Leo XIII explained, the common or social good is that which legitimates the new powers, since it created and sustains them, contributes directly to the said common or social good, reinforcing public peace and civil peace, and preventing the Church from experiencing any new persecutions, given that the direct result of the revolutionary disruptions is usually, commonly, the enthroning or exaltation of a government of men hostile to Catholicism to some extent; from which the conclusion is that the harm emanating from the greater bad, panacea of many blind people, is true and unavoidable, and the benefits that may result later from that greater bad are problematic and contingent. Let there be an end, then, forever to the new messianism that blinded so many excellent Catholics! Let us be practical; let us put to one side the fatuous fires of political questions, which divide, in order to study social ones, which are those of the future; let us copy Catholics in other places, Catholics in the Americas, Germany, and Belgium. The remedy is in our hands; with the arms provided by liberal constitutions let us fight Liberalism. Let us not be what the Jews are, who would open the doors and windows of their homes if a storm governed; the long-awaited Messiah will not enter therefrom, but only a bolt of lightning that burns and destroys everything!

Allow me, honorable representatives, to put an end to my words with those that the illustrious Cardinal Sancha pronounced in front of H. M. the Queen Regent. Therefore, the last impression you will receive from my lips will be agreeable: "Heaven wishes, my lady, that all honorable men, and especially those that pride themselves on being Catholics, renouncing changes and disturbances that can only result in benefit to the least number, instead of arguing, that they fulfil with loyalty and fidelity the healthy teachings of the Vicar of Christ."

Believing myself to have fulfilled these, and in any event aspiring only to fulfill them, I have verified the act that I have just exercised; which, on the other hand, could only with difficulty ever be directed at an object covered in clothing more appropriate to cultivate and win over hearts, as are: the pure innocence of a child, the wholesome virtues of a mother. May it respond fully to the wishes of the distinguished Pontiff who, with the austerity of a saint, with the depth of a philosopher, with the prudence of a politician, and even with the gentleness of a poet, guides Peter's ship and sheds torrents of light on the closed darkness of the modern world!

I have spoken.

Chapter 7

The Basque Personality in History, Law, and Literature: Lecture Given at the Basque Center of Bilbao on April 27, 1901

Gentlemen:

There is nothing more difficult than to give thanks. Because the simplicity of the expression could appear lacking affection, or the pristineness of the phrase could become a rhetorical subject. But if both defects are inevitable, I prefer the guilt of insufficiency than that of deception. Allow me, gentlemen, making use of cold words, to demonstrate a warm affect, and receive them, not so much as they are in themselves, but as I would have liked them to be to reflect with fidelity the vivid light of a gratitude without sunset.

It has been many years since I was last in Bizkaia. Then as now I came to give a testimony of adhesion to the cause of the Basque race and homeland, convoked fraternally by those here who shared such pure love. So great was the fervor of my enthusiasm, so intimate within my spirit the fusion of the ideal element and the reality of life, so complete—why not confess it, gentlemen?—the inexperience of my youth, that I thought the stay of the Basque Country in its sepulcher had to be very brief, and that the same eyes that contemplated it fixed to the cross would have to recover by drinking in the splendors of its glorious resurrection.

It was not like that, unfortunately. We continue to listen to the chorus of lamentations, but our ears do not perceive the Easter bells. The cross is hard; the shadows get longer. The heart of bad Basques deafens with Judaic persistence; the humble altar of the Basque tradition receives fewer offerings than the luxurious altars of the golden calf; alien immigration on all sides suffocates us, dragging us into the trance of being foreigners in our own land; the millenarian language, enforcer of immemorial liberty, retreats to the mountain summits in order to die closer to heaven; economic materialism drains our integrity, corrupts our customs, cools our faith, reduces the size of our thoughts, clips the wings of our aspirations, attracts the fondness of the rich for becoming richer and pierces the heart of the poor with the ulcer of envy... Under the weight of such multiple and efficient causes of annihilation the spirit collapses, terrified by the specter of the inevitable. We ourselves are sealing with our sins the sepulchral flagstones of our mother so that she will never be resurrected. And on seeing the homeland disintegrate and disappear; in which the level of Basqueness, on a daily, if not momentary, basis is disappearing on Basque territory and is deserving of that fateful sign with which Élisée Reclus, many years ago, described "a people that are disappearing," ah gentlemen!, the soul turns toward the past, and even acknowledging that then our culture, our wellbeing, our wealth were infinitely less, the price of the current progress drops, being equivalent to the jewels and silks that shroud a corpse, and we exclaim: Happy, a thousand times happy the rough warriors that on the slopes of Ibañeta or the crags of Amaiur succumbed to the banners of France and Castile! At least they, on exhaling their last breath, could cherish the generous hope that the homeland would remain unscathed!

But no. You and groups of patriots in diverse Basque districts are still here, capable of repeating the accents of the poet: "which although marked by vile chains, our souls have never been slaves." Distinguished children of the Basque Country that carry out the role of ancient vestals, safeguarding and nourishing the fire ignited for centuries. And from it you will extract the embers that must burn in every Basque home. Peoples, like individuals, are curable. I trust in the constant efforts of the good. I trust, moreover, principally, in the resources, in the abundance of qualities of the Basque personality, as the accumulated history, law, and poetry reveal to us. The Basque personality today resembles those imposing ruins that, because they were so well and perfectly finished by their makers, have not yet become rubble; rather, they shine with rich ashlars worthy of being arranged to reproduce the characteristic forms of the primitive building, and compensate for the irremediable destruction of time with new comforts and conveniences.

I

I want to speak to you tonight, gentlemen, about that Basque personality. Sketching the personality of a people is equivalent to describing its psychology and an ethnic psychology presupposes a set of minuscule explanations of al the past and present exteriorizations of social life. A people is a historical being, that is, a changeable evolutionary being, which elaborates familial, political, and economic institutions; which surrounds itself, like a mollusk in a shell, with a world of religious and patriotic traditions; which adorns and embellishes itself with infinitely more marvelous artistic works than the feathers and songs of birds.

This will indicate to you that I am not proposing developing in the brief space of this talk a topic so complex that it would require an awkward apparatus of tests and demonstrations. I will have to limit myself to what I take to be the dominant faculty of the Basque personality, the distinctive feature of its temperament, the internal motor on which the whole series of its movements depends and the transformations through the influx of changing circumstances. I will show it functioning in three or four great applications, leaving you to fill in the gaps, pull together the fragments, coordinate the details, bring together in one single focus the disperse beams of light. Do not call it cheating, gentlemen; I am not offering you a picture, but a sketch; less still, a rough outline; four nervous brushstrokes.

I lack the anatomical characteristics, without denying because of that their interest. Even supposing that science were to be in agreement with regard to the anthropological determination of the Basque ethnic group; even if it were to present them to us as constituting a *race*, or simply a *people* whose formative elements I had managed to condense, even then, those characteristics would not explain the differences and the analogies between the Basque group and other groups. We would know, to put it one way, the *animal*, but be unaware of the *man*. Man is known for his soul, and the people for those psychological characteristics that make up its personality.

The psychological characteristics, because they are dependent on moral and intellectual aptitudes, are hereditary; without this inheritance contradicting the minimum of free will, because it looks at the particular autonomy of the act and not at the possibility of the act itself. And individual blessed with an exquisite poetic imagination will produce exquisite poems, just as another whose imagination is prosaic will never merit the name of poet. However, both will be free to write or not to write, and to choose this or that issue.

The portraits that classical historians and geographers transmitted to us about certain famous peoples continue to be as precise today as they were then. Combine the features that they observed in the Iberians and the Gauls, for example, and you will have reconstituted the personality of the modern Spaniards and French, and moreover you will possess the key to the history they have lived. But as numerous and accurate as the cranial capacity, cephalic, basilar, frontal, orbital, nasal, facial angle, height, skin color, eyes, and hair, etc. data are, you will never be able to say anything about aptitudes and less still about the social evolution of the people under study, and you will have to turn to the ordinary information media: archaeology, written history, public and private documents, works of art, legal bodies, statistics, etc. Anthropology is very interesting from the phylogenetic point of view, an applied to historical study, when it manages to establish a *correspondence* among certain changes in the national temperament of a people and the preponderance or elimination of ethnic types that shape it, by means of so-called *social section*.

I have studied the Basque personality in the facts and phenomena of its social life and I have come to believe that its distinctive sign, the dominant faculty, is its *individualism*.

This is, gentlemen, a concept that today does not enjoy many sympathies, which has been called into question, and of which numerous responsibilities have been demanded. This stems from the fact that the term individualism, like most of those used by the political sciences, is confusing and misleading.

We find individualism in the two twilights of societies. The first is the child of barbarism; the second, egoism. Both reject and do not acknowledge social solidarity. The savage, who disputed the possessions of life with a weapon in hand and placed no limits on his satisfaction other than the appetites allowed by the physical extension of his strengths, was an individualist. The educated man, who directed all his resolve to increasing his wellbeing, avoiding all kinds of personal inconveniences and never listening once to the spirit of sacrifice, is also an individualist.

Yet what most contributes to discrediting individualism is the spectacle of modern society as it solidified in the molds forged by the French Revolution. The cornerstone of that edifice was he declaration of the rights of man, of the *abstract* man, without exception of time or place, the naturally good man free of original sin, as the false philosophy of that eloquent lackey who went by the name of Rousseau fantasized. That man, the product of rationalizing reason, who, through pure egoism, made a pact about social life as if with an insurance company, became the beginning and end of all things: he broke religious ties, he disowned traditional institutions, and to the extent that he erased in his soul the image of heaven, from it he took possession of a greed for the earth. Spiritual benefits gave way to their material counterparts. Producing wealth among the many and distributing it among the few was the hallmark. In this way, a pyramid was erected—at the base of which were the hungry masses and at the top the satiated oligarchy—divided and cracked by jolts of envy in the cement.

I imagine, gentlemen, that you are convinced, without any prior warning, that I do attribute any of these individualisms to the noble Basque people. The individualism to which I refer is a strength, a psychic energy, the feeling of personal independence, an estimation of their own personality with the firm resolution of keeping it distinct from others. I say personality and not individuality, because the content of personality is richer. The Basque never thought that the individual constituted an end in itself. He always tended to equip it with his natural complements: family and home. That is how Basque individualism, in its most perfect phase, in its highest demonstration, is a family individualism, the worship, to put it one way, of a *social cell.* This individualism transcends, it imposes a characteristic on the historical evolution of the people. It unfolds a principle of liberty that beats in legal and political institutions, and if we turn to the sphere of beauty, it produces the flowering of lyrical poetry, which is the poetry of *I,* and the flourishing of music, which is the most personal and intimate of all arts because in order to be objectified, it does not require any contest of *ideas.* On the contrary, the other individualism moves within the strict circle of the individual. The savage was subject to the ceremonial and despotic cruelty of his anthropological gods and petty kings. The modern individualist withstands with neurasthenic passivity the bureaucratic tyranny of the unitary state, the fiscal state, the Jacobin state, which is the most meddling, insistent, ruinous, and corrupting tyranny of all; the tyranny of unscrupulous deals, of civil governors without dignity, and *petty tyrants* without shame.

II

Let us speak, gentlemen, of Basque individualism, a formula that includes our whole way of being both for good and for bad, because if it gives us reason for our virtues to take shape, at times it also serves as a track for our defects.

I have described this individualism extracting from it my observations. Now it falls on me to demonstrate an exact description, adducing some facts that verify it.

Peoples usually take the name of some quality that they possess or that is attributed to them: from their habitual occupation, from some physical feature, from their form of dress, etc., and above all from the territory they inhabit. Basques, when they speak about themselves and express themselves in their language, they only accept one name, disregarding all others even though they may have received solemn and numerous confirmations. That name is that of *euskaldun*, the equivalent, as is well known, to one who possesses Euskara [the Basque language]. And in a generic way foreign peoples are designated, in their language: *erdaldun*, that is, the possessor of *erdara* [a foreign language].

Well, gentlemen, will you find a descriptive feature that more intimately corresponds to a person, that more intimately imbues and envelops them to the point of being the continent of all thoughts and volitions, the crystal that colors the imagination, the inclined arch between two realities, internal and external, an organ of active and passive information, the true robes of the soul, if not language? Well from this most personal note Basques have taken their national name.

The historically known Basque people are a small people. It seems to me futile to go into their numeric oscillation in diverse eras; for all that we may stretch out the account, it does not seem to us so different from the current figure, since in Navarre the population has decreased, while the Basque provinces and the French Basque Country have seen theirs grow. Thus, this people, a reduced islet that emerged in a foreign ocean allowed itself the luxury, the excess—no other name fits, gentlemen—of constituting six more or less complete political states; a kingdom, Navarre, which later split into two joining different nationalities; a seigneury, Bizkaia; two *behetrías*, Araba and Gipuzkoa; two viscounties, Lapurdi and Zuberoa. History records days in which barely a million people, linked by the most sacred ties of blood, were subject to five different sovereignties; those of Araba and Gipuzkoa to the king of Castile, those of Bizakia to their seigneur, those of Lapurdi to the king of France, the Navarrese to their own king, and those of Zuberoa to that of England. And if we delve deeper into each of these states, what a diversity of laws and fueros among the regions delimited by the borders themselves; what aversion to written law, the instrument of fusion; what attachment to custom, the differentiating organ! Each Basque state was a mosaic, and this not just in Navarre, a nationality formed b conquest, a land in which an indigenous race existed alongside invading races or simply immigrants: Romans, Germans, Arabs, Jews, Provençals, and French; Navarre, which in the same territory that is just a province in the Spanish monarchy outlined five miniscule provinces under the name *merindades*; this not just in Navarre, I repeat, but in all the most homogenously Basque states. How many centuries did Bizkaia need to provide itself with a common parliament, so that the holy branches of the oak of Gernika could extend the shade of peace to the whole Bizkaian territory!

Do you want, gentlemen, the most typical feature, the most undeniable signal of individualism? Do you not also imagine that there is something in excess here, a certain diversion from a good principle that, making us jealous of our siblings, subjects us more easily to outside influence? Does it not seem to you likewise that, without denying our past, nor attempting to erase the legitimate differences consecrated by time, the time has come to extol continuously, both in the practical spheres of politics and in the ideals of art, the concept or *race* or, more accurately, *family*, so that the hands of the Basque tribes may extend fraternally across the borders of the provinces and the contingent nationalities? Does it not seem to you that, after allying and federating ourselves with foreigners so much, it would be appropriate to reconstitute a common home? In order to do so, it is enough to listen to the clamors of blood!

If you examine, gentlemen, a map of Navarre, at first sight you will observe one fact. Toward the borders with Aragón and Castile, on the plains irrigated by the flowing rivers, where successive invasions took root and the primitive Basque topography by a layer more or less full of alien names, the historic town centers are few and dense. As you approach the central rugged massif and advance into the ravines of the Pyrenees, fully in the Basque country by race, although not always by language, one notes the opposite phenomenon. The size of the villages falls, and their number increases; municipal unity is the result of the federation of the hamlets, more accurately neighborhoods, that exist side by side in the same valley. The town council of Esteribar is made up of thirty-one places; the largest is Eugi, and it does not incorporate even four hundred souls; some of them, [such as] Tirapegi, despite being termed a council, had in 1892 less inhabitants than one house, six. The largest town in the Deierri [Yerri] Valley, made up of twenty-five places, is Lezaun: it has 341 souls. And many others like that. If you cross the boundary marked by the Belate dividing line, isolated homes appear that are called *bordas* there.

This fact is of great significance. The natural dwelling of the Basque, when the surrounding circumstances do not prohibit it, is the farmhouse, and, at most, the village. The farmhouse, gentlemen, how beautiful, how much those of us who love the Basque race should love it! It is the oyster that protects and hides the Basque pearl; the peace of the eclogues and the sweetness of the idylls reign; you perceive the murmur of the groves and the pleasant fragrance of fresh milk. The tight, stable, robust, industrious family, spread out in order of status and age, warming the stiff gray hairs of the great-grandfather with the golden curls of the grandchildren, comes together inside the smoky kitchen. In the poetry that the rustic home, the shady mountains, the approaching mist, and disheveled stables exhale, vibrates a serious note, the voice of a certain sentiment that ennobles and dignifies everything, never heard nor even suspected that home of Alpheus that Virgil envied: the murmuring of the rosary, the palpitation of Christian prayer. In this way, in a solitude that provoked boredom or sadness in the urban dweller, the *baserritar* [farmer] exercises sovereignty over the isolation, far from the irritating community of men, near the community of God.

It still seems to me, gentlemen, that this feature exceeds the meaningful value of the political division highlighted to verify the individualistic character of the Basque spirit. And how much, but how much does it say! Because living alone suits the strong and the brave. The eagle, the lion, are solitary animals. Whoever lives alone possesses within the loom and the thread that weave the plot of their own fortune; it reveals that this fortune stems from a sum of internal emotions, and not from a mechanical juxtaposition of feelings. Do you think that Beethoven, when he composed the *Eroica*, was remembering social gatherings? The emptier the man, the more he needs to fill himself with externalities. The fops, the snobs, the… I do not know what they are called, enclose within themselves an insatiable chasm: frivolity. And because they are frivolous they pursue endless amusement, without finding anything but eternal boredom. Inner wealth does not depend on the quantity, but on the quality of the content; two or three ideas or sentiments are enough, as long as they are felt truly. Love of God, love of the family, love of the native land that nourishes, amassed with the holy effort of work. This is the inventory of our rural workers: a reflection of the infinite on a small pile of dust. Now count, gentlemen, the heads of cattle in the pen, the chickens in the yard, the pigs in the pigsty, the apple trees in the orchard, the herbs in the meadow, the grains of wheat on the threshing floor; count the clothes, the furnishings, the implements, the furniture; all of it fills what? Half a sheet of paper? And exclaim immediately thereafter: how great are these men that are so happy with so little!

Etxeko jauna, the "master of the house," that is, "the master who comes from" or "originates in" a specific house, which equates him to the lineage or roots out of which that main branch or head of the family emanates. This simple phrase that, notwithstanding its democratic extension, retains a certain hint of the ceremonious and the solemn, as well as that of a noble title, although relating to the purely familial order, is extremely interesting because it provides us who a sociological concept of the Basque people. Note, gentlemen, that it does not mark a mere property relationship, ordered with the suffix *en*, but rather that of the extraction *ko*, the same one used to indicate that an individual is from this town or that district. In fact, the *etxeko jaun* is not even always the owner or landlord of the house he inhabits, and even if he were, he is always a native of it; indeed, it is often the case, etymologically speaking, that the soubriquet of the subject that possesses it is inadequate. Yet ideologically the match is perfect. Because the dominant and exclusive meaning of the notion is that the man, the family, and the house form a unit. The *ko* marks a natural, that is, perpetual, bond; the *en* would mark a legal, that is, weaker, tie. The individual is at the center of a dual moral and material circle of different radiuses: the family and the house. And the master, *jaun*, is, within the circle, that is, the head of a body, although elemental, perfect in its genre; the expansion or, better stated, the transcendentalization of the single central element. In this way, Basque individualism, so vigorous and pronounced, does not resemble modern *atomism* either from close up or from far away.

Let us speak now, gentlemen, about the house. Materially it is made up of a few cart loads of stones or bricks, but morally... the word "world" comes out from my lips! And why not? In order to live solitarily, on rough terrain, the house is *the* world; and even for he who lives among men, it is *a* world as well. It constitutes the loves of the Basque. He takes his surname from the name of the house; a surname and name not imposed by fantasy, but by nature. Basque surnames, as you know full well, are generally topographical. Within them the land and man marry. The four humble walls, naked to the eyes of indifference, are really full of tapestries that family tradition has woven and drawn with the yarn of the fiber of life. After so much association between family and house, the latter came to be the tangible symbol of the former, not at the actual moment of its existence, but during the immense development of generations. The noble organization of society contributed to extolling the importance of the house, converting it into the testimony of nobility by means of the concept of the ancestral home. The facades were covered in heraldic shields and personal privilege, tax exemptions, and political functions resided in the ancestral home: the right to sit in the Parliament of Navarre, for example.

The records of scribes and files in archives house thousands of most interesting and varied examples of the worship of the house among Basques, whose perpetual upkeep they always sought, reflecting that instinct of immortality that is one of the bases of our nature. The fact was attested to, in the name of everyone, by Doña Guillermina de Atondo, the paternal grandmother of Saint Francis Xavier, who, in her will of November 10, 1490, said:

> Furthermore, I order, wish, and mandate that Pedro de Jassu, my son, during his days, and his descendants who, in time, will inherit the said house and legal age, must always respect and maintain the honor of the main house and those that will be its masters, the aforementioned Don Johan de Jassu in his time and his heirs in theirs, as the senior relative and as descendants of that house; and likewise the said doctor in his time and his heirs, each in his own, may they look on and treat as sons of the house the masters who will be inheritors of the house of the aforementioned Pedro de Jassu; as long as everyone agrees with their duties and love, they will be seen as more esteemed and honored, may the homes last longer, everyone looking on this and functioning as descendants of a father and a house.

That society disappeared, but the sentiment that Doña Guillermina de Atondo expressed with such vividness lasts and remains currently, which demonstrates that it is not of noble or aristocratic origin, as others would contend, but is rather of an ethnic sentiment. In order to demonstrate this fully, gentlemen, permit me to sketch an outline of the Navarrese family organization, exactly as we observe it among rural workers in villages, among the owners of their own regular property, and from whom nor are the upper classes so removed that, while they disappeared in the ancient kingdom and maintained the characteristic of territorial owners, continue to live in the old fashioned way off the land. This old fashioned way is widespread, except in the district of Tutera.

The perpetuation of the Navarrese family or, put more accurately, *house* is achieved by means of applying legal institutions, the offspring, in turn, of the individualistic sentiment that pervades the concept of property: the free and absolute freedom to make a will, created, observe attentively, gentlemen, by *custom over law*, and universal donations on the occasion of marriage. I disregard the other two other interesting, but not key from my point of view, institutions: direct family inheritance and right of first refusal.

There is less use of the freedom to make a will because its essence, which is the free disposition of possessions, is exercised with absolute amplitude in marriage contracts or donations *propter nupcias*, in which not only is the family organized during the whole life of the donors, but even after their days, by means of the express designation of a person to receive the possessions, becoming a piece by way of the joint will and contract.

There is nothing comparable, as I understand it, in purely civil life, to that great spectacle. The parents of the future bride and groom having met, the mutual affection of the latter having been examined and verified, and likewise the closest relatives having come together with the idea that the sacrosanct notion of the family fits all these acts under its amorous wings, they organize the new family, extend their request to the other children, and look toward the glow and perpetuity of the native house. They choose and older or younger son or daughter, since neither age nor sex enjoy any preference, and that choice, when the only things to bear in mind are the personal qualities of whoever is favored and the circumstances of general coexistence, common language defines it with the expressive phrase: "make a child for the house." A pact is made over common life, and the parents reserve the *mastery* and *rule*, that is, the authority they received from God, as regards people; and as regards possessions, the faculty to refuse agreement to levy or transfer them. Likewise they reserve a small sum in cash in order to be able to make a will in their day, retaining in a symbolic way the characteristic faculty of the father of a family: the active making of a will. Children that receive the donations are obliged, for their part, to feed and assist their parents and siblings, stipulating the conditions befitting of the different states. With respect to the parents, in the event of separation on account of incompatibility of personalities, the bulk of the possessions that must be divided is established, and the main rooms are reserved for them, with the remaining rooms given to those who received the donations, and when this is not possible in a house, the latter leave, taking with them the portion highlighted. With respect to the other children, the siblings of those who receive the donations, they must be fed and clothed in health and in sickness, until they contract marriage, deciding on dowries or advance inheritance gifts. It is agreed, finally, that one of the children of the future marriage must be, in turn, the heir, deciding on dowries or advance inheritance gifts for the others, without this being understood as a prohibition of selling possessions; and in the event that the parents die without having designated an heir and the decision about dowries, this function is entrusted temporarily to the two closest relatives, one on each side of the family, and a third in case of discord; and in the event that the parents do not make a will about their portion, it is declared included within the donation; and in the event that there is no offspring, new class are established. The door is closed to all legitimate or potential legal expectations by means of the institution in foral lawfulness or the form of *sueldos* or *carlines* or paths stolen from common mountains, being an act so complex, with similar prescriptions, perfect, finished, and irrevocable.

I have stopped, gentlemen, to trace this outline of the Navarrese family, even at the risk of bothering your attention with too many details, because in my opinion it expresses in a *representative* and absolute way the spirit of Basque family individualism, without the obstacles that inhibited its complete flourishing in other districts of the Basque Country. No one would deny, to be sure, that this system is only possible on the basis of a cooperation of neither small nor unstable virtues. Oh, the day Navarrese heart was empowered with egalitarian envy! Oh, the day the notion of family solidarity became blurred! Oh, the day that the concept of a merely "economic" life came to predominate! Oh, the day that paternal authority was not the direct reflection of God's authority, and that respect for old age waned, and the elderly, the poor elders, instead of being venerable were rendered useless, their feeding and clothing constituting the most insufferable chapter of tasks! That day, every Navarrese home would be hell, and every marriage contract a sinister evocation of Cain!

But in the meantime, gentlemen, I must confess that I have spoken to you about a great matter, despite the defects and inconveniences that may in fact diminish it. At the end of the day, men and not saints are the beings that make up those families. But because they are men, they suggest a noble, comforting, and exemplary spectacle. Parents abdicate at that age, they mature but they do not expire, so that hearts typically adhere to landed possessions more tenaciously. They lose their importance as salient figures in the picture and resign themselves to occupying some small corner in the shadows. The tones of authority deafen into insinuations of advice. The activity of the *young masters* transcends all orders. The customary tasks proceed ceaselessly, with the addition of the soft note of love to the sharp note of work. The house benefits from the new energy and enthusiasm. Although the property of one, it continues to be everyone's, and the sibling mistreated by misfortune finds refuge there, in order to recover and to gain encouragement, like a fisherman returning to port in a damaged boat. And when death calls for the parents, no spirit of greed or indiscreet curiosity stalks their final anguish, nor casts on the portentous irradiation of the eternal the thick shadows of the world. Everything is prepared and anticipated in advance by a law that everyone has known and followed for a long time, resembling, from this point of view, the transmission of goods from the humblest farmer to that of a king's crown.[1]

And for that Basque who lives among wolves and forests more happily than among men; who has transformed his home—often a humble shack—into an inestimable jewel whose unscathed transmission is ensured, through the generations, making all those laborious efforts and all the resources of the law meet that key goal,

---

1   This whole picture of the constitution of the Navarrese family by means of marriage contracts is taken, with the exception of slight modifications of form, from a report on foral codification in Navarre written by the chair of the Committee of Codes, my honorable friend Don Antonio Morales, a distinguished legal counsel and most eloquent orator who in the first parliament after the Restoration defended, with noble words befitting such a just cause, the rights of the ancient kingdom, denied by Mr. Cánovas del Castillo.

to the point that today there are houses that have survived the devastations of wars and the modifications, a thousand times more deadly, of society, therefore being examples of a true petrification of time; for that Basque, such an individualist, so personal, such a lover of the sovereign "I," does he want to be imprisoned by the irons of socialism and collectivism? Making him a "workmate," registered by order of number, putting a value on the hours he works, rewarding him with stamped vouchers, replacing the *etxeko andrea* with whom he shares the rights and duties of domestic sovereignty, for a woman who is also registered, assigned the animal functions of reproduction; depriving him of the ration of paternity that God assigns each man so that, by which, they may exercise the most noble virtues and benefit from the softest comforts, snatching his children away from him and submitting them to the horrendous promiscuity of universal *socialization?* This is not possible, gentlemen! You would sooner uproot Gorbea!

There is absolute and irreducible repulsion between the Basque spirit and socialism. This explains why the propagandists, instigators, and followers of those ideas, the shame of Bizkaia, are outsiders, nomads of servile immigration. This is the latest foreign invasion that we are suffering. And in the same way that they attack the purity of our race and the integrity of our untainted physiognomy with their waves of ethnic *detritus*, a hybrid mass of bastardized Celts, of decadent Latins, and corrupted Moors, they are still attempting, gentlemen, to cause us greater harm, poisoning our souls with a vulgar ideal, befitting of jealous slaves![2]

---

2   The tendency of workers to improve their economic conditions is honest, legitimate, and laudable. It deserves all my sympathy as long as this improvement is considered a means to acquiring greater intellectual and moral perfection, and not to enlarging a narrow margin of material pleasures.

The fulfillment of duties that Christian morality imposes on the rich is, now, more pressing than ever. We must ensure that it rises continuously from the dead precept of routine exhortation to a living percept in deeds.

It is not enough for Catholics to ponder the wisdom of the teachings of Leo XIII on the social question; it is necessary, moreover, and mainly, that we set to work. Our Lord Jesus Christ said that there would never be a lack of poor people among us (and there will be, despite the modern redeemers); yet for the resignation to which they are exhorted to not sound like sarcasm, it must be accompanied by the self-denial of the rich.

I think I have outlined, gentlemen, the innate tendency of the Basque to live isolated and in small population settlements: the farmhouse, the hamlet, the village. Just as the exception proves the rule, the foundation of cities and towns, in pointing out a new current of ideas and sentiments, underscores that primitive tendency. The foundation of cities and towns responded to new and external needs, of a general nature, which say nothing about any particular Basque tendency, but is instead part of the phenomena of civilization, common eras and interests. For example: the collection of ranches of *Iruña* had to be elevated to *Pompaelo*, as *Lutetia* was to *Paris*, merely on account of its topographical position; it suited the Romans to possess and fortify it in order to dominate as much as they could the restless Basque Country; gradually converted into a military, administrative, and religious center, it received the seal of capital for ever and ever. The desire to foment navigation and commerce presided over the foundation of Bilbao, a poor neighborhood of the village of Begoña. Few are the cities and towns in the Basque-Navarrese Country—if any indeed exist—whose foundation cannot be connected to a strategic, administrative, economic, or political reason. This instinct to establish towns is an *imposed* instinct, as Taine would say. Several of them were just renovated settlements, on which Roman urbanization had exerted its influence. Sometimes they absorbed therein diverse villages and scattered places. Such was the case, for example, when the

---

If you break the natural and divine laws of society, there are many legislative reforms favorable to the welfare of the greatest number. Combined individual and public action may, in large part, redeem some of their excessive wealth and others from their extreme poverty.

The censorship of the text is aimed exclusively at militant socialism, led by *politicians* who, when they were not born *bourgeois* and seek ways to obtain public office, aspire to live in the bourgeois way, handling, instead of the tools of the trade, high-sounding phrases of socialist rhetoric, while continuing to pursue the aforementioned positions like others; against all that accumulation of errors, delusions, lusts, and blasphemies, invented by the most perverse revolutionary radicalism, which proclaims not social harmony, beneficial to all, but *class struggle*, deadly for everyone.

Do a lot, but much good to the workers; combat mercy without socialism: this is the program. By design, the current ruling classes are unable to show the generosity and energy required. The lack of strong religious convictions and the practical materialism that corrodes them have made of them a flock willing to enter the slaughterhouse. With the coldness of the stupid or selfish they listen to the most horrendous denials and contemplate the most threatening movements. Their philosophy is that of Louis XV: *après moi, le deluge.*

inhabitants of the land of Aranatz, during the fourteenth-century border wars with the Gipuzkoans, took refuge inside the *bastide* or fortress called Etxarri, and founded the current town of Etxarri-Aranatz.

In the Basque provinces the foundation of towns was linked intimately, to the point of constituting a chapter therein, to the history of the factions. And the war of the factions was a sinister outburst of the individualist spirit, free of any religious or moral curbs to ennoble it. Lope García de Salazar, in relating the origin of the struggles between the house of Urtubia and that of Ugarte, with the greatest naivety, declared: "and it is said that the cause of that was jealousy, and which was worth more." And much the same in referring to the feuds within the Seigneury of Bizkaia: "In the year of Our Lord 1425 there was a war and much discord between Ochoa de Butron and Iñigo Ortiz de Ibargüen his cousin, over who was worth more in land…" The foundation of towns was a reaction against unstoppable individualism, and contributed effectively to that sentiment being clarified, eliminating the dregs of antisocial passions that it contained.

Basque individualism was evident equally in the two forms of political organization that the Basques adopted when they were in control of realizing their natural tendencies spontaneously, because outside ideas applied little to them, because outside laws did not restrict them from their free movement. These two forms, gentlemen, were feudalism and democracy. At first sight, it seems absurd to fit such diverse ideas together; but on closer inspection, we see two correlative ideas, owing to an identical cause.

Feudalism stems from the bond of personal ties that make up an objective hierarchy. The benefits and the domains ceded brought with them the fulfillment of certain obligations or services, with such express preciseness as accepted free will. Loyalty, fidelity, honor, purely individualist sentiments were the base and guarantee of those obligations. They do not stem from the concept of homeland, whose material base is a land enclosed by borders, but from swearing oaths and contracts. For that reason, the clause in which the obligation was consigned to help the seigneur against men from all over the world, except against him and them, was so typical, since another previous feudal link prohibited it. This, for example, in the year 1234 Raymond Guillen, the Viscount of Soule, paid homage to King Theobald I of Navarre, in Maule Castle, telling him:

> I become your vassal My Lord Don Theobald, by the grace of God, the honorable King of Navarre, and Count Palatine of Champagne and of Brie, in such a way, in good faith and without any deceit, that I must be obliged to you to serve against all the men of the world, as a loyal vassal must do service to the Lord . . . except for that land that the King of England has in his hands and in his domains.

A similar system of organization, so different to the classical Greek or Roman city, in which man was a mere political unit without his own value, appears to have been invented to order by the Basques, who did not know how to create the greater concept of a common Basque nationality. That is how it developed widely, where the historical circumstances favored or did not impede it, for example, in Navarre, whose "rich men or minor nobles," according to the old general fuero (bk. 5, title 2, chap. 5) find us aided by a "trust," in which perhaps the vestiges of the primitive disorganized clan are transparent:

> All rich men or minor nobles of powerful gentlemen that had sons and daughters, and vassal gentlemen and squires who may receive a salary or other benefits, and salaried apprentices, watchmen and plowmen, cattlemen, shepherds, and pig farmers, and many others contracted on a salary, and looking after their close relatives giving them food and clothing and everything else that they need, and also aiding many other foreigners that come and go, eating in their home, and the "mutton, barley, or moneyed vassals," whom are defended in the market court or in any other place...

What profound harmony in the institutions! You can see it, gentlemen, sought out in the most abundant quarry of the Fuero, worthy of being exploited by a Thierry, the highest personification of the noble classes. What have we found? The Basque patriarchal house.

The feeling of personal equality—another individualist sentiment—abandoning its own inspirations, among all the possible political forms, chooses naturally democracy. In the same way that feudal organization in Navarre led to the individualist branch, democratic organization flourished from the same root in the Basque provinces, without this implying that these provinces have not known feudal elements in their constitution, or the Pyrenean kingdom democratic elements in its constitution.

Since nowadays so much is said about democracy, without the anthems and dithyrambs of its official and officious panegyrists managing to hide what stem from it, those decadent governments, a field of manoeuvers for professional politicians, and prizes to foment all manner of mediocrity and corruption, I wish to pause a moment to salute Bizkaian democracy, a prototype and model of Basque democracy. Proudhon, in one of those bouts of tremendous sincerity that he used to endure, defined contemporary democracy by saying: "democracy is envy."

Such is, in effect, all political democracy that resides in personal egoism, I the eagerness to make all classes equal, not managing to raise, but to lower those ho are at the top. But Bizkaian democracy was not a "political" democracy, a dynamic commotion that destroys an order of things; it was a "social" democracy, the static formula of an almost homogenous society that took its natural seat. It was not the product of a philosophical theory, but the expression of facts.

The proudest kings bowed their heads on their knees before the oak of Gernika, the sparkle of their crowns warmed by the verdant reflections of foliage. In its beneficent shadow grew, like the grass in the meadows, laws of *free will*, if not of *subtlety and the rigor of law*. Agreements to die for religion and the homeland sounded out, with Thermopylaean fortitude maintained, and the Christian fraternity carried out the miracle of constituting a natural aristocracy, without any decrease in democratic equality, entrusting the ordering of public things to the best citizens. The envy of the poor, the insolence of the powerful, the avarice of the rich, the brutality of the strong, the bribes of ambition, the bastardy of private interest, or the perjuries of infidelity never infected the agreements of the foral councils; nor Shylock's money bag, filled by hands tainted by the minerals of Somorrostro, bought at an ignominious auction those in charge of the Republic. Bizkaian democracy, I bless you! You are the oldest and, therefore, more illustrious than Helvetian democracy! Your faith remained pure without any Calvin corrupting it. While your valleys lack the dazzling resonance of the Alpine snows, in contrast they hear the sublime somber song of the verdant ocean frosted with spray. The five sirens of Oiz, Sollube, Kolitza, Ganekogorta, and Gorbea answer the trumpets of Uri, Schwyz, and Unterwald. And while Schiller communicated his prestigious poetry to the Rütli confederation, another no less celebrated poet, Tirso de Molina, sculpted in his immortal verses the austere freedom of the Bizkaians.

III

I warned you, gentlemen, at the beginning of my talk, that its material was most vast in itself, and that I proposed to touch on only some points. I have said something to you about Basque individualism in history and in law; but the material lack of space obliges me to restrict my observations about Basques and their use of arms, which would have only illustrated the matter more clearly, explaining the apparent antinomy that is observed between the profound repugnance of the Basques toward conscription and any form of collective military service, and the great number of men that distinguished themselves under the flags of the kings of Spain and France. You would also have seen why, in the civil wars ignited by those two grand plagues on our society that are called the Liberal and Carlist parties, the transformation of militias into regular armies was accompanied by the crystallization of the progresses of fighting. While *guerrillas* may have fight, is it still discrete to ask: when would they win completely? But scarcely had the *generals* begun, and the question was something else: when would they be defeated definitively? Despite that, an entire section of my program, "the Basque personality in poetry," will not appear in the project. Nor do I propose demanding too much of your attention, courteous and benevolent as it is, nor would it be forgivable that, when it came to the moment I should bring my words to an end, I began developing a topic that would double the length of my talk.

A basic idea will suffice for today. Among all the genres of poetry, that best felt and expressed by the Basque is the lyrical genre. You all know that lyrical poetry is subjective poetry, the poetry of "I," since although the poet launches into describing the external world, or narrating external events, what he really demonstrates is the impression this makes on his soul. How few are the "literary" pretentions of the Basque poet, I mean, greater are the preferences he expresses for the lyrical genre. This fact is revealed with midday clarity by noting the poetry that, in the form of short songs, they met to compete for the prizes offered by Monsieur d'Abbadie for so many years. The winners were, usually, men of scarce education and therefore in the most intimate of harmonies with the Basque popular consciousness.

I estimate that the poetry entitled "Solferinoko itsua" [The blind man of Solferino] by the French Basque Salaberri, is characteristic. It is a gentle, sentimental poetry in which the inconsolable sadness of its author, who goes blind after the Battle of Solferino, moans. Do you think that for a moment the poet lifts the veil of shadows to show us at least a small corner of the epic clash, or that the idea of having written with his blood a page in the history of Europe serves as some consolation? There is no trace of military pride, nor vestiges of patriotic exaltation. While the Basque was able easily to remain silent before French exploits, he was able in contrast to feel that his blood had not been shed in the defense or for the glory of the Basque Country! He referred to everything in terms of himself; and with what grief!

Ene amaren begi samurrak, betiko zaizkit estali.
Maiteñoaren begithartea behin betiko itzali...
Behin betiko itzali.

My mother's soft eyes are concealed from me forever,
My beloved's face obscured forever...
Obscured forever.

Herriko bestan, gazte lagunak kantuz plazara dohazi,
Eta ni beltzik, eche zokhoan, irri egiten ahantzi,
Irri egiten ahantzi!

In the village festival, young friends go out singing in the square,
I, shrouded in darkness, in a corner at home, have forgotten how to laugh,
I have forgotten how to laugh!

Other poets sang about home, about the herd of sheep, the freedom of the charcoal burner in his shack, the solemnity of the woods, the anxieties of jealousy, the delights and torments of loving, the beauties of nature, the nostalgias of the emigrant... lyrical sentiments, in sum, or aspects of the world and life contemplated through a lyrical temperament.

Gentlemen, individualism is a salient feature of the Basque moral physiognomy. From it flow, like a spring, the qualities and also several of the defects of the race. Religion corrected the ferocity of that sentiment, stopping it from degenerating into an antisocial instinct. Before embracing the Christian religion, the Basques were ferocious and heartless men. Each eclipse of Catholic influence has marked a horrible relapse in customs. Let us love, above all and against everything, the sacrosanct religion. It is the truth and it places the honeycomb in the mouth of that lion called the Basque people. For that reason we are a beloved and honorable people. Impiety, gentlemen, is "foreign." Let us correct the defects of the individualist character: the tendency to isolation and particularism, obstinacy dressed as coherency, vitreous self-love, an excessive attachment to particular judgement, envy, which ignores the enjoyment of applause and of admiration. But let us fight to preserve our personality, into which so many influences run and dissolve. Let us look out from the banks of the Ebro and contemplate, new Spartans, the spectacle of inebriated helots; do we want to be assimilated in *that*? Let us ensure we remain Basques, and continue to be yourselves, gentlemen, those that walk at the head of those that achieve.

I have spoken.

Chapter 8

Speech at the Basque Festival of Azpeitia
on September 30, 1901

Honorable gentlemen:

Invited to say a few words during the act of awarding prizes recognizing the merit of Basque poets and writers, I did not even attempt to restrain myself, stating before the council of the floral games in Donostia-San Sebastián the good reasons that surrounded my refusal. I suspect fundamentally that the courteous hosts will have dismissed them and that, stressing their original tone of courtesy, they would have gone out to lock up some of those "tasks" that are invented for similar cases. And instead of such surly words being heard, I preferred my enthusiasm and joy to be given free rein in communicating intensely with this select part of the Basque race known as the people of Gipuzkoa.

It ignites the singular brightness of my affection—as well as the concurrence that, among my rural pastimes and those elevated mountains and those shaded valleys populated by idylls, establishes and solidifies my sense of an external nature, and of the enchantment produced in me by the gentleness of your customs, the Georgian beauty of your women, the loyalty and courtesy of your men, the Catholic aroma of your social being—a unique and precious circumstance intensifies my ignited affection: that of the fact that all the peoples that make up the noble Gipuzkoan home *still* speak the millenarian and marvelous language that, since the time immemorial of the race, with the exception of atrocious catastrophes in which the greatest empires of the West and East ended up being involved, has come down to us today without blemish or error, frivolity or blasphemy, always worthy of transmitting even on the throne of the Almighty, the requests of prayer. In this way, if the dust of native sepulchers were to be animated with the breath of life, Gipuzkoans today could converse with those remote ancestors of theirs whose dates time has forgotten. An enviable perpetuation of the ethnic soul, which almost all the inhabitants of Araba, many in Bizkaia, and too many in Navarre interrupted, condemned to claiming the titles of their historic independence in a language learned from their very hereditary enemies and tormentors themselves!

You will have observed, gentlemen, that I used the adjective "still." Not without sadness, to be honest. Because it indicates how much I fear and suspect that soon, too soon, some Gipuzkoan towns that defend their own language, and isolated villages, may follow zones and districts in repeating the unfortunate replacement that many districts and zones in Araba, Bizkaia, and Navarre already carried out: a replacement to which pariahs have not rendered, serving as an example and reproach to all, the Basque territories located in France.

Someone will suspect, perhaps, that I come to repeat or reflect certain omens of death that, recently and in solemn festivity, some scandalized and embittered the country. Let us hope, gentlemen, that in the speech to which I allude there would have been nothing else except an allusion to precise, observable, and clear facts, which are put forward, in the way of facts, pitilessly: the twilight, dusk, late afternoon of the Basque language, after which night falls.

I myself, and in Bilbao, had just declared that the Basque language was retreating into the mountains to die closer to heaven. No one took it badly or censured that declaration. It is because they saw in me the son that holds a vigil at his mother's bedside, who would give his blood to keep her life going, and who, far from proclaiming that she is an inadequate, burdensome, decrepit being that should be buried ostentatiously, cries out ceaselessly that she is curable and deserving of living perpetually, and that she would take with her to the grave the meaning and even the name of the house. Yet in the speech to which I refer, next to the truth of the facts slithered and crawled rumors of all kinds, the sterile fruit of a great but wayward inventiveness. It was deemed that a Basque, worthy of being so, cannot contemplate with stone cold impassivity the agony of the Basque language, as well as the fact that the "science" of a wise person, even though great, is worth infinitely less than the "love" of a patriot.[1]

Those that equate languages with a living organism, that of a plant or an animal, necessarily believe that they are subject to the universal law of death. I do not accept this comparison unless in a metaphorical, analogous, or merely explanatory sense. But let us suppose that I am wrong: observation teaches us that, just as a lesser number of organisms perishes by natural death, that is, from old age, and that generally they succumb to the misfortunes of an accident or sickness, so history, likewise, reveals that the immense majority of disappeared languages did not die, but were killed off. External causes or, put another way, sicknesses and accidents ended the plots of their lives: the ruin of nationality, the loss of political predominance, and, principally, the degeneration of patriotic sentiment. For a people to lose their language it is necessary, to some extent, for them to begin by looking down on it themselves. Language, gentlemen, is the externalization of the ethnic soul, and conquerors' chains and the tyrant's knife do not reach into the soul.

Nor do the Basque people belong to those that suddenly come into contact with civilizations superior to their own, such as the Australian tribes next to their European discoverers. They coexisted with the Roman Empire, with Visigoths, with Franks, with the Arab Caliphate, with the great Spanish and French monarchies, to whom they were federated. Nor is the practical use that knowledge of *other languages* yields a thing of today. Nevertheless, the Basque language has been spoken through an

---

1 Mr. Unamuno himself, years later, has appreciated in the following terms certain effects of his discourse: "...in the compliments that have been lavished on me by that act, there is a disgusting, foul-smelling background. They do not praise what is called patriotism, not saying serenely and calmly the truth, no; they were delighted to see that a people was wounded in its vital sentiments, my Basque people, whom they could save. I was, unwittingly, an instrument of their petty passions" (Paragraph cited in *Euskalduna*, July 29, 1905).

indeterminate series of centuries. Why, gentlemen? The answer is easy: because Basques loved their language and wanted to speak it.

This factor of sovereign will would contradict the enemies of the originality of peoples, those who try to convert nations into a kind of human "jumble," a cadaverous "detritus," where it may manage to cloak in suitable form the infernal spirit of demagogy. And they seek a way of hiding it beneath the sinister veil of sophisms, with the aim, by showing our minds the concept of some inevitable laws, of weakening our spirit and that we capitulate without a fight.

For that reason they tell us that the Basque language is of no use for official purposes; that the educated classes of the country practically disdain it, in conversing always in Castilian or French; that it is the speech of ignorant rough people; that if some loftier idea must be expressed in it, there is no remedy but to invent words that turn it into a hieratical language, inaccessible to the masses; that works of literary pretensions require the "enlightenment" of a small attached vocabulary; that the literature of our floral games is abstract, cold, sterile. The conclusion of these and similar reasons is that Castilian and French, civilized, administrative, political, and literary languages, will suffocate *fatally* Basque, a purely common language.

Ah, gentlemen, this conclusion would be true if it were not a lie! If man were reduced to the role of robot subject to determinist evolution! If man lacked will!

It is not true that, in the "struggle" between two languages, one civilized and the other common, the former should triumph fatally over the latter. In the appendixes in my *Gramática* [Grammar] I included several memorable examples that demonstrate quite the contrary. I refer to the examples from Romania, from Finland, from Hungary, from Croatia, from Germany itself that I mentioned there. But observe that all of those are imbued with the concept of struggle expressed by me; and they are not when one of the parties resigns softly to losing its language, or seeks criminally to lose it. What is the case of the Basque people? Formulating the question comes with great pain for me, and even more answering it in the terms you are going to hear.

The Basques, in regard to the survival of their language, are divided into three groups: the enthusiasts, the indifferent, and the enemies. The first and third groups—the former select, the latter degenerate—make up a minority; the predominant one is the second group. This is made up of people who speak Basque because they learned it in the cradle, and who still prefer it for family conversations over any other they may possess. Do not ask anything more of them; their mentality is incapable of taking in the idea that the loss of the language is a transcendental fact added to the life of the people that speaks it. If you repeat to them my old axiom, that changing a language is changing a soul, they would shrug their shoulders, considering from the first moment that it was insubstantial and vacuous hot air. Because those people do not experience any variation, they do not realize what is happening around them or, perhaps, because of its gradual nature, they do not even notice. They are witnessing, with cold insensitivity, the installation in their homes of generations that are absolutely alien to them through their way of speaking; the family, previously linguistically homogeneous, has been replaced by other dualist forms in the intervening period, of which there are so many unfortunate examples in Navarre: grandparents speak exclusively in Basque, their children badly in Basque and in Castilian, and the grandchildren exclusively in Castilian; a rough incorrect Castilian, with touches of Barbarian; the Castilian of Aragón and La Rioja; a vehicle for coarseness, obscenity, and blasphemy.

Let us leave this sphere of unconsciousness, in which due to a lack of willingness to carry out acts the only deplorable thing is that unconsciousness itself, and examine, containing my natural indignation, the third group, the group of ungrateful Basques, unworthy of belonging to their race. Imagine that, among the diverse varieties of this kind of ignominious person, two are especially worth highlighting: the variety of the "intellectuals" and that of the "utilitarians." Consider, gentlemen, how this description of intellectuals, in itself innocent and even praiseworthy, is gradually acquiring everywhere a meaning that would denigrate all truly honorable people. In detail, it designates today the delinquents of the pen, enemies of Christian civilization, who to the cry of different principles and without principles of any kind, for pure nihilism and moral anarchism, combat it satanically. I now observe two nuances among Basque intellectuals: that of simple pedants and that of sectarians. The pedants stress the poverty of Basque literature, and therefore the impossibility of the Basque language contributing to the culture of the country. But from this scarcity, it is noticeable that the language is not guilty, and one does not deduce the consequence that may proceed to contribute to its extinction. Why don't these intellectuals write masterpieces in Basque? But the thing is, nor do they do so in Castilian! The same thig happens to them that happens to liberals, that after attributing intellectual backwardness in Spain to Catholic unity, with irreligious freedom now obtained, nor have original works of consequence been produced, but just miserable translations of the most commonplace books in Europe.

Sectarian intellectuals proceed in a different way: they do not adorn their hostile sentiments with philosophies of any kind. They detest the Basque language because they esteem it to be an obstacle to the diffusion of ideas that they profess, opposed, it is worth noting, to some extent to those that predominate here. Theirs is a utilitarianism that does not look at personal gain, but at that of ideas: for that reason, I refrained from including them in the same identical denomination.

Basque is an unusable organ for the diffusion of culture: this is the main thought of our prestigious intellectuals, and that of those more parsimonious others that, for five cents a day, buy modern wisdom in the "newspaper" store. Thanks to such a short formula, which a parrot would repeat, it is possible for them to repeat, without any anti-patriotic affronts, the scorn of the wise man for our tendencies debated in the open. Just a few days ago, speaking to a respectable Gipuzkoan gentleman who holds an important position in the province, the conversation turned to the Basque language. Said gentleman expressed affection for his maternal language, but esteemed any number of attempts they may carry out to rescue it useless: "It is impossible to write in it," he added by way of victorious conclusion—a treaty of differential calculation. "The same thing," I replied, "as in the Castilian of shepherds, farmers, and fishermen in Castile." I assume he did not understand the scope of my objection.

The Basque language is an exclusively common language. It lacks, therefore, the technical vocabulary of the arts and sciences. But if, instead of undervaluing it, it were used for artistic and scientific aims, the vocabulary that it lacks today would emerge: it would be given neologisms and metaphors distinct from direct borrowings, which do not have to be prohibited from Basque as they are not for any other language. If you were to close off the import of Greek, in particular, to it, the Castilian technical vocabulary would *ipso facto* be equivalent to that of Basque.

The Basque language possesses a rich variety of endings whose enumeration does not make the case. It is also susceptible to combining its words: nouns with nouns, nouns with adjectives, nouns with verbal nouns, adjectives with verbal nouns, nouns with verbal adjectives, adjectives with verbal adjectives, and nouns with numerals, freely, without any other limits than those of the clarity and property of the language. From the point of view of composition and derivation, the grammatical sources of neologism, Basque rubs shoulders with more glorious languages, hovering above Castilian and French. The great writer will create expressive and profound words, the skillful body of thought.

Metaphor consists of translating the sense or meaning befitting objects of one order into others of a different order, in accordance with the specific participation of properties that the spirit discovers or imagines between both. Locke demonstrated, and comparative philology confirms its demonstration, that all words meaning immaterial concepts stem, by metaphorical transformation, from words that express clear ideas. This being the case, the most feared objection that, against Basque as a language of culture, could be formulated, remains peremptorily destroyed. Without metaphor, as Mr. Müller observes, no language would have been able to leave the rudimentary stage.

From that same word "calculation," which came from the mouth of the aforementioned Gipuzkoan gentleman and possesses today such an abstract, immaterial meaning, what was the original etymological meaning? That of "pebble, tiny stone," which is still used today by pathology. You all know the Roman numeration system. It does not lend itself to the regulation of figures in the way that we are accustomed for arithmetic operations. Addition, for example, is the simplest of all. Let us write in Roman numerals the quantities, seven, five, nine, fourteen: VII, V, IX, XIV. If we were to place the additions beneath the others and add them up in our manner, taking each figure for its absolute value, regardless of that of the composition, we would see that because the figures of the same order do not correspond, the result of the addition is erroneous: 1051 instead of 35. Beating the Romans was very difficult. They turned to two methods: the purely mimicked digital one and that of the abacus, which was a stone, metal, or wooden board on which pebbles (*calculi*) were placed that served its functioning and that have given the name to this. If one wanted to subtract 18 from 35, one placed thirty-five pebbles, removed eighteen, and the remainder was the quantity sought. If dividing 408 by 31, four hundred eight pebbles were placed and one thirty-one removed as many times as one could until the remainder was less than thirty-one. The number of times provided the quotient, 16; and the remainder, when there was any, the rest of the division, 2. And all the other operations were like this. If such key words in brilliant culture as "calculation" and "calculate" derived from those pebbles that had been trodden on, imagine, gentlemen, what we could extract from those enormous mountains that surround us on all sides!

In the example proposed we have seen metaphor formed by virtue of a physical act. But the spirit, blessed with unflagging spontaneity on account of the principle of analogy, whether its own or borrowed, essential or accidental, permanent or transitory, transmutes and transfigures meanings continuously. This is the variety of senses that the same word usually has, leading to much confusion for those learning the language. Metaphors make up this diversity, and when the analogy that gave rise to it is obscured by the passage of time, different meanings are many other petrified or dead tropes. The study of metaphorical expressions is one of the most entertaining and pleasant ones in linguistics. It provides us with curious details about ethnic psychology and it reveals customs, institutions, and even hints of history. Mr. Müller took to Rühn a curious list of savage metaphors; on seeing that among them, for example, "hit" was equivalent to "punish," and "dog" to "inferior person," "to be seated" to "live," and "to eat something" to "confiscate goods," I imagine that we do not need to know the savages to portray them. How much does the fact that Germans call "society, company, or a social gathering" *tisch* (table) or "food"? The dual meaning of the Basque *horma*, "wall" and "ice," goes back to the prehistorical perspectives of the Basque people.

The Basque language is today a relatively uncultivated language, there is no reason to hide that, just as a diamond is uncultivated until the jeweler cuts and mounts the lapidary; but being capable of culture on account of possessing its own grammatical resources that many other languages lack, as well as common and ordinary ones, imposes a very distinct conclusion to that which the intellectuals support. The conclusion from logic and patriotism is the following: instead of sidelining and leaving Basque to die, it is necessary to cultivate it faithfully and piously. Good sense came out of the mouth of the celebrated Axular when he wrote the following words: "*Baldin egin balitz euskaraz hanbat liburu nola egin baita latinez, francesez edo bertze erdaraz eta hitzkuntzaz, hek bezain aberats eta konplitu izanen zen euskara ere, eta baldin hala ezpada, Euskaldunek berek dute falta eta ez euskarak*" [If as many books were published in Basque as were so in Latin, French, or any other language, Basque would also be as rich and complex as they are, and if it is not that way, Basque-speakers themselves are at fault and not the Basque language].[2]

---

2   *Geroko gero: Irakurtzalleari.*

Beneath the intellectuals—who do not fly especially high—shuffle the coarse mob of utilitarians. They do not entertain themselves by creating systems or coordinating general ideas; their empiricism does not go beyond the line of feelings of a social kind. There are few that speak the Basque language; those that do not, many; Basques like going to foreign countries, or house in their own foreigners; for the relations that in both cases must be initiated, the Basque language is useless; one must speak Castilian, one should speak French, one should not speak Basque: then one must not speak. These syllogisms of tutors, from their point of view, are invincible, as from theirs were those of the pigs of Epicurus. The idealist Unamuno, without proposing so, would insufflate new energy into the followers of Alberic and Fafnir; and those that have adorned their intelligence with money for their pockets, dressing up now as "educated people," will have at their disposal new reasons to persist in removing the Basque language from the country.

Perhaps you are waiting, gentlemen, for me to refute such cowardly effects and such despicable thoughts. You are wrong. If I were to be presented with a child stripped of his nature, urging me to convince him that he should love his mother, I would not know what to say to him; but I am sure that public reprobation would envelop him. I invite you to burst out against bad Basques

I have spoken.

Chapter 9

Speech at the Basque Festival of Oñati on September 29, 1902

Honorable Ladies and Gentlemen:

A contemporary poet, seeking to ponder the highest meaning of "silence," said that, "from the very instant that something really important would have to come out of our mouths, we find ourselves obliged to shut up . . . souls weigh heavy in the silence." In effect, between the profound sentiment that flutters around in the most remote insides of life, and words, material and concrete in themselves, there is no appropriate concurrence. This is the reason why I am searching now and not finding any way of externalizing verbally my gratitude to the Honorable Provincial Council of Gipuzkoa for the honor of summoning me to the Basque festival that is being held under its illustrious defense and patronage.

If I were to manage to achieve a concurrence between my affection and my words, I would communicate the relief of the sculpture to the praise that so many who know the intelligence and honor of its administration offer to the provincial corporation, at all times and in all exemplary places, but above all in an era and in a nation in which those administrative bodies are marked with the stigma of incapacity and even with that of delinquency.

That is a lot; but still the Honorable Provincial Council of Gipuzkoa esteems it to be little, and adds to the duties emanating from its constitutive law others dictated through the concept of being the material successor to the venerable and never sufficiently mourned general provincial council, a form of executive power thought up by the Basque people when they were in possession of their own destiny. In a word, the Provincial Council of Gipuzkoa considers itself to be the depository of a glorious tradition, as the personification of an ethnic spirit, as the organ of a collective life that nature and history wove in their resounding looms. Good evidence that this is how the Provincial Council of Gipuzkoa feels and thinks is the program of the current festival in Oñati, in which the worship of authentically Basque popular customs and in the old-fashioned foral way join forces; and in particular the act that we are celebrating in honor of the millenarian and marvelous Basque language, a vibrant herald of our innate independence; and if it does not appear bad to mix things of such unequal value, likewise this is demonstrated by my presence in this place.

Note, ladies and gentlemen, that the custom is to give the greatest possible grandeur to the holding of the floral games, conferring the title of their chairman on one of those personalities that, in letters, and still more in political activism, enjoy national renown. And the Provincial Council of Gipuzkoa would have obtained the cooperation of a prince of Castilian letters, or the leader of a Spanish political party, the moment it made the request. But why did it not do so? Undoubtedly, because those illustrious personalities would have encompassed all the merits that in any peninsular region are appreciated, but lacking at the same time that hint that is only valid in the Basque provinces: the exaltation of their race, the veneration of their language, the love of their fueros, with the eternal hope and irrevocable decision to recover them.

II

Now it is my turn, after soliciting your benevolence, to contribute to the patriotic goal of this festival, which is that of maintaining and even increasing the Basque spirit. Last year in Azpeitia I spoke about preserving the Basque language, a point brought into debate by Mr. Unamuno with little filial piety. The same practical tendency that consumed me then demands of me today, obliging me to disregard a matter that offered narrow margins to my pastime, to sketch out, although in general terms, the most curious history of this noble and loyal town of Oñati, which dates specifically to the harsh struggle of feudalism and the municipality, and in the truly tragic conflict sustained by the opposition between law and nature, the former insisting on imprisoning the town within the iron ring of the seigneury, and the latter insisting, equally, on incorporating it, by the inexorable law of blood, into the Gipuzkoan brotherhood. A history that provides serious lessons for the legal advisor and the politician, one of whose most important chapters would be, without any doubt, that which explains the psychological evolution that transformed the lair of the ferocious medieval factions into a temple of universal wisdom. And given that I have alluded to the university, allow me, ladies and gentlemen, before proceeding, to salute with the sweet respect befitting of someone who took the first steps in his educational life on its floors.

But that story would be a point of erudition, and there is no longer time for us to be erudite. We are contemplating the decline, the twilight of the Basque Country, and the terrible sphinx asks us: will it be resolved in a radiant dawn or, on the contrary, will it thicken into a sinister eternal night?

I looked, then, for another kind of topic, capable of interesting all god Basques, and the aspect that public life in Spain presents provided me with it. The general formula of our situation is the word "problem." There is the religious question, the military question, the question of the navy, the question of international alliances, the workers' question, the question of changes, the question of Mr. Sagasta's heir… an infinite number of questions; some real, others artificial, some grounded in profound needs that have not been met, others fixed arbitrarily by the political trash that lurks about. The only thing that does not exist, ladies and gentlemen, is the Basque question.

In other words, while everyone in Spain is convinced that we lack stable or definitive solutions, and believes that the reality of one or the other order must be modified by some quantity of an ideal that is deposited in it, and exercises its critical faculties in order to declare that the national mechanism is imperfect, outdated, or defective; while regions, classes, individuals utter complaints, formulate protests, demand reforms; while the sick body of the Spanish nation asks for a change in posture that usually serves as momentary relief for those who are suffering an incurable illness, the Basques, from whom was seized by force the most invaluable possession that a people may possess, the faculty to regulate and govern oneself; the Basques, with more justice to allege grievances than anyone, are the only Spaniards that seem, I do not know whether it is resigned or satisfied.

The Basque question, that is, that of restoring the foral system, does in fact not exist. Yet it should exist, because it is the most transcendental of any to affect the Basque people. Any other question would have to exhibit beforehand the qualifications or reasons that may justify its posing; but the antecedents of the foral question are so clear and well-known that it is not necessary to either recall or explain them. Purely and simply, it is a question of exercising an act of reclamation. Since when did outrages of brute force attempt to be eternal? The anomaly would not be that there is a Basque question here; the anomaly, the inconceivable, the ignominious is that it should not exist. The honor and interests of the country demand it.

The reasons for said question not existing and for not making the most of a very opportune moment to reproduce it with the greatest splendor, on the accession of the new monarch, so that it was clear that this "separated" land did not recognize the note of intangibility in solutions that, in order to the existence of its rights, were dictated during the reigns of Isabel II and Alphonse XII; these reasons are very complex, but can be defined with sufficient precision for our objective, classifying them as the apathy of Basque patriotism, directly favored by economic and industrial progress that was emphasized on the end of the last civil war. Peoples habitually suffer crises of energy, eclipses of the ideal, bewilderment of consciousness, at the same time as material prosperity puts itself in a position to satisfy the demands of egoism. The Basque people—I do not want to, nor must I, hide it—are going through a period of serious moral depression, which must be combatted with all kinds of counterirritants, tonics, and stimulants. The most powerful dissolvent of civic virtues is the worship of wealth, the immoderate yearning for the common good, diffused by all social classes. Athens, Rome, Byzantium, the most illustrious cities and the strongest empires on earth perished, not because the light of their intelligence was switched off, but because the character of their citizens was corrupted. Understand me well, ladies and gentlemen: I am not arguing that Basque patriotism ceased to exist. It exists, yes, but in the background of the soul, like an image that remains latent on a photographic plate, until the reagent comes to develop it. And it must reach the background of the soul, transforming all of us who do not tolerate the anti-foral fact into just as many trumpets of Jericho that can bring down the inert wall of Basque passivity.

III

The current spirit of the Basque people must provide the elements in this current of opinion to which I refer; and we will not know this precisely except via previous study of the legal concept that through its relations with central power the country has possessed for several centuries, constituting, therefore, the main political tradition.

Since Araba, Bizkaia, and Gipuzkoa were incorporated, in the shape and way that history dictated, to the crown of Castile, the nucleus of condensation of the Spanish monarchy, the legal doctrine of the country, expressed in countless documents and declarations, is that it lived subject to the system of pacts or contracts: so that the country retained its old jurisdiction over privative matters, it continued to enjoy a specific amount of exemptions and rights that the other party had to respect, and it was obliged, in regard to the other party, to fulfill certain tax obligations.

It is clear, ladies and gentlemen, that according to pure logic, this contractual or agreement-based system implied the faculty of rescinding the contract on incompletion of its clauses. And even if one of the parties was materially much more powerful than the other, and the powerful ones routinely abused their strength, it is evident that the weaker party had to be assisted in the right to seek a divorce on the grounds of "cruelty." But one thing is logic and another is life. It is true that, indeed, the parties never assumed ostensibly that it would arrive at this extreme. The weak one feared, yes, that the strong one may mistreat it, and the strong one agreed with the plausibility of that assumption. And it resorted to an opportune remedy, establishing the "foral pass," which in Gipuzkoa authorized even on the death of a minister or official of the king that anti-foral measures be carried out; so that, ladies and gentlemen, since the aforementioned incorporation, it was "obedience without compliance," that is, the non-observance of the law or damaging provision, but not secession or separatism. The Bizkaians, on occasions of great pressure, turned to the supreme recourse of contractual logic, and threatened the king, not with separating Bizkaia from Castile, but with them, the Bizkaians, leaving to populate new lands.

The Basque Country fulfilled with distinguished loyalty, and often exceeding, the duties joined to its incorporation; not so central power, still more perjured and unjust. But these old-fashioned anti-foral measures fell, to put it one way, on particular matters; but the system, the organism, remained unscathed in everything else. It woke up, nevertheless, one day on which the state rejected the system and destroyed the organism, invoking a new law, although in reality availing itself of its force; and that day, ladies and gentlemen, led to the most profound anguish for the Basque consciousness because it altered substantially the terms of the relations under which that consciousness had been conceived for several centuries, the union of these provinces and Spain. The old traditional formula of national integrity and the fueros was replaced by this other one: national integrity, but without the fueros. The difference, as you see, could not be greater.

There are three logical positions of the public spirit in this country, since the day on which the transcendental event referred to happened: accept the mutilation of the annexed formula, sacrificing the fueros to Spanish nationality; on the contrary, sacrifice the nationality in favor of the fueros; and finally, pursue secular harmony and concord, by means of restoring the abolished system, within the national state.

The false men of state that abolished the foral liberties did not just injure the Basque Country but they created a new danger for the nation, whose strengthening they spoke about. Because if they thought they were able to declare the incompatibility between national unity and the fueros, without, one day, the consequence stemming from that of attacking the nation in the name of the abolished system, in truth, ladies and gentlemen, those men were affected by a blindness of which the Scriptures speak. They and no others are the ringleaders, the accomplices of the separatist tendency in a country whose façade of Spanishness is the heroic city of Hondarribia. And will they oppose it, tell me, in the terrain of ideas and of sentiment? The voice of nature and of blood? Well, both shout that the Basques are the children of the Basque Country! The moral obligation to love the homeland? Well, they will answer them that homeland is the land of parents, and that the homeland is the Basque Country! The laws of the state? But if these expired on eradicating the laws, no less evident, of the Basque Country! In this way, so many arguments they will use must be twisted easily, and the only ways at their disposal to counteract Basque separatism will be repressive and punitive measures, that is, the art of making martyrs today, procreators of heroes tomorrow. And even for this they would have to violate the logic of the political principles that they may support and apostatize once more from them. Because if it is fair to reject God, and mock his ministers, and combat property, and attack the monarchy, and disseminate socialism and anarchism, and ignite the class struggle; because if this can be done, and it is done within the law, under the aegis of liberal freedom, using constitutional rights, without any basic principle of the economic, political, social, and religious system remaining, the overcoat of contradiction and insult put on, can an exclusive privilege in favor of national unity, the daughter at the end of the day of historical circumstances, and as such changeable and unsteady, be maintained? No. He who allows God to be debated is condemned to permit anything being debated: from the money he keeps in his pocket to the homeland of his loves. I only know one rational, fair, and efficient way of cutting separatism at the root: reestablish the old, authentic, traditional, venerable brotherhood of the fueros and the Spanish monarchy.

How eloquent are the lessons of providence, ladies and gentlemen! Those that abolished the Basque freedoms concealed the ugliness of their designs with the apparatus of maxims and precepts taken from political philosophy; they were going to complete the work of the Catholic Kings, to perfect established national unity by these monarchs, with the political unity that declared equality in the rights and obligations of all Spaniards. In this way, the integrating elements of nationality founded more intimately, the activity of the propellant and coordinating center strengthened, the national Spanish organism would enjoy all its potential strength without this being lost amid frictions of complicated adjustments and machinations. The fueros were abolished ladies and gentlemen. And the strength that Spain acquired? Go and ask about that on the beaches of Cavite and in the waters of Santiago de Cuba. A strange aberration that of our times! While every facility was offered to destroy the moral unity of peoples and to increase the predicament of meritorious work, they seek to replace it with all kinds of mechanical and purely external unitarianisms, fabricated in a Jacobin workshop, expecting from these and not from that power and grandeur. Previously, the sun never set on the dominions of diverse and varied Spain: now the sun asks where is unified Spain to send it some of its beams.

IV

Because of the colonial catastrophe, to which I have alluded incidentally, a phrase was uttered that is like a tombstone over the announced regeneration: "nothing has happened here."

May God not allow such a phrase to constitute a motif for the Basque people after the abolishing of the fueros. Beforehand, on the contrary, let it be extended and persuaded that a lot has happened: how much can happen to a people, such as the loss of its personality. Lift your hearts to the level it was in better times, and work like someone caressing a superior ideal to that of transforming the country into industrial exploitation, or that of stirring up opponents along the lines of Monte Carlo, competing for the title of "roulette" and European brothel.

It is enough for me, ladies and gentlemen, that after having increased the need to promote a public opinion movement in favor of the foral system, the method would demand that I indicate to you the way of achieving it, removing the obstacles that until now have closed off the route. But this would lead me to the terrain of current politics, from which I am distant on this occasion and in this place. Nevertheless, to conclude and without departing from the general approach of the politics of principles, and since we are in the noble town of Oñati, allow me to evoke the most glorious and noble pages in its history: that of its patricians of Marulanda, who, dismissing all the hatreds and quarrels of the Oñacinos and Gamboinos, so stubborn and ferocious, by means of union for the sake of the common good, restrained the excesses of the House of Guevara.

Jaunak: alkartasuna indarra da; ezta egia egiazkoagorik (Gentlemen: unity is strength; there is no greater truth).

I have spoken.

Chapter 10

Speech at the Basque Festival of Irun on September 27, 1903[1]

Honorable Ladies and Gentlemen:

I understand that the solemnity we are currently celebrating possesses a more profound meaning and greater importance than that of a mere literary competition. We do not come here to fight for culture; we come here to fight for life. The emulation that, through prizes and laurels, is sought to ignite among the writers of the Basque people does not tend, initially, to enrich the pages of future anthologies, although it is interesting to discover and reward the merit. The imitators and sponsors of this competition seek, initially, to give public testimony that the country possesses its own language, so that patriotism demands the love and respect that the illegitimate children of the Basque home reject. In this way, the native language reverberates where, ordinarily, it is prohibited, and the barely tolerated beggar rises to become king receiving honors and respect.

This transcendence of the competition established by the council of the floral games of Donostia-San Sebastián connects perfectly with the character of the Basque festivals that the illustrious Provincial Council of Gipuzkoa sponsors, as well as the competition. Since these festivals, out of all of those in their genre, are distinguished by a noble memory that, like a soul, invigorates them: the memory of the foral system, wickedly eradicated from reality, but not from our hearts. And when the provincial council, in its festival program, prints the phrase "according to the foral way," it is not suggesting the representation of archaeological "simulations" for the entertainment of fickle crowds, but saying to

---

1   The *Diario de Navarra*, November 17, published a letter from Ituren in which, alluding to this speech, I was called the champion of barbarity.

178 | *POLITICAL AND LITERARY SPEECHES* | *ARTURO CAMPIÓN*

the Basque people, with all the solemnity of Charles I of England before the executioner's ax, "remember!"

Do you not think, ladies and gentlemen, that I would have sent out a dissonant note if, amid such grave concerns, all in the interest of the common good, were I to speak hypothetically about this or that literary genre, about the importance of this or that poet, or about the directions they are following or that Basque literature should set forth on? It is not that I undervalue such matters; not at all, in fact, because I am personally extremely interested in them: not in vain, with varying degrees of success, I also work in letters. But since the moment I was convinced that in this festival everything, directly or indirectly, ensured the preservation of the Basque personality and the integration of its substantial elements, I was obliged to add my humble pebble to the building of the defensive wall.

Ah! If that wall were to be raised against external enemies, how easy it would be to construct! How pleasant the work, joining hands at tiring moments to revive the collapsing tense strength, in the sentiment of Basque fraternity! How many chords would those mountainous chants resonate, expressive in their virile joy, with their misty melancholies and sea depths! But the enemy that annihilates us, the enemy that seeks to erase even the name "Basques," the heartless attacker of our traditions, the sacrilegious violator of the native sepulchers, is a domestic enemy: he lives among us, he is named like us, he belongs to our people and family. It seems as if the land, tired of drinking the blood of Oñacinos and Gamboinos, of Beaumonteses and Agramonteses, of Liberals and Carlists, is boiling, contracting, and forming the body of a new monster. Now Cain is not killing his brother; that is too little: now Cain is murdering his mother.

Few peoples I know that resemble the Basque people in the number of qualified motives to, without puerile boasting, show that they are proud of themselves. It is a fact that, however many men of worth studied them, sometimes examining their history, sometimes their foral organization, sometimes their public and private customs, sometimes the physical type of the race, they praised them without reservation. These testimonies constitute a splendid *Book of Gold*, absolutely unimpeachable. Flip through its pages and you will find the signatures of politicians, legal consultants, historians, sociologists, publicists, poets, celebrated travelers of universal renown; those not blinded by national love, because they were foreigners, nor astonished at the communion of political and religious ideas, since some were Catholics, Protestants, and others freethinkers; and if some gave luster to traditionalist and conservative parties, others were ornaments of more radical and revolutionary ones. What a marvelous phenomenon! Men that disagreed on everything, coincided, nonetheless, in celebrating the Basque people!

Against this unanimous and prestigious praise, however, protest was raised. By whom? It is chilling to say. By Basques. Because protest is the inextinguishable desire of novelties that, in a kind of epileptic aura, agitate the country; that desire for exoticism that induces one to model oneself on inferior social types and go through phases of a true regressive evolution; protest at the disdain for the modesty of the ancient customs, the coarseness of manners and expressions, the unseemliness of popular modern dances, the diffusion of ideas opposed to the Christian constitution of the homeland, industrialism that removes the farmer from the farm to submerge him into a workshop, degenerating rural democracy into urban demagogy; the indifference toward foral restauration, so hated in itself, that those that are its prisoners attempt to cover their renegade faces with a mask of love for the fueros; protest, finally, at the forgetting, the abandonment of the Basque language, an inexplicable apostasy of the quality of being Basque.

I

It is not the occasion to repeat what, as regards the national importance of the language, I explained in books and talks. In order to justify before you, excluding other proof, the constant equation that, between the Basque homeland and the Basque language, my words must be based on, it is enough to observe that the Basque people did not take their name from the territory or physical or moral features, but from the language. Speech is eponymous of the ethnic group. That is how it is termed *"euskaldun,"* that is *"euskara-dun,"* or he who possesses Euskara, the Basque language, the collective consciousness of said people believed that with the language on the same level Basquism, that is, the distinctive and characteristic feature of race, evaporated. A judgement worthy of a great psychologist and a great politician. The seriousness of the current crisis resides in the fact that relinquishing the Basque language is being transformed from an unconscious, involuntary fact into a voluntary, conscious fact perpetrated with a deliberation that seeks the ignominy of applause. In this matter, as in many others, a sense of the just and unjust has been lost. Work on the bad is carried out while arguing that it is good.

I will cite three typical cases, and luckily exceptional, of deliberate repudiation of the Basque language, occurring in Navarre, Bizkaia, and Gipuzkoa. The Navarrese case is as follows: a lady, whose name I regret forgetting at this moment, instituted a school foundation in Ituren, putting down a relatively extensive amount of capital to construct the building and pay the salaries of the teachers. That lady, contrary to what happened to the benefactors who created pariahs to "school superstition" in what I will discuss later, remembered that she was Basque and in appointing the schoolmaster and schoolmistress, in the hands of the municipality of Pamplona-Iruña, made a provision that preference be shown to those candidates who spoke Basque. Time passed and the position of schoolmaster remained vacant and the city council of the capital filled the vacancy with a person that did not speak, nor even was Navarrese, even though among the candidates there were those fulfilling both criteria. A dear friend of mine, Mr. Aranzadi, protested in the newspapers against that crime of patriotic harm, and I, sick at the time, sent from my bed a few lines adhering to the protest. Do you know, ladies and gentlemen, what happened then? From Ituren a counter-protest was sent to the press applauding the appointment, supporting it fully so as to produce as much impact as possible. "This city council," it said, "the local council, the parents, have always recommended that their teachers do not allow their pupils to speak the Basque language either in or outside school, since we are disillusioned if we do not realize that what the young people need is to learn Castilian, the universal language of Spain and the Americas, which is where the children of this town must develop in the study of their careers and professions." Thus, as you have heard, brutally, clearly and frankly: the most pedestrian and coarse utilitarianism; the utilitarianism of avaricious rustics. The children of Ituren were declared a kind of overseas export, whom had to be put into exceptional conditions for the market. Consider, ladies and gentlemen, what would have been, with some major encouragement, the work of that schoolmaster who left the high plains of Castile to harvest the "plums" that sometimes grew in the "uncivilized" Basque mountains! The honemoon between villager and teacher ended soon, only God knows why: according to what I have read, So-and-So gave up the school in Ituren and went off to "Europeanize" other places with his Castilian.

Undoubtedly, the same utilitarian spirit that stirred up the Basques of Ituren against Basque would instigate the "beating" organized in Busturia against that language. This is the Bizkaian case. The schoolmaster in that town—for greater ignominy, a Basque in race and language—stood out for the cruel punishments meted out to children who spoke in Basque in or outside school. The provincial public education council, on the proposal of the representative Don Sabino de Arana, warned or reprimanded him severely, and the teacher, in order to apologize, published a letter in the *Noticiero Bilbaíno*, stating that he was following the orders of the pupils' parents. To my knowledge, no rectification has been forthcoming.

Now let us look at the case of Gipuzkoa, not as outrageous, to be sure, as the previous ones. And I say it is not so strange because the profession of certain ideas leads logically to a rejection of the homeland. The case consists of the following words by socialists in Eibar, published by some newspapers in Donostia-San Sebastián: "We speak Basque because we don't know Castilian. We would speak with much more pleasure in that language, but wanting to is not being able to." True; but wanting to stop being Basque is already not being so.

We would be ignoring justice if we did not attach responsibility for these most hateful infidelities to the villagers of Ituren and Busturia, and the workers of Eibar. Behind them, in the guise of prompters, we would find the rural jauntxo [local powerbroker], a graduate doctor in the universities of daily newspapers; the returning *indiano* [emigrant who had made money in the colonies and come back home], who in his village represented the role of donkey laden with offerings; behind them, the *industrialist* of the class struggle, the owner of bars in which "good news" is imparted to everyone through glasses of wine. But it is not my intention to determine responsibilities, but rather to extract from these typical cases the suggestive teachings they enclose. And it is the following: the declared enemies of the Basque language make up two groups: that of the utilitarians that believe Basque should only be provided with the minimum facility for providing the business of life; and that of the politicians, who mistrust Basque as an obstacle to the rapid diffusion of their ideas. And it is the second: that there are Basques for whom possessing their language implies a certain state of intellectual and social inferiority, that hope to redeem themselves by renouncing the speech of their parents; an easier and more expeditious procedure than that adopted by all the modern peoples of Europe, cultivating and perfecting their rustic languages until they are elevated to the status of educated and knowledgeable languages. Thus, I do not know any example of peoples that have thrown out their own national language as old and unusable clothing. In order to find a similar mentality, one must turn to Aguinaldo and his Tagalogs, who, in their tirade of grievances against Spain, included that of the fact that they had not been taught Castilian. Do you see, ladies and gentlemen? The enemies of Basque in Ituren, Busturia, and Eibar are "loincloth" people, they are the Tagalogs of the Basque Country.

Our beloved language runs the risk of death. The steps separating it from the sepulcher can, seemingly, be counted. The place in which, in batches, the Basque festival is being held this year invites us, more than any other, to meditate on this death. Irun is suffering more than Donostia-San Sebastián from the de-Basquizing of its inhabitants. Anyone would say that the old quarter of the town is an alien colony, inhabited also by a hundred Basques; but by timid spiritless Basques who are either ashamed or do not dare demonstrate their own nature.

Children do not speak Basque in the street. What have these children been taught? That Basque is "crude"? That Basque is obscurantist? That Basque is not listed on the stock exchange? Cold, indifferent, without love or hatred, the parents are witnessing the breaking of this golden chain, the native language, which links generations and makes the modern fisherman a "compatriot" of Elkano. The Basque Country reappears on the slopes of those hills where people walk over gorse and ferns. The farmhouse, the mother from which the renovation of the race flows perennially, carries out the task of the ancient vestals. Whenever the farmhouse, in turn, defeated by the bad example of those who should give better ones, should give in and capitulate, it will no longer be the daybreak, but instead the night, closing over a degenerate Basque Country.

Irun, Irun! Why are you collapsing in your Basque loyalty? Do not fear, ladies and gentlemen, that it will rant and rave anathema. Anger does not breed anger. Pity, which no one is affronting, a reward worthy of received hospitality, is opening up its torrents. I would love the progressive people of Irun to stop executing at all costs their Basque nature. Because Basqueness, as regards its most exquisite and agreeable features, is being diluted including in the air we breathe here. Observe the circle of mountains that, from the peaks of Aia, Jaizkibel, and Arkale, staggers down the hills to the plains below; the placid course of the Bidasoa and its serene waters, which do not reflect aggressive cliffs but rather accessible riverbanks, demonstrating, in its way, the unity of the Basque people, since if God raised the Pyrenees up between France and Spain, it was to reduce them to piles of sand in these confines of Lapurdi and Gipuzkoa; the placidity of the humid environment; the tireless verdure of the fields; the beauty of the women from whose throats comes a Basque intoned so sweetly that it promises all the tenderness of a wife and a mother; the honesty, industriousness, courtesy, jovial and open spirit of the men. Observe, ladies and gentlemen, these physical and moral features, and tell me if Irun has not been, and may continue to be, a model town in the Basque Country!

More demonstrative than accumulating laudatory epithets, I believe, is narrating an event that provoked the admiration of all those who were aware of it. It was the year 1895, if I remember rightly, and the day of the Saint Martial festival. Among those taking part in the "spectacle" a serious quarrel erupted, and despite the fact everyone was armed with a rifle and bayonet, the only arms used were fists. As such, whereas in countries in which the cowardly knife and ignoble conceitedness reign, in those countries from which they bring us schoolmasters entrusted with taking a fetid sponge to our authentic physiognomy, there would soon have been a bloody fight, in this noble, in this honest Irun land it did not go any farther than a fist fight among young men.

I am listening to the excuse that those from Irun who love the old days in their town, but not enough to perpetuate them, would claim if they were to answer me now: "Irun, due to well-known circumstances, possesses a significant foreign population, and through contact it has been tainted with new colors other than its own." This excuse, which other localities also claim, is a skimpy fig leaf that does not cover the nudity of patriotism. Have you seen, by any chance, any of those Castilians, those Andalusians, those Aragonese that come to live among us adopting the customs and the language of the Basques? Why, then, must Basques, in their own home, adopt their customs and language? I will answer frankly, but bitterly: it because such foreigners see themselves as superior to the Basques, and do not believe in imitating them. Basques do not mock foreigners that ignore the Basque language, but foreigners make fun of Basques that do not speak Castilian. The most raggedy "rascal" from the heartland, who in the Basque region looks for and finds a daily wage that he cannot in his village, harbors only disdain toward those he calls *sagardúos* [provincial Basques]. He will demand with insults and invectives that he be spoken to "in Christian," and only with great difficulty will he put up with locals, nearby, expressing themselves in their mother tongue. I have witnessed events of this kind a thousand times, and I still have not come across any Basque who has said: "it is you that should learn my language, because you have come to my land." I will not hurl insults at the foreigner who keeps and propagates his ethnic personality; I reserve them for the local that, imitating him, becomes less authentic.

If the growing alien immigration, and the facility of communications and the growth of foreign contacts must erase with denigrating ease the physiognomy of the Basque people, the final page in its history will recount a great shame. Because History will say, and say it clearly, in part: "the so admired preservation of an original people for countless centuries in the ravines of the Pyrenees, surrounded by powerful nations and peoples, was not due to valor, to resolve, to patriotism, no; it was the simple result of an isolation produced by the topography. That preservation was not an epic feature; it was a simple geographical accident." Is this, ladies and gentlemen, the epitaph that modern Basques, their minds blurred by certain second-class progressives, are trying to record on the sepulchral tombstone of the Basque Country?

II

I suspect you will have noted, ladies and gentlemen, in several paragraphs of my speech, how obsessed I am with primary schools. In effect, teaching exclusively in Castilian leads directly to the de-Basquizing of the country. In its present form, this education is he most damaging and efficient enemy of the maintenance of the Basque language. By virtue of legal dispositions, the Basque patriot sees himself restricted forcibly to looking more favorably on ignorance than instruction.

I am scandalizing you, am I not? You would not be of your times if you were not scandalized. For me, of all the reproaches that may be aimed at me, that of being "old-fashioned" pleases me most by a long way. Popular instruction is the great contemporary social panacea. All that about it not being the generals, but the Prussian schoolmasters that won the Battle of Königgrätz; all that about opening a school being equal to closing a prison; the famous exoneration that Victor Hugo placed in the mouth of the *communard* during *L'anée terrible*, rebuked eloquently by the fire in the Paris Library: "I cannot read;"[2] so many set phrases, the obligatory repertory of insipid sociologists and visionary regenerators, repeated daily all over the place, without any consideration, by newspapers, journals, parliaments, and athenaeums, have created a special mentality, an extraordinarily diffused Chinese or Siamese mentality, which can only be classified as is fitting, terming it "school superstition."

Given that typical primary schooling is, clearly, a weapon of war forged to cause us greater harm than that deriving from ignorance, it is now time to replace it and bring it to account; not to deny its benefits, in other ways undoubtable and desirable, but to reduce them to their proper proportion; destroying in passing the human respect that inhibits our defense, with the absurd assumption that at any time and in any place the benefits of instruction outweigh and exceed generously any disadvantages being held to account. It would be something to see that, on fleeing from the grotesque stigma of being "illiterate," we would cease to be Basques!

The benefits attributed to public education, by their impulsive and impressionable panegyrists, cane be summarized and reduced to two: the morality of individuals and the cultures of nations. Is this right? Let us see by examining both points separately.

---

2   Several of the arsonists lacked education. Yet Victor Hugo, a tarnished courtier of demagogy, remained silent over the fact that the leaders of the infamous communist uprising, Delescluze, Flourens, Blanqui, Pyat, Pigault, Ferré, Malon, Vallés, Courbet, Vermorel, Rossel, Arnould, etc. were not "illiterate."

That instruction does not exercise any beneficial influence on morality, or in other terms, that good or bad conduct is completely independent of the scientific notions possessed by the individual and the collectivity is, *a priori*, evident in itself, and the existence of an opposing conviction a marvel. Yet the latter dominates; and well before statistics with its impassible numbers had demonstrated its unsubstantial nature, a dignitary of free thought, an Anglo-Saxon and a positivist, blessed therefore by grades that confer the greatest authority within the schools and political groupings that defend the stated chimera, Herbert Spencer, in his notable *Study of Sociology*, had communicated the certainty of a true mathematics to its refutation. And not long ago, on turning eighty-two and publishing his *Facts and Comments*, observing that the stupid superstition survives and is gaining new proselytes, he attacked it with vigorous insistence: "Everywhere the cry," he says,

> is—Educate, educate, educate! Everywhere the belief is that by such culture as schools furnish, children, and therefore adults, can be moulded into the desired shapes. It is assumed that when men are taught what is right, they will do what is right—that a proposition intellectually accepted will be morally operative. And yet this conviction, contradicted by every-day experience, is at variance with an every-day axiom ... Though in presence of multitudinous schools, high and low, we have the rowdies and Hooligans, the savage disturbers of meetings, the adulterers of food, the givers of bribers and receivers of corrupt commissions, the fraudulent solicitors, the bubble companies, yet the current belief continues unweakened; and recently in America an outcry respecting the yearly increase of crime.

The old philosopher argues that identifying the human spirit with intelligence and devaluing feeling is driving us directly toward the "re-barbarization of Europe;" and he says so without any qualms, calling for intellectual education to be replaced by moral education. I will sum up, in order to simplify them, the arguments of thirty years ago. To certain supporters of progress, such news will be of interest.

First, let us note that the problem of whether education moralizes or not is of a psychological nature. Psychology teaches us that man does not decide to work or abstain from work according to the *ideas* stored in his mind, but by the *motives* that canvass his will. Thought is the light that illuminates the way; volition, the motor that passes along it. A book came into my hands about Shakyamuni. I read it; I understood it even in detail. Does that mean that, from that instant, would adjust my conduct to Buddhist doctrine? No, as long as this does not receive the consent of my will. There is an abyss between doing and understanding. Very clear notions leave us indifferent; we would not even lift a finger in support of them. Confused, perhaps unintelligible, notions but that are, at the same time, profound sentiments, sometimes obtain the sacrifice of our lives.

Herbert Spencer expresses these truths in greater detail than I do:

> To argue that feeling and reason maintain a constant relationship is to enunciate a proposition that demands restrictions. In effect, automatic actions that are verified independently of sentiment appear in one of the extremes, and at the other extreme feelings; so intense, that they mess up the vital functions and, therefore, they upset or suspend their activity. Yet generally speaking, action and feeling adhere to the same variations—one must add to this indisputable truth in its generality the principle that knowledge *does not produce* action. If I prick myself with a needle, or inadvertently put my hand in boiling water, I shake: the strong sensation produces a movement without any intervention by the faculty of thinking. On the contrary, the proposition that the needle pricks and hot water burns leaves me apathetic. It is true that, if to one of these propositions is added the idea that my skin will be pierced by a needle, or sprinkled with hot water,

there will be a more or less pronounced tendency to back up. But this action is due to ideal pain.

Spencer's most typical and suggestive idea is something else:

See this group of persons clustered at the river side. A boat has upset, and some one is in danger of drowning. The fact that in the absence of aid the youth in the water will shortly die, is known to them all. That by swimming to his assistance his life may be saved, is a proposition denied by none of them. The duty of helping fellow-creatures who are in difficulties, they have been taught all their lives; and they will severally admit that running a risk to prevent a death is praiseworthy. Nevertheless, though sundry of them can swim, they do nothing beyond shouting for assistance or giving advice. But now here comes one who, tearing off his coat, plunges in to the rescue. In what does he differ from the others? Not in knowledge. Their cognitions are equally clear with his. They know as well as he does that death is impending; and know, too, how it may be prevented. In him, however, these cognitions arouse certain correlative emotions more strongly than they are aroused in the rest. Groups of feelings are excited in all; but whereas in the others the deterrent feelings of fear, &c., preponderate, in him there is a surplus of the feelings excited by sympathy, joined, it may be, with others not of so high a kind. In each case, however, the behaviour is not determined by knowledge, but by emotion.[3]

The supporters of the "curative virtues" of education should have started by demonstrating the causal relationship between knowing geography and arithmetic, and abstaining from stealing or killing, I offer as a case. I will add an example of my own. I am going for a solitary walk. In front of me, there is a man going

---

3   *The Study of Sociology*, 260.

through some papers; a monetary note falls out from among them and the wind carries it to my feet. I pick it up. No one has seen me. I am broke, up to my neck in debt, and needs. Do I keep it? Do I return it to its owner? What do I do? In my conscience there is a face-off between honesty and wickedness; my religious and moral principles struggle over part of that; and over another part, my passions, the certain impunity of the crime... On the contrary, my notions about carbonic acid or the campaigns of Seti I do not take any part in the troubling colloquium.

Moralization by means of education attempted to base itself on events taken from statistics. The intended demonstration was based on applying gross sophistry: *post hoc, ergo propter hoc.* Sixty, seventy, eighty percent of delinquents—they used to say loudly, with incomplete or badly observed data—could not read or write; hence, ignorance is the mother of criminality. But if another point of comparison had been taken, weekly changes of shirts, a season ticket to the royal theater, attending Wagner's lyrical dramas in Bayreuth, owning an automobile, the hobby of fly fishing, etc., etc., those percentages would have risen markedly, and the causes of criminality would have been even more amazing. The comical note of those well-worn statistics resides in the fact that, ordinarily, they referred to countries in which most of the inhabitants were "illiterate." Obviously! The criminals were as well. Yet at the same time that the proportion of the uneducated was reversed, so was that of criminals, increasing the number of the educated without the coefficient of total delinquency decreasing for that reason. Previously, on the contrary, criminality was increasing, particularly in Western Europe, which provided the raw material for these statistical conjurers.

The inefficiency of education is a patent fact, ladies and gentlemen, which no publicist of worth and good faith puts in any doubt, even though they may profess other erroneous ideas in sociology and criminology. "On sees clearly," says the celebrated and most original sociologist Mr. Tarde, "the influence of education on madness and suicide, which increase simultaneously to their advances; but nowhere does one note any restrictive would-be effect on criminality. Official reports confirm and deplore it." Now let us listen to Baron Garófalo: "Italy, where education became quite widespread after 1860, has witnessed an increase of grave proportions, precisely since then, in the numbers of its criminality." France, adds the same author, where in the year 1826 out of one hundred criminals sixty-one were uneducated and thirty-nine more or less educated, has witnessed the proportion reverse, with the former falling to thirty-eight and the latter rising to seventy [sic]. Mr. Fouillee, who in his *La Science sociale* [Social science] followed Victo Hugo's nonsense of "he who opens a school closes a prison," some years later wrote, with sadness, the following words: "Scientific education, increasingly widespread, has not raised the moral level; on the contrary, it is low." Spain demonstrates how exaggerated the supposed proportion has sometimes been between ignorance and criminality, since when the former affected two thirds of the total population, "illiteracy" barely provided half of all delinquents; with the result that in the penitentiaries there are sixty-four educated murderers next to sixty-seven uneducated ones.

Criminality is on the rise in most European and American nations: this is an indisputable fact. And it is on the rise despite the development of education (I do not want to say now on account of it): this is a fact as indisputable as the former. And in some places the increase masks a nature that provokes extraordinary sadness. In France, for example, it relates to the precociousness of the delinquents. Of a skill that, in increasingly less time since boys left school, they were closer to prison. There exist, meanwhile, very extensive categories of crimes, rarely punished, which only people with a regular education commit: such as those perpetrated by industry and commerce, sophisticating the quality, subtracting the quantity, and falsifying the brands of merchandise, defrauding the state of customs dues, presenting deceitful accounts, inflating artificially stock quotes, truly ruinous, in order to launch them on the market and dispose of them, etc., etc. If education does not diminish the number of crimes and misdemeanors, it facilitates significantly their undertaking and impunity. The day that toxicology and microbial cultivation become more widespread, the new criminals will roar with laughter at the old inexpert poisoners. Gustave Humbert understood procedural law better than all the courts put together: for that reason the discovery of his colossal scam was so difficult and late in coming. Education would decrease the number of violent criminals in order to increase that of the more astute ones. Science without any conscience is the greatest punishment that God can unleash among a people. In a word, the school as an instrument of moralization has failed.

And it could not help but fail, ladies and gentlemen. To marvel at that, one must lack a sense of causality. Education works on the mutilated man. It proceeds, as if it were pure intelligence, disregarding will. Ideas do not influence conduct but insofar as they are transformed into feeling, because only then do they integrate character, which is the "constant" of the moral man. Character has been defined as, "the stratification of unconscious ideas," that is, descended from the mobile region of thought to the stable region of feeling. Will is manageable. Its manager is called "education." But in order to educate one must arrange in the name of principles higher than human nature. This is why only religion may educate and why only religion may moralize.

III

Let us now study, ladies and gentlemen, the second of the supposed virtues of primary education. Just as, in declaring it an agent of morality, imagination and fantasy roam ceaselessly, it is impossible to ignore a certain positive relationship between education and culture, the former being the first of the steps one must take to lead to the latter. The error consists of identifying both terms as one and the same, or in supposing that ordinarily one climbs the whole ladder.

Culture is not a common ordinary state; it stems from personal vocation. Derived from the word *cultum*, supine of the verb *colere* (to cultivate), and meaning the cultivation of the most preeminent faculties of human, intellectual, and sentient nature, following a general tendency and completely selfless. A specialist, although eminent, and for all that his specialty is important, is not someone befitting of the title of cultured. He requires, to some degree, culture, the appropriation of heterogeneous knowledge, a sharp esthetic receptivity, the refinement of tastes; in other words, the constant aspiration to enjoy the true and the beautiful, achieving the greatest possible splendor when he obtains, likewise, possession of the good. Cultured men usually acquire, the adjective being imprecise on account of exaggeration, the description of *universal*. Those of the Italian Renaissance were, for example, within certain limits, such men.

Culture, therefore, is not the typical clothing of the masses, but the jewel of true intellectual aristocrats. Assuming that education, not just primary, but professional, necessarily produces culture is ignoring what culture is. I was speaking with a very well-known publisher about the works he published and I asked him why he did not prefer manual editions, elegant and cheap at the same time, to the enormous luxury folios that come out of his workshops. Do you know, ladies and gentlemen, how he replied? "Cheap books, except those about mere current affairs, do not sell. People want luxury books in order to put them on their living-room tables." In effect, that is how it is. You will find the poor books on tables, printed *bibelots*, without anyone touching them except the maid with her feather duster. Because the thing is that the owner, a doctor, a lawyer, an engineer, a businessman, an industrialist, a property owner, barely finishes up his work before going to the casino, the social gathering, in search of something common to distract him, incapable of finding intellectual recreation. That is the main state of foretold culture.

There is more; educated people who appreciate education as an instrument of productive work—who are and *a fortiori* must be the majority—look, above all in very utilitarian countries, sideways toward the higher education of the spirit. Mr. Carnegie, the possessor of hundreds of millions of dollars earned in commercial companies, said: "Given that in the areas of business none of the men who achieved a high position had received any academic degree, there is a basis, it seems, to draw the consequence that college education, as it is today, is an insurmountable obstacle to that kind of success. The graduate who at twenty is engaged in business will be inevitably supplanted by the young man who has swept the warehouse floor." How much those in Ituren would appreciate this criterion! Another millionaire, Henry Clewes, expressed himself even more disdainfully: "I don't employ anyone in my bank that has been to college. They are tainted when it comes to a life in business. Their thoughts are not resolved toward commerce but to books, literature, philosophy, Latin." Note that the United States is one of the most passionate peoples in favor of education; that it spends enormously on disseminating it; that around eighteen million Americans (a quarter of the total population) sit down at school and college benches; that those same millionaires favor, through donations and sumptuous legacies, teaching centers, managing to put them on the tracks in a utilitarian direction. Well, with all this, there is no possibility for true culture to flourish. Compared to that of Germany, the American people are barbarians. University reform in the great republic consists of accentuating the practical and technical dimension, so that education serves as "entertainment" for future men of business. This is how they can shake hands and, in fact, extend both instruction and a lack of education.[4]

The Yankee, through utilitarian prejudice, scorns higher education. Its enemy in Europe is political passion, the growing democratic envy that invades and destroys everything thanks to the disastrous progresses of socialism. The advanced parties reclaim universal integral education. By integral; understand, ladies and gentlemen, limited, restricted, extremely incomplete education, without any subjects that ennoble and adorn the spirit, irreligious, amoral, and utilitarian; an education of foremen and, exceptionally, technical directors of rural, manufacturing, and commercial endeavors. But, above all, a uniform education, arranged

---

4   John Van Vorst, "La nouvelle Amerique," *Revista de Ambos Mundos*, September 15, 1903. The comparison to which the text refers must be understood from the perspective of intellectual and artistic life in the countries alluded to.

as a gift of the greatest number that, since the time of Solomon, has been made up of fools, until the result of China is repeated: masses that can read but cannot think.

It used to be said: how many men of marvelous talent, and even genius, remain submerged in the underground of society, without ever seeing the light of day, with widespread and intrinsic prejudice, for lack of schooling and other gratuitous means of education! These are indeed reproductive expenses. The money-capital squandered will soon be replaced by intelligence-capital believed in. This prophecy is also pure rhetoric, ladies and gentlemen. The number of educated people is growing; that of eminent, or simply notable, individuals remains stationary. The horde goes to school stupid and leaves it stupid. There are regions, specifically in northern Europe, in which general education coexists with general ordinariness and insignificance. Not even the faintest spark has emerged from those brains. This question of superior men is not a school, but ethnic, question. Each people, each race, yields a certain percentage of eminent men that demonstrate its psychological capacity. Tiny Greece in the century of Pericles was infinitely more important, in the spheres of thought and art, than the gigantic United States, despite the fortunes that are squandered on public education. If it were to disappear from the globe, no intellectual light would ever be turned off. Yet what would the inexistence of Greece mean for the world, but a thick cover of darkness that had not been torn up?

I do not deny that, through an abnormal combination of unfavorable circumstances, some men whom nature prepared to carry out primary roles in the world, will have sprouted up, without luster, from the corner of some village or workshop; but this, far from being frequent, is a very rare case. Do you think that the divine Plato and portentous Aristotle would have lived in a cobbler's hovel, moldy with ignorance and banished perpetually from the city of ideas? The man of great ability experiments within himself the impulse that pushes him to climb up the deserved post. He does not crawl along the loops or the filth of worms; he flies with the wings of a dove or an eagle. And he climbs to the most unforeseen heights: as Sixtus V rose from the pigpen of Felice Piergentile to the Crown; as Robert Burns rose from the frozen Scottish earth, manured by his own hands, to the aristocratic salons of Edinburgh.

What is the social value of democratic education, or rather, of education extended to the greatest possible number of citizens? I will say it without beating around the bush, concentrating my thought, even though the issue deserves careful study and there is a copious body of work about it: such education, *a fortiori*, is most deficient and only produces the "half uneducated." With the result that the most eminent and modern thinking Mr. Michel Breal pronounced the acrid statement: "The half-knowledge offered by these schools is as dependable a recruiter of soldiers for rebellion as ignorance." More precisely, adds Gustave Le Bon, commenting on this: the advances in criminality, alcoholism, and anarchy among choirboys confirms it. Unruliness, immodesty, the ridiculous conviction of possessing knowledge that is lacking, the tedium of manual labor, the worship of verbalism become more widespread. And if that education is completed with it being accompanied, jointly, by means of decorous subsistence, and the graduated and diploma holders find themselves in the middle of a river, gorged on science but starved of bread, ah! Then ladies and gentlemen, the maladjustment between individual and social environment is absolute, and demagogy acquires, *ipso facto*, drivers and head that will drive it to combat, and perhaps victory.

Let us ignore this, to some extent, philosophical aspect of the issue and let us inquire into, however superficially, what the "useful" effect of the scholarly machinery is on the popular masses. And I invite you, ladies and gentlemen, to check with your own observations the level of precision in mine as regards Spain, and especially the Basque-Navarrese region. I am going to speak about what happens ordinarily, avoiding exceptions, whether few or many, confirming of the general rule.

Let us question a day laborer or farm worker two years after leaving school. Immediately, we will note that all notions of scientific or literary order (history, grammar, geography, arithmetic, etc.) have been erased completely. He only retains those of a practical order: reading and writing, and the four rules. Even these notions, through a lack of practice, above all among the rural classes, are reduced little by little to working out a calculation on his fingers, writing a letter without any orthography or punctuation, in coarse handwriting that wears out the pen used, and to spelling out a form.

Most of the urban workers and a minority of rural ones usually stay within that *minimum* of education described above, without diminishing it, and still enjoying exercising their knowledge of reading providing fodder for a certain intellectual pastime that, through imitation of what is seen, they have acquired. We will not come across intellectualism, extremely meager among the high and middle classes in our society, characterized by their de facto lack of culture, as thriving among the popular classes. They would seek "culture" that is spoken about in streets and squares, cheap daily print culture. So that, ladies and gentlemen, the useful effect of education, summing up, is just that of being able to read and, in fact, read a newspaper. If this were good! But only God knows what it will be!

Without entering into an elucidation of what is the good press and what is the bad press, an elucidation that is linked to militant politics, I will limit myself to formulating appraisals of a general nature, related to the common effects of reading newspapers. The first is: the choice of newspaper is a free act, determined by the particular opinions of the reader. Each citizen buys a daily that matches his ideas, whether true or erroneous, and his passions, whether good or bad. As such, instead of opening up intelligence, the newspaper closes it, period, crystallizes it, stunting the faculty of thought any critical sense to adopt new and diverse orientations. The newspaper, partial in its judgements, partial in its information, partial in what is says, partial in what it keeps quiet about, provides incomplete fragmentary notions, often deliberately deceitful, and deforms and disfigures, even without wanting to, reality. The assiduous reader of a newspaper is confined; he ends up delegating his discursive operations to the editorial staff, incapable of forming his own opinions. Modern nations are a theater of this extraordinary spectacle: an unconscious mass brought and led according to the whim of a group of irresponsible people.

Besides the relatively scarce public, who profess specific ideas and only read the newspapers of their party, there is another group of readers saturated with a circumambient spirit, but without any fixed criteria or definitive orientation, impertinently curious, for whom household, neighborly, or neighborhood "gossip" is not enough, but who reclaim global "gossip;" the "neutral masses" in popular speak, whom all the newspapers attempt to capture by multiplying and widening the means of information. Insofar as more and more common people can read, the press has transformed, by means of distancing itself from general ideas and its literary form, in order to cultivate news and the telegraphic style. The "reporter" unseated the old-style journalist, who used to rite doctrinal articles with a care demanded by a work of art. The modern industrial press, the journalistic factory, is relegating to a secondary level the press of ideas, obliging it to adopt new procedures.

The industrial press, as a first measure, studies the "market" mentality; it does not suggest modifying or combatting it, but courting it, adulating it, and pleasing it. The book of subscriptions and sales is the sphygmograph that reveals the pulse of opinion. Its goal is to sell the greatest number possible of copies; its artifice, the well-known rhythmic shovelfuls of quick lime and sand; its exclusive finality, to distribute grand active dividends. I say exclusive, with one restriction: except the not infrequent cases in which industrialism and the sectarian spirit walk hand in hand to dump out ideas hypocritically that would be rejected if revealed clearly. And as each public, or each fraction of a public, possesses special tendencies, the newspaper, above all else, must know how to serve the appetizing feast. In Spain it would cultivate gossip, news, that is, vulgar inconsequential facts demanded by decadent reality and the lack of culture among people; and in France, the feuilleton, fodder for Gallic imaginations and sensibilities, and at the same time the maximum exponent of a democratic literary level.

A very talented writer, a sharp observer, Mr. Maurice Talmeyr, noting that the first thing townsfolk look for in opening a newspaper is the feuilleton, concentrated on reading those published in the popular French newspapers. The result of his investigative work, extremely well documented, was: that the feuilleton, starting with *The Wandering Jew* and the *Mysteries of Paris*, and finishing with the atrocities of Bouvier, Hector France, Boulabert, et cetera, painted systematically priests, monks, friars, and practicing Catholics of all kinds and conditions as true monsters, the authors of terrible crimes and prisoners of degrading vices. You know, ladies and gentlemen, for whom the feuilletons reserve flares and scents of adoration? For single mothers: such unexpected and suggestive examples of virtue!

The "useful" effect of popular education, the object of such sonorous dithyrambs, does not exceed that of multiplying indefinitely the number of readers of useless gossip columns, immoral feuilletons, and political articles. The mountain aborts the ridiculous fake mouse... But you know, ladies and gentlemen, that modern science has demonstrated mice to be the most active transmitters of pestilence. How, then, must we marvel at the fact that the reaction against school superstition, initiated thirty years ago by Herbert Spencer, is being opened up among sociologists, for all that those in Spain continue to publish evidence of that vague *cliché?*

Vainly those encomiasts of education propose the fantastical panacea, feigning an exclusive zeal for the culture and moralization of the people. Others may fall into the absurdity of believing them, yet, thanks be to God, I am years away from their propositions and true intentions. Most of them could care less about science, culture, moralization. Proof is provided by the fact that when schools and educational centers are run by collectivities that are usually disagreeable to them, for example religious orders, if they dare to, they close them, and if not, they put up as many hindrances and obstacles as they can imagine. The true aim of the apostles of education is political and not scientific; sometimes because they assume that the little knowledge communicated will predispose the intelligence of the favored to receive certain ideas via the press, other times because, being universal, the tendency of modern states to take control of education, they expect an identical result in official influence.

In fact, school education has come to be a mere *instrumentum regni.* I will enumerate its types, as if they were presented isolated in practice, overlooking their frequent combinations. Where military conquest annexed new territories, the school is dedicated to their *moral* conquest; to de-Polonize Poles, to dye the Irish English, et cetera. Where nationality is the federation or conglomeration of other smaller nationalities, and of diverse and anciently separated races, the school puts itself at the service of national division seeking to exercise hegemony over all others: at the service of the Germans in the Austrian Empire; at that of the Castilians in the Spanish Monarchy, etc. Finally, where all regionalist resistances were beaten and local souls died forever, the school is the conduct by which political, philosophical, religious, and social (understood as antireligious and antisocial) ideas are distributed, from the party or faction represented by the government. As an example, France, whose schools are auxiliary organs, publically and officially declared, of the "Jacobin conquest."

The teaching state, that is, the state that monopolizes education and teaches the "doctrine" to its liking in order to maintain, as it says, the moral unity of the homeland, an inept falsification of uprooted Catholic unity . . . is here, ladies and gentlemen, the final word, the conclusion and whereabouts of so much hypocritical declamation about science and the freedom of science and the freedom to teach science; an "official" truth, promoted by professional politicians from the Sinai of budgets. At exactly the same time that the state declared the legality of all opinions and all propagandas, of all beliefs and of all "misbeliefs," without any other argument in favor of that monstrous inhibition than that enounced from the lips of the Pilates on asking Our Lord Jesus Christ *Quid est veritas?* (What thing is true?)!

The teaching state requires the transformation of the schoolmaster, the delegate, and the technical substitute teacher of the father of a family, into a public functionary; in other words, the complete subordination of the schoolmaster to power; or put another way, to politics: an abstraction that the minister, the governor, the inspector, the overlord make sure to specify. This is what we have in Spain, and part of the other, too, and the rest will come in due course. In order to know how we should dress at the next station, it is enough to look at the figurines of Paris.

IV

Excuse me, ladies and gentlemen, for the tiresome extent of my speech, which is, despite that, a mere indication of ideas, without due prior development. And even when it may seem, perhaps, that such arguments belong to a general and non-Basque topic, I assure you that I did not forget for even one moment what was palpitating through my initial words: the de-Basquizing of the country by means of the school.

What is the attitude that Basque patriots must adopt with respect to the Castilian education to which our country is subjected? Fight it by all means, including to the extreme, where, rationally, school absenteeism fits, limiting ourselves to the strict fulfilment of the current laws, without facilitating their implantation or extending their effects, and reclaiming tenaciously, by means of the provincial bodies and parliamentary representation, bilingual primary education, at the least, achieving, while it is obtained and the state does not prohibit it, the opening of free schools in which teaching is done in Basque.

School absenteeism and the observance, reluctantly and to a minimum extent, of the current school legislation, which I extoll, assuming the harm that would temporarily be caused to the diffusion of primary letters, would seem unacceptable to many of our locals, shocked by fashionable sophisms. School-mania, or whatever it is called, is a nice idea in our country, I do not disagree, and contradicting that lends itself to easy attacks and diatribes. They would come at a good time. Few of those that would hurt me would have a practical advantage over me in my love for the culture of intelligence and of the heart. The only punishment that I would place on them would consist of them exchanging reading their newspapers for that of my books. But at the end of the day, I should take charge of the governing opinion, and I have made sure to prevent it from reducing to more precise limits the benefits of the school, and stripping education of its sequins and theatrical glitz.

I wish above all that such opinion, certainly well intentioned, might be convincing that the main need of a people is its existence. The ignorance of the living dissipates easily; that of the dead is irredeemable. Why, then, if the school destroys our personality, do we not repel it as we would reject poison? Why, then, if the school is the *instrumentum regni* par excellence, do we not take control of it in order to establish the control of the Basque Country? This is what common sense and patriotism dictates with one accord

I have spoken.

Chapter 11

Address in Basque to the Bascophile Association in Irun On September 29, 1904

Gentlemen:

Our norms or regulations state that the general assembly of the Bascophile Association should meet on August eighth. But because this year the eighth falls on a major holiday in Spain, it did not seem like an appropriate day to meet. Against my wishes, because of some secrete issues, we have reached the final days of the month without meeting. I believe, gentlemen, you will forgive me if I say I am in violation of the norms.

My initial words must be dark sad words. We have lost a dear friend, an honorable associate, and we, together with the Basque Country, have lost a most beloved illustrious son. The sweet name of Salaberri from Maule is flying across your lips or, stated better, your hearts. Mr. Salaberri was always ready, anywhere, to express his love and affection for the Basque Country, and he has left us believing in that affection, for his laudable work: a collection of songs about our mountains, prettier than the most beautiful garden flowers. As long as Basques persist, the name of Salaberri will never be forgotten, because there are songs in which mountaineers keep our race or people's soul, essence, and trace. That is enough, gentlemen; we are Christians, and we are not charmed by flattery, but by what prayer offers.

And now, welcome gentlemen. Let us remember, that our solidarity worked out something to do, from the beginning to the present there is no job we have not done. Our beloved Basque Country is getting sick and dying; we see its pure customs decaying; its unique language declining; non-Basque languages

204 | POLITICAL AND LITERARY SPEECHES | ARTURO CAMPIÓN

conquering and oppressing Basque, and if things continue like this, nothing else will remain in our towns, just a few old words in the mountains. And so, who knows? Full of shame, like our foreheads, those mountain peaks will also be flattened.

We must erect an altar in the heart of the Basque Country; an altar to the ancient customs and language, and offer or sacrifice all kinds of disagreeable non-Basque languages before that altar. That is the work you must do, gentlemen. There is nothing that cannot be done with the aid of God, and you will be the liberators and life-givers of the Basque Country

I have spoken.

Chapter 12

Lecture in the Basque Center of Donostia-San Sebastián on May 29, 1904

Gentlemen:

The foundation of the Basque Center demonstrates before my eyes the value of an extraordinarily important fact. It has been a while since it was verified here, in Gipuzkoa, that one can compare it with any other. Because many societies, yes, have been founded with all types of uses as their aim: material societies, which hurl their black clouds into the sky so that they thicken the longed for dividends; societies that even in wildest corners of our mountain valleys make contact with the exotic, often bad, with the authentic, almost always good, in conditions of "let things alone, let them pass" that, if the unfamiliar is not rectified, the familiar is corrupted, and we proceed along the exclusive path of industrial and commercial progress, of factories, trams, and spas, to the complete degeneracy of the Gipuzkoan personality. Yet societies whose "value index," by the way not tradeable on the stock market, is made up of physical and moral features that communicate to a people its particular nature, a kind of fixed loom by which history stretches its fibers in order to weave the narrative of national life; and the treasure of truths acquired by experience, which the generations of yesteryear transmitted to those of today by linking them together, so many invaluable pearls, in the golden thread of the national language; and the profound consciousness that individuals are members of a historical community that summarizes and completes them, identifying them among themselves and differentiating them from others with the same sovereign efficiency that nature forms and preserves *species*; societies that in Gipuzkoa may write their value index of the Gipuzkoan people and raise it aloft, gesturing like Moses, in the center of this most beautiful Donostia, which is troubled by the tendency toward cosmopolitanism and the conquest of pleasure, I have not seen, as I said at the beginning, gentlemen, until the foundation of the Basque Center.

During the most raging revolutions, when the destructive movement crushes all obstacles and overcomes all difficulties, the solitary serene thinker contemplating such destructive activity may prophesize, with fear of being contradicted by what will come: "the reaction will come now." This time of reaction, but of Basque reaction, is that which marks and heralds with eloquence the foundation of the Basque Center. The Gipuzkoan body seemed pleased to ingest all kinds of venoms and poisons, so long as they carried the label of "from elsewhere." But, without doubt, the moment of saturation came and the heaving antecedents to being sick began that, at the time, would expel the harmful foreign substances, the instigators of death.

It is well known that among Gipuzkoans, as among all factions or families of the Basque people, there are men who love their land, in their own way; who, enumerating the transformations that the country is experiencing, and thinking of them as progress based on the only reason that they are new; adding up the increases in public wealth and private savings; measuring the kilometers of roads, tramways, and railroads that are constructed without pause; enumerating the beautifications that the cities and towns are experiencing; inventorying the factories that are being operated and the merchandise that is being bought and sold, declare that these are the best times the country has ever known, and consider themselves extremely happy and fortunate, with an optimism that not even Dr. Pangloss outdoes. Our sad note bothers them like a brutal dissonance, and they see us as shy hypochondriacs tormented by imaginary illnesses, whose symptoms are not found in the statistical tables that so delight and please them. However, such happiness leaves us indifferent: it appears to us like a temptation of the flesh in order to defeat the spirit. And they call dreams and fantasies what we term supreme realities, by whose virtue life is worth living… You will search in vain for the formula that may reconcile these opposing criteria, the highest synthesis that may destroy such antinomy. It is impossible to find it. Because they are supporters, consciously or unconsciously, of a certain doctrine of progress that, so long as this is carried out, they do not care if ethnic and historic types disappear—when they do not make that disappearance a fatal and healthy effect of progress—and always seeking broader groupings, streams that penetrate creeks, creeks that disperse into rivers, rivers that are lost in seas, seas that are submerged in the deep ocean: a terrifying image of that humanity destined to dissolve races, homelands, and states into its impassible essence! Whereas we, distinguishing between the *life* and *culture* and *civilization* of peoples, seek to perpetuate the life of ours, because life is the first possession and the condition of all other possessions, even though, by living our intimate and own people's life, that civilization and culture may be weakened or hindered or deferred, or we may reject any culture and civilization that may kill us.

I understand the Basque reaction, that is, the movement of return to a Gipuzkoan Basque type, which does not exclude the progressive movement within the identity of the species, but is opposed to its transformation into another, to be formulated in article 2 of the rules of the Basque Center: "the society proposes to foment Basque culture, which must multiply the love for our land…"

The aim of Basque culture that must be fomented is that which intensifies love of the land, or what amounts to the same thing, love of the homeland. In such discrete terms any other culture that may propose the merely human cultivation of intelligence and sentiment is excluded; the cultivation of which, because it is carried out by Basques, would perhaps claim the title of "Basque culture." A healthy restriction in these times when intellectualism and "dilettantism" are shiny perfumed precursors of an international sewer. "The Republic does not need sages," said the French Jacobins, contradicting themselves. You, gentlemen, practicing your principles, could declare: the Basque Center rejects sages that do not love the homeland.

Love for the homeland, gentlemen, is like the love for a mother. Whoever does not feel it is a monster. All climates, all eras, all peoples know that feeling and revere it. The eyes of those who die for the homeland, contemplate it as equally beautiful to the cold light of the pole, under the glowing radiance of the tropics. Just as children do not judge their mother, or note her defects, or suspect her of any vices, in the same way citizens adorn the homeland with all virtues and perfections, considering it impeccable. This is a providential sentiment; since God having created man for him to live in society, love of the homeland is a very strong link of social life. For that reason, it is only lacking in two of man's lineages: in the hordes of primitive barbarianism, when civilization had barely dawned, and in the hordes of decadent civilization, when barbarianism once again approached its dawn. Savagery and internationalism shake hands; with one difference that I note: the former often leads to life; the latter, always to death... but via the path of ignominy.

What is the homeland [*patria*]? Its very name tells us: it comes from "father" (*pater*), derived in turn from the Sanskrit *patar* or *pitar*, in which the root *pa* (protect) functions. Homeland is the land of the fathers, the birth territory; the land of cribs and graves, watered with tears of pain and joy. It is formed by two elements, one material and the other human, which were joined together, rocking, in the arms of time. Homeland is not improvised, like anything grand and lasting; neither geological terrains, nor forests, nor mountains: the little flower in a field could grow in the space of a day; the oak demands years and then more years. The land, before being a "homeland," begins as *ground*. The nomad plants his tent there and unhooks his cart; and, then, he goes, leaving behind as a relic a pile of dry ashes. When the cement thickens to some extent, and the house darkens the sky on a daily basis with the smoke of home, and the ditch becomes a grave, and the temple or church extend their roofs over the altar table of the altars; when the same horizon and the same landscape tinge the imagination and sentiment of man with their sad or happy reflections, and "surround him as if in the beloved arms of a mother;" when the voice of the dead speaks in the whirring of the wind and the groans of the ocean, and the past is the greatest quantity in the present, and memory even sweeter than hope… then, gentlemen, the homeland has been born and man conquers a new being for his love.

Like the mother, the homeland is unique. This is a self-evident truth, often forgotten. One hears it spoken, with every step, and we ourselves will even have spoken, about the small homeland and the big homeland. The thing is, there is a desire to mark out a certain existent gradation on the basis of the point or locality of mere birth, up to the highest and widest sphere of political organization. But such locution is faulty, it goes against the characteristics of the terms; doubly improper, on account of the concept that it contains and the expression it masks. I have said that the homeland is unique; I should now add another note. The Greek at Thermopylae and the Russian at Yalu, on succumbing to being overwhelmed by enemy forces, represent a feeling hose intensity is not measured by the number of square leagues in Russia and Greece. The homeland—and this is the second point—the homeland, gentlemen, is always large!

The homeland of the Gipuzkoans is Gipuzkoa. Physically, they can have no other; morally, they can want no other. Big and small homeland, just homeland, in sum, which fathers amassed through the sweat of their brows and the blood in their veins; received by their children, obliged to maintain and honor it, under threat of infamy. I would like to invoke its image before you: to open the profound furrow of its valleys, peel back the veil of its melancholic mists, crown the steep mountains with the cresting of its crags, to repeat the sublime maritime song of its waves… I would like to count the crosses in its fields and the bell towers in its churches, and reproduce the divine dialog that the celestial lady entrusted to the consoling echoes of Arantzazu, Itziar, and Guadalupe … I would like to evoke the peace of its farmsteads, in which righteous poverty knows no envy, nor surrenders venerable tradition, to the present, to the brutal theft of modernism… Above all, gentlemen, I would like to evoke, alongside that profound image of Gipuzkoa, the soul of its ancestors, that soul of good sense that inspired the agreements of its councils, the soul of integrity that rejected the flattery of power and repudiated servile compromise, the soul of austerity that did not become a prisoner to the degrading bonds of economic enrichment, the soul of permanence that preferred constantly that which lasted over that which changed, custom over fashion, tradition over revolution, the rights of God over the rights of man... the heroic, bold, and religious soul of Churruka, Elkano, and Ignatius of Loiola. And when that evocation were complete and enthusiasm were to overflow from your chests, then, deducing the response in advance, I would ask you: "Is it true that you love your homeland and that you love above all its growth?" Ah, well, if you love it so much, you will sit on the throne of its rights!

I said before that the distinction between small and big homeland contains a certain dimension of reality. In my view, it expresses imperfectly the possible dualism between homeland and state. I say possible, because ordinarily the homeland tends to become a state; but in fact it does not always achieve that; or perhaps with the passage of time it loses that degree of organization. I will raise an example a very important segment of the Basque people, the Navarrese. The Navarrese homeland condensed into a perfect state, stocked with all its constitutive elements and essential organs. United to another state according to certain pacts and contracts that respected the integrity of its constitution, but losing its international personality; and after a thousand vicissitudes, to which there is no need to refer now, the ancient and glorious Kingdom of Navarre degenerated into a third-degree more or less autonomous province. Has Navarre, for that reason, ceased to be a homeland? Ask the Navarrese if we are ready to die for it!

The Basque people did not constitute a single state, because their individualist spirit emptied the feeling for homeland into small territories, without losing for that reason the consciousness of original community, to which the names Basque and Basque Country, the totality of the Basque people and country immemorially applied, attest. There was as many Basque states as the feeling of homeland produced condensations, and their historical curve was identical: primitive independence, a contracted union with other states, and, finally, the destruction of their own state through tyranny and injustice of the outside state. Yet the homelands live on: Araba lives, Gipuzkoa lives, Navarre lives, Bizkaia lives; and likewise I believe, although asleep or disturbed, the patriotism and self-love of the people of Bizkaia, Navarre, Gipuzkoa, and Araba live on; and while the homelands live, so the potential to create states will last. It would be more difficult for the Basque homelands beyond the Pyrenees to achieve or even attempt that, being too small to file their nails and bear their teeth at the despotic French state, conceived by Caesar within the core of the masses... But they will continue carrying out, as they have done up to now, the sublime role of vestals of the Basque language, and against the socialist and Jacobin assassins of the Republic of the three lies, they will celebrate in their millenarian language the two supreme possessions of the race: God and Freedom!

My ears already perceive the spiteful term that clear or hidden enemies of the Basque people do not cease to aim at me despite realizing, now as well as before, that I desire and hope for the resurrection of the Basque states. Yet the essential incompatibility that they assume to exist between what they defend and I defend is unsustainable. Because no one that possesses notions of political rights ignores that there are *simple* states and *compound* states, particular states (the *Landerstaten*, of the Germans) included in a collective state (*Gesammstat*), which is the public and international personification of the component historical-juridical elements. A complex formation that is not against, in itself, the intelligent, cultured, and honorable administration of Switzerland, or the economic development and global power of Germany and the United States. While other more uniformly constituted nations, according to the canons of political rationalism, may be recreated contemplating the unity of their despotic de-foralization, and the unity of their progressive corruption. Everything therein is done uniformly badly. And if, to the force of tightening the mesh of political unity, they boast about maintaining the cohesion of the national territory, they can also be recreated by confronting that hope with the possibility that, any morning, they may awake to see a foreign flag on their ocean islands, their Mediterranean islands, or their Galician estuaries.

The geographical reality and the historical reality placed the Basque states within the orbit of two nations that preceded the rest in the conception and realization of the unitary national state. The classical conception of the *respublica* was communicated, from the thirteenth century on, to the policies of the French monarchs by legists whose gospel was the *lex regia*, providing them with the necessary arms to defeat the underlying three political ides of the Middle Ages: the Catholic idea of the institution and consecration of principles by the Sovereign Pontiff, the feudal idea of the solemn investiture or pact between lord and vassal, and the juridical idea of inheritance of territorial property as source of public powers. Thanks to the specific aim, always present, of resolve to act and the ability of the means, the French monarchs managed to impose their absolute supreme power, but erasing any egotistical features that tend to degrade the Asiatic powers of a similar nature; since so intimate was the penetration of the artifice and the work, that French nationality, fit together piece by piece, with infinite patience and tenacity, is considered justly the personal creation of the House of France. Louis XIV represented the unity of power, the unity of the nation, the absolute affirmation of sovereignty; a formula that the Revolution accepted and sharpened, and that the Empire perfected and concluded, elevating it to a definitive and tangible institution. "I am the state," said Louis XIV, "I am the state," repeats the democratic Caliban that has succeeded him. And the day will arrive on which the forced heir of these tyrants, the bestial socialism, that is spreading to the horizons of its future harpy wings, will exclaim: "the state is the individual, the family, the homeland; the state is work and capital and wealth; and the distribution of wealth; the state is God; the state is everything." An unhappy day on which it will be worth envying the nomad that roams the steppes, fleeing from the chimneys that blur the horizon, a thousand times more destructive of liberty than, not now the often defamed feudal turret, but the monstrous palaces of Babylon!

The formula of the political evolution of the French state is the destruction of centrifugal forces instead of harmonizing or subordinating them; a formula that likewise presided over the destinies of the Spanish state, although here the confrontations and resistances were greater, and the less propitious historical circumstances. The method of forming said state has been that which those in political science term secondary, through pacts of incorporation, such as those of the current Basque provinces; matrimonial alliances, such as that of Ferdinand of Aragon and Isabel of Castile, and combinations of conquests and pacts, such as the annexation of Navarre. Monarchical absolutism gained ground, developing somewhat behind the political stages in France, until the detail of the revolutionary contagion accelerated the progress of the uniform spirit, with the new system arriving to supersede the old one in its usurpations. The Roman imperial tradition and revolutionary principles are the premises of that consequence that is termed the modern state; but the historical syllogism would never have arrived at its conclusion without the egalitarian and dominant spirit of certain ethnic elements in Spain and France, on account of their extremely important density, which applied the doctrine to the world of deeds.

Whatever the method of forming the national state, it is undeniable, gentlemen, that its organization can be shown as either *simple* or *compound* form. In other words, the notion of the national state does not connote necessarily a unitary or centralized idea. This is the essential point that I am interested in emphasizing. The cohesion of the state is greater or lesser according to specific cases. First, we find the *personal* union of two states, by means of the community of a governing prince and the law of succession that regulates the transmission of the crown within the dynasty. More intimate is the so-called *royal* union, which presupposes, as well as that community, that of the guiding principle and the state government, and even of certain legislative functions. The dominant nature of the central state is unitary, but subordinate states enjoy widespread relative independence. Within these forms of union are those that owe their origin to the *federative system*, or those in which the union is carried out by means of a *constitutional link*, freely established or contracted. The two main kinds within this genre are the *confederation* and *federated state*, or federation. The confederation is born out of a pact among states, which agree on a federal constitution; sometimes the government of the whole is assigned to one of the particular states possessing hegemony, and other times to an assembly or representation of said particular states. The confederate state is founded on the idea of a preexisting single nation, or a people, and is a general, central, complete, and independent state; blessed with its own bodies, which are national and possessed exclusively. With his habitual lucidity Mr. de Tocqueville discovered the characteristics of both federative formations, before political science would systematize them. "This Constitution," he says,

> which may at first sight be confounded with the federal constitutions which preceded it, rests upon a novel theory, which may be considered as a great invention in modern political science . . . In all the confederations which had been formed before the American Union the Federal Government demanded its supplies at the hands of the separate Governments . . . In America the subjects of the Union are not States, but private citizens.

Excuse me, gentlemen, this dry digression. But I did not want the enemies of the Basque people to take up positions and from there admonish us with the rigors of the Code, insofar as we reclaim the absolute reintegration of the Basque states: if they enunciate the disjunctive between unitary and separatist ideas, it is my responsibility to reply to them that such a disjunctive is the child of ignorance, or of bad faith. The Basque states formed part, until recently, of compound states, formed historically. The sovereignty to which they were subject was a contracted or conditional sovereignty. That is how it was recognized without any qualms by those great monarchs that were called the Catholic

Kings, Charles I and Phillip II, more powerful and feared than the kings of unitary Spain. From which I deduce that if there exists currently any lineage of separatism, it is the separatism of the politicians that altered the terms of the incorporation pacts and wickedly destroyed them; the separatism of the politicians that, *a priori*, declared the coexistence of the Basque states and the Spanish national state incompatible, because the coexistence formula did not appear in the manuals of Jacobin law; the separatism of the politicians that proposed locking up in the pigeonholes of their elections independent Basque voters, assuring, in order to achieve this, the all-embracing supremacy of central power; separatism, yes, the separatism of hatred for law, anti-foral separatism, the separatism of perjury, the separatism of an eternal rejection of justice! But they should be aware in advance, and listen, from our loyalty, to the warning: the day will come—that I hope—when the Basque people, after vanquishing the parties, a bunch of vipers at the heart of the Basque Country, will reclaim, with the intention of recovering it, the restoration of the Basque states; and that day politicians will need to look for and find a formula for coexistence, because as regards what we must do, we must offer them nothing else than what the centuries have shown us!

And I must not discuss separatism, gentlemen, because I have proposed overlooking certain principles, the professing of which is down to the individual, according to the regulations of the Basque Center; and separatism, gentlemen, is not a principle, it is a consequence. It is the result of bulldozing politics, the systematic infringement of the rights of the peoples that make up the nationality, the exploitation of colonial territories in the name of the nation and on behalf of corrupt employees... That consequence in the history of Spain is called the Flanders uprising, the separation of Catalonia, the loss of the Americas... But that consequence does not emanate from our principles; it flows from opposing principles. The politics of the Basque states is the politics of harmony, of concord, of mutual respect for law; the politics of loyalty, which with meticulous scruples fulfills, not just the letter, but the spirit of the pact of union with the Crown of Spain, and which exceeds in this fulfillment: the secular politics of our land, written in irrefutable documents, which only the accomplices of separatism have the audacity to call separatist!

This is not the appropriate occasion to narrate, not even in general terms, the history of relations between the Basque states and central power, under its two absolutist and revolutionary phases. The struggle against the monarchical spirit was detailed, comprehensive; the words "anti-fuero" and "affront" summarized it. It was a simmering procedure on the grill. In the same rhythm that the old monarchy was becoming corrupted by absolutism, its unitary and centralist tendencies were affirmed. Charles IV and Ferdinand VII cherished the project to complete the ignominies of their reigns with the abolition of the foral constitutions. But the tragic conflict from the beginning coincided with the establishment of a new law; the grill was replaced by the guillotine. The henchmen of the absolute sovereignty of the people received the password of the halberdiers of the "net" king, and the liar Llorente was the oracle of the twelve-ists. The two muddy cataracts of royal supremacy and popular supremacy, one tumbling out of the Versailles of Louis XIV and the other from the Rousseauian Convention, blended and mixed together in the estuary of identical tyranny!

Studying the question in "abstract" terms, no reason can be given for whose effectiveness it is forbidden for homelands to form states. And looking at the question "specifically," or relative to the current Basque-Navarrese provinces, the question is not even a question. Since the unions of Gipuzkoa, Araba, Bizkaia, and Navarre to the Crown of Spain, the rule of law in those territories was constant and invariable, without those events that often tried to modify it prevailing. An enlightened French writer, Mr. Louis Lande, sent by the *Revue des Deux Mondes* to study the foral question at the end of the civil war, expressed rather accurately the juridical aspect of the problem:

Certainly, the free institutions, placed in comparison to the laws that govern a despotic country, may seem like privileges; but in the precise sense of the word, there are no privileges when a people, at one with their native soil, inherited from their ancestors free institutions: then they are true rights and it is permitted to maintain them and defend them. This is what happened in the Basque Country; the autonomy that it possessed was not due to anyone; it is what always existed, without there having been any concessions or cowardice committed; and when it was annexed to Castile it was proposed, not to transfer that, but to guarantee it better. Today then, Basque autonomy, founded on tradition and on treaties, is an existing fact, the prevailing law against which there can be no prevalence of the will of kings, or the example of other nations, or new principles of modern legislation … From the dual historical and legal point of view, its rights are indisputable; today, however, no one wants to accept it because [the Basques] are not the most numerous or the strongest. But were they to possess just the material power of Belgium, Portugal, or Switzerland, there would be no diplomat who would not rush to recognize its official existence in all treaties.

In effect, gentlemen, there were a complete lack of any important reasons or laws to oppose the rights of the Basque-Navarrese Country. For that reason, the Spanish politician that, in the year 1876, completed the work that started by the legislators of 1839, Mr. Cánovas del Castillo, believing it unworthy of his admirable talent and his elevated nature to appeal to sophisms, good for Alonso Martínez and the other majority lawyers, he raised the debate from the subtleties of the legal profession to the sovereign decrees of destiny, opposing the irrefutable reasoning of the Navarrese representative Mr. Morales, the steel knife that cuts Gordian knots: "a fact of force," he said, "is what comes to make up law, because when force leads to a state, force is law." Are you listening, gentlemen? The only reason he prevailed against us was the savage injustice of force. Oh force! I do not believe in the sempiternity of your works! I contemplated you a thousand times freely all over the world, like a lion in the jungle; but other times, discharged high up, the golden arrow of justice pierced your heart!

Spanish politicians, gentlemen, have no failed to destroy Basque liberties, those commentaries that history writes to government acts, demonstrating their uselessness and inefficiency. Because they ensured that the party resentments, regional jealousies, and school prejudices that made up the substance of the abolitionist movement were disguised as lofty reasons of state: the need to pursue a policy of national assimilation and erase even the last semblance of contracted or agreed sovereignty. "The national unity that the Catholic Monarchs sought to establish here," said Mr. Cánovas del Castillo, "was the national unity of today, but the unity of royal power as opposed to the feudal powers . . . I have defended constantly to date the need for power not to be decentralized, for the principle of government to reach everywhere, for no government agents anywhere to be against stimulating, promoting, the direction of royal power exercised by its ministers responsible for doing so." And Senator Acapulco said: "The nation refutes the idea that there may have been a pact within the law of 1839 . . . one of the ideas that [at the time] prevailed, it was just legislative power, and wherever there is just legislative power there is the faculty, not just to make laws, but to change them, modify them, and even annul them." And Mr. Navarro Rodrigo:

No, Cisneros and Richelieu did not take into account interests that could damage in order to constitute their glorious and great nationalities; Bismarck has not been stopped in the work he has carried out before the eyes of modern Europe, the complaints of the small kingdoms and the small principalities that had to merge into the great melting pot of German unity . . . The criterion must be inspired by that most noble and broad criterion of homeland that has inspired the great and true men of state, the policy of Cisneros and Richelieu, which were based on the whole to constitute the great nationalities of Spain and France.

And Mr. Mena Zorrilla: "the law of the Latin peoples has been a condition to which they seemed condemned, the coming of national unity to the realization of progress, through the enhancement of royal power, through the infringement and annihilation of provincial liberties." All of that, gentlemen, in order to tighten up the ties of Spanish nationality, to enhance it, to strengthen it, to fortify it, in passing making the rest of the world believe that the kinglets of the parliamentary taifas were Bismarck, Richelieu, and Cisneros... Yet here, precisely, history came to write its comments, measuring the vigor acquired by the most complete unification of Spain, with the capitulation of its armies, and bottling of its squads!

The struggle to the death between the Basque states and the central state, as I pointed out to you earlier, was carried out through installing new laws, conceived by rationalism as an abstract absolute principle, that is, unconditional, which did not recognize the sovereignty of God or respect the legal states that did not emanate directly from that. The more radical the parties of liberalism, the more intensely they expressed the absolute nature of the new laws, as one can see by studying the socialist schools, for whom the only body and only function of law is the state that controls totally the very functions of individual, family, and social life, raising stone pyramids from grains of sand. For the same intrinsic reason that rationalism, in the philosophical sphere, led fatally to pantheism, so political rationalism constructed the omnipotent state, the only substantial reality of legal life. For that reason, Hegel, the greatest and most logical of modern rationalists, summed up the immanent doctrine of all rationalism when he considered the current state to be like God, and argued that it was a divine earthly thing and the absolute and immovable aim of its own substantial unity, with supreme rights over individuals. We should not be amazed that in the years that followed the law of July 21, 1876, the then head of the great liberal reptile, that is the party termed democratic-progressive, which was the grouping of all the active or militant revolutionary elements, as is said now, even though they did not know how to do anything except shameful military rebellions, publishing new editions of "liberating" sergeants and generals; we should not be amazed, I repeat, that this democratic and progressive grouping should sponsor the absolutism of H. M. the nation with more insolence than any "sycophant" of the old regime of H. M. the king: "The Spanish nation," they said,

> as the single and supreme power, and meeting in parliament, the product of universal suffrage, will dictate laws; laws in which the sovereignty of the nation is accommodated, must also accommodate, without any subordinate body, whether it be termed province or municipality, may oppose one law against another, one precept against another, the creative will of positive law to that other superior will.

That was the simple and most correct formula of the new laws; that the fullness, the unconditional nature, and the absolutism of the new sovereignty, the perfect equivalence of the "net" king, adopted by the royalists of Ferdinand VII. How must we feel about the new idol? The same as our grandparents thought about the old one: we should not give him any right to break the foral idea, we should not award him that privilege, being resolved to hurl him over to the other side of the Ebro!

I say hurl, and I pronounce that word hardly with any enthusiasm, I am overwhelmed with anguish. Because before, when the king committed anti-foral acts, the Basques and Navarrese, whatever their theoretical ideas about sovereignty, did not disagree when it came to the rights of the Basque people, nor did they dissent of their love for the homeland. But now, since anti-foral acts have been committed by the nation, or more accurately parties, the "moral unity" of the Basque people broken, as those parties extended their tentacles over the whole country, and they have fellow believers and newspapers and overlords, and they are a garbage dump for exotic ideas that cloud the intelligence, and they incite passions that poison the heart, and they satisfy greed that corrupts characters; as there is no longer in Spain anyone making a living from politics that Basques may follow, not with stones, but applause; as here all "obstacles" have been established and all the flags of the contemporary political Gomorrah fly, the forces of preservation and reconquest are disintegrating, and their effective action is made impossible, and the most destructive means of our rights find a "claque" to applaud them and "sipahi" to defend them. A terrible spectacle, from which our eyes will not be freed until the day that exclusive love of the homeland, disseminated by the Basque Center, occupies a place that may usurp that of love for the Spanish parties!

I have spoken.

Chapter 13

Nationalism, Foralism, and Separatism
Speech given at the Basque Center
of Donostia-San Sebastián
on the evening of January 7, 1906

The incorporation of the Kingdom of Navarre into the
Crown of Castile was by the way of principal axis union,
each one retaining their ancient nature, both in
laws and in territory and in government.
(Law 33, title 8, bk. I of the *Recop. de las Leyes de Navarra*)

Gentlemen:

The first time I had the pleasure of directing my words to the
Basque Center, I spoke about the homeland, I made sure to define
it, to enumerate its constitutive elements, and I enunciated the
fundamental truth, looking at the place in which I was speaking:
the homeland of the Gipuzkoans in Gipuzkoa. When I broke the
spell that subjugated me with the memory of physical beauties
and the moral clothing that this noble land possesses—a spell that
attempted to place on my lips some babbling poetry in order to
celebrate them and extoll them—I drew a dividing line between
homeland and state, I affirmed the historical existence of several
Basque states, and I traced the curve that led them, in flights of
time, to become harmonized with another bigger state, under the
protection of federal pacts that respected their full personality. And
hand in hand against that odious and dishonest alternative from
which, from very opposing camps, either centralism or separatism
were formulated, I resorted to the arsenal of political science and

provided a testimony about our history, demonstrating that a third term exists, the organization of compound or collective states, at the heart of which the Basque states lived and prospered while monarchical absolutism, first, and later liberal absolutism did not alter but reduced and dissolved our own constitutions, and brutally cut the link that united the Basque states to the Spanish state. Answer me, gentlemen, who are the true separatists?

Today I propose to continue studying questions that were omitted from the first speech. Not just the issue, but even the way of explaining it will differ, because in speaking about the homeland I touched on your sensibility and your imagination: now I am aiming for your intelligence to listen to me. Everyone gathered here feels and wants unison: that is why my task yesterday was so easy and pleasant. I aspire to this communion lasting in the world of ideas, whose subtle loose nature, whose propensity to take on changing colors and nuances, is usually the reason that terms that take shape by force only with difficulty acquire the firmness of signs of invariable notation. The idea imprisoned by the external façade of the word, when it does not manage to alter that form, is obliged to fill itself with diverse meanings. This is the source of mistakes and confusion that politics, the fertile mother of passions, exacerbates and profits from, separating that which, by another kind of chance, would have remained together. I do not pretend to elaborate programs, or define dogmas, or outline directions; I come, requested by polite invitation, to explain my intimate thoughts on very controversial and important subjects, and on such vast matters that, not even treated superficially as I do, are compatible with brevity. The certainty with which I am going to test your patience almost takes away my hope that you will indulge me.

The Vagueness of the Technical

Race, people, nation, foralism: there are just as many other words in popular language that are used to discuss, applaud, or attack Basque nationalism. Words furnished with multiple meanings, which people use by investing in them their ideas at a given moment, and that at other later moments express other very different ideas: the ambiguity that is likewise spread to these other words extracted from political vocabulary, such as autonomy and autonomism, adopted by those dedicated to prescribing a *succedaneum* for the country for its historical constitutions.

Let us extract the meaning of those words, not with the aim of crystallizing it for everyone, but with that of providing the technical dimension of politics with Basque claims, terms that do not add fuel to the fire of merely *verbal* divergence among their devotees; terms that may exteriorize clear defined ideas, whose profession or rejection, and not in the vague sense of their terms, may constitute the *real* matter of possible discrepancies.

The Race

When one speaks about the *white* race, the *black* race, or the *yellow* race, it is undeniable that that word evokes a very different idea to that which we attribute to speaking about the *Semitic* race and the *Aryan* race. In the former case, the differences are so salient, so pronounced, that common people perceive them just by looking at any of the examples: physical features dominate the picture. These persist in the latter case, but are lessened, and in order to maintain the classification other, less patent, ones must enter the account, which require more acute observation, more of a scientific than a merely impressionistic criterion. And, instead of the Aryan and Semitic race, we were to speak about the *Celtic*, *Germanic*, *Latin* race, or, if exaggerating the differentiation, we award the qualification of races to the whole set of Spaniards, French, and Italians, contrasting them, we observe that the number of physical characteristics employed diminishes while the number of historical characteristics used rises, to the point that the latter almost exclusively dominate when one terms races those observable varieties within a broad national political community, such as Galicians, Aragonese, Catalans, and Andalusians.

Adjust yourselves, gentlemen, to the dilution of the concept of race by comparing the image that, in your intelligence, the following extreme phrases conjure up: black race, Castilian race. The noun in both cases is the same; but its content differs enormously. This reveals that the term race is erroneous, used all over the place, according to the aims of whoever writes or pronounces it. The same people that, under the generic name of French race, include the descendants of prehistoric tribes, of Iberians, Celts, Gauls, Greeks, Latins, and Germans that, in various doses, are distributed throughout French territory, will speak to us, immediately thereafter, about the Breton race and the Basque race, in enumerating the components of the modern French race. How is possible for the same word to serve to amalgamate such heterogeneous ethnic elements, and then to disassociate them again by separating the previously Armorican from Basque, which were previously mixed together?

I will answer: because the word race, which in the natural sciences has an invariable meaning thanks to certain details that make it up, is one of many in common speech subject to the arbitrary nature of use. And what from use has happened is: the replacement of the details in the natural sciences by others, mainly taken from political geography and linguistics.

Language and Nationality in the Concept of Race

It is enough for a human society to speak a specific language or constitute a specific nationality for such use to be deemed authorized to classify it as a race. Even more if the tow circumstances, however unequally, coincide! Because the French language predominates in a certain territory, and because that territory is the seat of a nationality, the name of French race rings out.

Language and nationality are terrible instruments to determine races, and the results obtained through their manipulation do not stand up to the lightest of examinations. I will cite some examples. The Semitic languages that, already in very ancient

times, took control of the region of Assyria, stifling the agglutinant
language of pre-Semitic settlers, had the good fortune that one of
them, Arabic, was implanted by Muslim scimitars over immense
spaces, which extended from Spain to the banks of the Indus:
to enumerate the peoples, races, nations of Europe, Africa, Asia
that learned, through the pages of the Quran, the mother tongue
of the Prophet, would be tiring to your ears. The Normans, an
illustrious tribe of Danish people, by the third generation had
adopted in Normandy the French language, a language that,
among the folds of the flags of Tancred of Hauteville, was taken
to Sicily and southern Italy, and which stirred up people in the
strophes of the *Song of Roland* during the conquest of England,
where, after two centuries, they adopted the English language, a
near relative of the Norse their ancestors spoke on the beaches
of the North. Numerous Celts in Germany were dispossessed of
their language by German; those of France, by Latin, which also
erased the language of the Iberians and Celts in Spain. Castilian,
a Latin *patois*, took possession of significant terrain in Araba,
Bizkaia, and Navarre that a century ago spoke Basque: a mournful
list that embarrassment and shame impede me from reading out,
but in which soon would appear, oh! Gipuzkoans! Many of you.
But did that loss change the race? Basques are divided into two
nationalities; the Poles, into three; there are French in Switzerland,
Belgium, and Germany; Italians, in Switzerland, Austria, and
France; Germans, in Russia. If we look from the perspective of
history, there are an amazing number of variations: the Roman
Empire, the Empire of Charlemagne, the British Empire are true
global syntheses that reduce the best raised external borders to
internal borders. In more modest proportions, the variations are
continual: compare the limits of France in 1551 to those of 1791.

The Scientific Concept of Race

No; the criterion to determine races by language and nationality
is inadmissible. Since the notion of race has been elaborated the
natural sciences, let us go to them for the clarification we are

missing. They tell us that race is, "the hereditary variety of the same species." But they also say that it consists of fixed and variable characteristics. The confusion we sought to avoid surfaces once again in the latter, since the variables are apparent and visible characteristics. In the human races, stature, jaw shapes, hair, eye, and skin colors are all variable characteristics; fixed, skull shape and orbital index. Fixed characteristics appear hidden; they are only discovered by means of technical procedures.

Having said that, gentlemen, the notion of race has been transplanted to the field of tumultuous politics; national claims, yearnings to conquer, excuses for dominating, are based on it. The only title that some concede to peoples in order to organize themselves nationally is that of race. This is embracing the absurd, the ridiculous, and the impossible. Can you imagine Germany, still brushing off the dust of Sedan, Metz, and Paris, stopped in its triumphal tracks by the sage shouting: stop! Your soldiers' heads, crowned in laurels, are in places long and narrow and in others short and broad! Your terrible armies line up, in a fraudulent unity, dolichocephalic Scandinavians and brachycephalic Celts! You are not a pure race, you are a mixed people; I deny you the right to national existence. History, through the mouth of Germany, would reply: I am the true matrix of nations!

Purity of Race

Nevertheless, this idea of race with which so many of us are obsessed, which is troublesome and sometimes still, in fact, impossible to determine, contains a positive reality. In comparing extreme examples, it shines with midday clarity: no one would think of denying that the black, the white, and the yellow are races: the difficulties begin in proposing which are the yellow, white, and black races, whose mixing, whose crossing, which is the law of biology, produced that immense number of white, black, and yellow, of often mistaken characteristics, grouped into different tribes, peoples, and nations. The study of races, *a fortiori*, registers in its program the determining of pure races, factors in a subsequent ethnic combination. A messy problem like few others. I said that race is a hereditary variety of a species. What is the mechanism of its production? A preexisting type must begin to vary in a certain way, crystallize into a certain degree of variation, and transmit the characteristics acquired to its descendants. Individuals that together experience this variation constitute a race. In order to experience this variation in unison, individuals must receive the same differentiated influences. So that in the formative period of the race, many individuals stemming from the original type, on receiving other influences, or on account of not receiving all of them, remain outside it: loose rings outside the central nebula.

It is not enough for race to form; it is necessary for it to perpetuate by withdrawing from the penetration of foreign ethnic elements, which would alter it, making it degenerate from pure into mixed. Theoretically, the existence of pure races is impossible, because all that is needed is an accidental mix to infect them. In practice, the accentuated predominance of an element can be equated to purity of blood. A sixteenth part of foreign blood is not very much; a hundredth does not count (Lapouge, *Les selections sociales* [Social selections]). Even races that, on account of their high numbers of mixings, barely deserve that name from an anthropological point of view, would receive it legitimately from the political perspective, as long as a certain number of natural characteristics were added to historically important other ones. And this how many, with due caution, without immoral latitudinarianism, use the concept of race, not to construct exclusively nationalities, which would be absurd, but to deem it an expression of one of its most transcendental *physical bases*.

Basque Race and Basque People

A race is not just whoever, gentlemen. Basques, singular for the marvelous fact of their language, a "linguistic isolate" in the sea of inflected languages in Western Europe, owed to this circumstance the constant possession of an ethnic civil state. Science came with its analysis, not so much to clarify the problem, but to complicate it. But the latest research recognizes the existence of an original native element that is not shared by the people who surround them; an element that has combined with others gathered at random, without dissolving it. And while some attempt to disassociate the ethnic singularity from the linguistic singularity, arguing that they do not match one another, the shrewdest inductions reestablish the association of both. The result of which is that the Basque race exists, whose language is Basque, and as well as an externalization greater than the latter, the Basque people, in whom are personified combined ethnic elements by means of a common consciousness that reduces them to unity, through the deeds and grace of, especially, the language. If the Basque race, a *substratum* of the Basque people, and the Basque people, an amplification of the Basque race, organized states and formed nations, and they are perfectly within their rights to restore them, it is not because of their skull, nose, jaws, and faces are like this or that, nor because their eyes, hair, and skin display this or that coloration, nor because their size reaches a certain height, but because Basques brought into play their natural qualities, and practiced the heroic art of making them worth something, and they loved independence, and they did not fear death; that is to say, because they knew how to, wanted to, an could represent a role in history, which is what definitively joins foreheads to the crown of sovereignty, or subjects hands to the chains of slavery.

The People: Disparity in its Concept

The concept of people, in fact, gets confused with that of nation and even with that of race, and does not even enjoy identical acceptance in the educated countries. Bluntschli highlights the disparity one observes in this regard between Western and Germanic languages: "When it comes to the word *nation*," he says, "German, in the same way as the Latin of Ancient Rome, indicates a notion of *spirit*, of *culture*, while the French and the English prefer a popular expression, *people*. In contrast, *as a notion of state*, Germans use the term *Volk* (*populus*); the Western countries, more that of *nation*.

The etymology favors the German use: nation, from *nasci*, refers in effect to birth and to race; people and *populus*, from *polis*, *res publica*, more to collective public existence" (*Theorie generale de l'Etat* [General theory of the state], bk. 1, chap. 2).

The famous German professor to this point. Let us expand on his etymological and lexical indications. Strictly speaking, the Latin word *plebes*, besides its juridical sense, means crowd. It comes from the same root that has given *pleo*, the primitive form of *compleo* (to fill), *plenus* (full), *plerique* (the greater part), a meaning that palpitates in *populus* (the group of citizens as a whole, the crowd, the public). From "people" derives the verb "to populate." All these words do not go beyond the limits of a material meaning of number and group, without any other determining note. The word "nation," taken from the Latin *natio*, which means "tribe" or "race," either comes from *natus* (born) or, in a more roundabout way, from the Sanskrit *nah* (to sew, to tie), expresses common origin, and therefore the unity of the group. Between people and nation would be the difference that separates the organic from the inorganic, and the juxtaposition of assimilation. But one thing is etymology and another thing is use.

Typical Definitions of the Terms Nation and People

The Royal Spanish Academy dictionary defines nation as: 1. The state or political body that acknowledges a supreme common center of government; 2. The territory this comprises, and even its individuals taken collectively; 3. The group of inhabitants of a province, country, or kingdom; 4. That same country or kingdom. As you see, the dominant concept, applied to human beings, is that of people: in one case the notion of common origin has been replaced by that of political dependence. Thus, we should not be surprised that one of the definitions of the term "people" [*pueblo*], according to this dictionary, is the fourth of nation; the remaining ones attributed to people are: place, town, or city that is populated by people; a group of people that inhabit the place; common and ordinary people, the opposite of nobles.

Littré, in his admirable dictionary of the French language, approaches the Germanic sense without avoiding confusions. He defines the people as "a multitude of men in a country that live under the same laws [this definition does not take into account the community of origin, but rather the political and territorial connection]; a multitude of men that, although they do not inhabit the same country, possess the same religion or the same origin [now he dispenses with territory and laws in order to focus on race or, alternatively, religion, so that as people profess Christianism, Buddhism, Islam, etc., so they constitute one single people]. We can overlook the remaining definitions and move on to that of nation, since it is of interest to us: "The gathering of men that inhabit the same territory, subject or not to the same government, who have possessed, for a long time, fairly common interests through which they can be seen as belonging to the same race." The government connection is relegated to a secondary position; territory occupies first place, and the old community of interests is adorned with such extraordinary importance that it is even valid for constituting the concept of race. The *community of interests* is equal to the *relationship of spirit and culture* in German authors. Littré recognizes that people and nation are synonyms, but, starting from the basis of etymology, manages to Germanize its meaning: "nation," he adds, "expresses a common relationship of birth, of origin; people, a relationship of number and group. Use considers nation, above all, as representing the body of the inhabitants of the same country, and people as representing that same body in their political relations. But use often confuses these two terms…" This is Littré's conclusion, the simple recognition of a fact.

Official political technicality has not managed to disentangle these confusions. The constitution of the German Empire and that of the United States use the term "people;" Switzerland, that of "nation" and "homeland." The Basic Code of Spain is termed: the Constitution of the Spanish Monarchy. Its article 3 imposes the obligation of defending the *homeland* with arms, 11 proclaims that the *nation* is obliged to maintain the worship and minsters of the Catholic religion, 14 alludes to the rights of the *nation*, 62 to coexistence in the *nation,* yet 75 goes back to using the word *monarchy* to specify that the same codes will govern there. Based on these texts, homeland, monarchy, and nation are synonyms.

If, avoiding use, etymological value, and official political terminology, we were to consult the technicality of authors, seeking greater precision, we would experience major disappointment. The words race, people, and nation change sense in flying from mouth to mouth; and the concept of state, with which all of them are combined, only clouds things more. Of everything that I have said and omitted, I only want to draw one conclusion: the imprecision of the terminology, and therefore the faculty that helps us to define terms that the fitting enunciation of our thought demands. I will use this freedom, dispensing in my definitions with etymological value and maintaining, as much as I can, that of use among the Western countries to which we belong.

Establishing the Concepts of Race, People, Nation, and Tribe

I say, then, gentlemen, that people is the group of ethnic elements, of a single or varied origin, capable of *historical* life through having arrived at establishing within that group, more or less intimately, a certain community of aspirations or ideals, and of culture or spirit, fully conscious of its connection, manifested externally by language. The *substratum* of the people is the race, whether pure or not. In this case it is necessary for gentilic heterogeneity to not go beyond physical nature, or to be so noticeable as to prevent the appearance of a dominant average type. The people are differentiated from the race, and more still from the progenitors of the latter, the horde and the family, by their aptitude for *historical* life, that is, to affirm their own personality in the internal and external order against other peoples or nations.

The nation is the people itself, or a part of it, which is subject to an external, sole, and sovereign power that is the state, a means for common ends, the organ of social solidarity and of spiritual unity, to whom it personifies publically and internationally.

So that, gentlemen, referring to the same group, we can denominate it diversely, according to whatever our points of view may be, *race* when we are dealing with the simple physical element, to blood and its origins, *people* when our attention is called to the dual *psychic-physical* element that unravels in history, and *nation* when we are interested in emphasizing the *juridical-political* element, the finalizing and perfection of the whole series.

The race preexists in the family, in the horde; pure or mixed, it is expressed in the people on ascending into historical life. In that race, for multiple reasons that do not need detailing, varieties of little importance stand out, which we will term *tribes*, which are ineffective when it comes to impeding the unity of the nation. There are peoples that make up a nation, and peoples that make up several nations; and likewise we know that several nations can combine and make up a *nation of nations*, whether in an equality of its components or with a clear hegemony of one of them, and whether they are all formed out of violence or they amalgamate through the destructive virtue of time. All this movement, politically, translates into the organization of simple and compound states.

The Large Nationalities: The Law of their Decadence

If race, according to anthropologists, is rarely if ever pure, imagine, gentlemen, what will happen to the larger nations with their long histories, which reveal so much, ordinarily, about cruel histories, immense ossuaries of peoples, and small nations assassinated. Therein, ethnic types, which barely reached the four points of the horizon, overlapped and overlapped again, using up all the different kinds of mixing; in the end, the citizens of these distinguished nations usually resemble, in the terms of purity of blood, street dogs, and when ethnic cohabitation has been practiced to its limits, the time of inevitable or irredeemable decadence has come for them, as it did for Rome, the victim of colossal *hybridization* so strikingly described by the great Count de Gobineau.

Eugenics[1]

Just as individuals, within the substantial unity of human nature, may differ qualitatively among themselves, so do ethnic groups within the unity of the human species. In the scale of perfection, some occupy the higher steps, others the lower ones, many in the middle, and the equality attributed to men and races is such a lie.

There are groups that stand out for the assertiveness, energy, resolve, and consistency of their character; for the faculty of pursuing sublime aspirations and cultivating magnanimous tendencies and propensities. These groups, insofar that their aptitude to produce a certain average of superior beings is obvious, have been classified justly as *eugenics*.

The gift of intelligence to an exceptional extent must be considered a sign of eugenism; yet intelligence is the most liberally distributed quality in all groups. Alone, it does not imprint quality. The primacy belongs to will. Each people, each nation possesses sufficient intelligence to exist. Neither the Romans nor the Persians were inferior, from the intellectual perspective, to the Germans and the Arabs that destroyed them. The leaders of internal barbarianism that approach belong to the intellectual class. In full social decay, the arts and sciences still shine as spook lights in cemeteries. But a people without will are lost irresistibly. Even reduced to their psychological and not metaphysical extent, we can repeat Schopenhauer's maxim: "will, as a thing in itself, the only true and indestructible essence of man."

All this about eugenism must be understood in two ways: respect for the families that make up the ethnic group, and respect for the ethnic groups that make up the people or nation. In the pure races, supremacy is settled by means of families; in peoples or nations, and especially in the nations of nations, by means of groups. In effect, these contain groups that are eugenic and groups that are not or that are but to a much lesser extent, whose role is to receive and imitate the ideal that the former elaborate.

---

1   From the Greek *eugenes*, noble, brave, honorable, of illustrious lineage, of good race or caste.

The decadence of pure races is more visible earlier; it looks like a straight line that goes askew: that of ethnically heterogeneous nations is angular, it rises and falls like the course of a fever. While the nation possesses reserves of *eugenics*, even of an uneven quality, it is capable of illustrious deeds and of regenerating itself in its decadence; but it barely exhausts them, through the hospital of *sick nations* it enters the cemetery of deceased nations. Eugenics can be compared to the usable part of nourishment in the body: combustion, organic oxidation destroys it, and it is indispensable for another of the same quality to replace it. Here the analogy ends; since even if social combustion burns the eugenics, the ingestion of new ones occurs rarely, and the *detritus*, far from being eliminated, remain active without ceasing as lethal social toxins. Everything conspires within the large nations to make the eugenics disappear: first, internal mixing, which degrades the superior types; second, historical selection, which functions contrary to natural selection; since through this, what are superior beings, as well as embellishing them generally with less of a natural reproductive capacity, they pay more from their person and diminish the common probabilities of reproduction and perpetuation.

Two Historical Problems Explained by Eugenism: The Disappearance of Medieval Literature in France; The Decadence of Spain in the Time of Charles II

This doctrine of the diversity of ethnic groups included in the nation, and that of the hierarchy of natural aptitudes and excellences, explain many until now unsolvable historical problems. I will cite a couple of them. For example: that which Gaston Paris, in his admirable lesson on *Les contes orientaux dans la littérature française du Moyen Age* [Oriental tales in French literature of the Middle Ages], classified as an "extremely curious and important phenomenon for the history of literature and modern civilization" and what the celebrated Menéndez Pelayo contended so vividly in a volume of his *Historia de las ideas estéticas en España* [History of esthetic ideas in Spain], dedicated to "El romanticismo en Francia"

[Romanticism in Spain]. Let us listen to him: "No nation in Europe can compete with France for the glory of having created, in the twelfth and thirteenth centuries, romantic literature and art par excellence." Recall the prodigious efflorescence of the *chansons de geste* in their three fundamental cycles: the poems of the *Round Table*, the first appearance of the novel of love and adventures, the satirical cycle of Reynard; the picaresque world of the *fables*, the incipient wonderful dramatic literature, enormously prolific, of the liturgical dramas (miracles, mysteries, and moralities); the two lyrical schools, of the *trouvères* of the North and the *trobadors* of Provence; the series of ingenuous picaresque chroniclers; "and if all this were not enough," he adds, "ogival architecture that, for more than one hundred years, was an exclusively French art." Enthused, he exclaims: "What more splendid crown could adorn the figurehead of any people, if all of this had continued its natural progressive evolution, if all of the seeds had flourished at the right time, matured by the soft breath of the national tradition..." But that was not the case, and Menéndez Pelayo sums up everything by saying:

> There was just a people, precisely the first of the peoples of the Middle Ages, the leading people of the rest in Europe and its darkest periods, which practiced on its spirit that kind of mutilation, as painful as it was imprudent, dividing its history and its literature into two completely different halves. There occurred in France a veritable collapse of the national consciousness: the history of the Middle Ages was forgotten, its institutions were almost completely forgotten, its art and its literature were forgotten, even its language was forgotten.... *Old French* is a completely different study to the study of Classical French. . . . when one wants to popularize a text of the Middle Ages, a *chanson de geste*, one must begin by *translating it!*

The divorce was so absolute, gentlemen, that modern France is incapable of understanding and loving its older counterpart, that it devotes all its efforts to rejecting and eliminating it. Outside the reduced illustrious coterie of Paris and Gautier, all the other writers, even the most celebrated, even those that boast the most about having purged the spirit of kind of prejudice, dismiss and affront the tradition of the French Middle Ages, despite it being "the richest and most glorious of anywhere" (*Historia de las ideas estéticas en España*, vol. 5, pp. 2–6).

Mr. Menéndez Pelayo limited himself to pointing out the fact, leaving the French to the task of figuring out the reasons. I am unaware whether they have figured it out truly, although there is no shortage of explanations. In my opinion, gentlemen, the explanation is to be found in the disappearance, by selection or by social reabsorption, of most of the eugenics of that most glorious epoch. The collapse of the national consciousness reflected the collapse of the most select ethnic elements that had produced it. A collapse that was repeated when the choppy waves of the egalitarian ocean eroded the islets on which the last survivors had taken refuge. That is when the final and decisive national excision took place. The bloody Republic, so that no one may have any doubt about its apostasy, began to date chronology since its establishment. The nation that organized feudalism, that which constructed the cathedrals of Reims and Paris, that which always carried in its soul the distressing echoes of the *olifant* of Roncevaux, that which with a cross on its chest rescued Christ's sepulcher, that which spread the chivalrous ideal and condensed the spirit of its monarchy into the figure of Saint Louis, fulfilling greatness with the saintliness of the King of France; that nation is not the same ethnically, it is not rationed ethnically in the same way as that in which Mouquette's bottom shone blood red in the last rays of the setting sun, it demands of its supreme judges the democratic gift of the "average," it uproots crucifixes from schools and official buildings with the same hands that received "checks" from Panama bribery, and resolves to lock up the herds of its debased proletariat in that barracks lacking honor, in that convent lacking holiness that is called collectivism![2]

---

2   The matter (like many that so-called sociology studies) is so complex that it would be necessary to contrast skillfully that picture with an antithetical one, denouncing mine as artful. Mote that my objective is to characterize the evolution of France by

The second example I propose presenting you is taken from the history of Spain. The Catholic Monarchs ushered in a period of unprecedented splendor. In three generations, the Castilian-Aragonese Monarchy incorporated into its states Granada, Portugal, Navarre, Roussillon, Artois, the Franche-Comté, the Low Countries, the Duchy of Milan, Naples, Sicily, Sardinia, and the Canary Islands. In the New World, from tropic to tropic, it took control of territories that measured fourteen million square kilometers, by means of military and maritime expeditions that eclipsed all others carried out to that time by men: Mexico, Central America, Venezuela, New Granada, Peru, Chile, Cuba, Santo Domingo, and Jamaica. In Africa, Ceuta, Melilla, Oran, Bougie, and Tunisia. In Asia, part of Malacca, the Philippine archipelago, and the Moluccas. One of the Kings of Spain wore the crown of the Germanic Empire; another married the Queen of England; Lepanto buried in its waters the formidable Turkish fleet; the French were defeated at several battles with the Spanish; Francis I was taken prisoner at Pavia; Paris, made Spanish, suffered a tight

---

means of *representative* examples. The chivalrous ideal emerged spontaneously at the heart of that society; today, poets that adopt it would be expressing a personal taste. There were incidents and coarseness equal to or greater than those of the foul Zola in the Middle Ages; but this does not prevent the naturalism, realism, and sensualism of art from expressing fittingly the current decadence of idealism and spiritualism: an important meaning that they lacked in the Middle Ages, being the mere manifestation of the scarce policing of customs and the eternal sinful tendencies of man, but not of the system and concept of life—Materialism, sometimes dressed as transcendental pantheism, sometimes as mechanical monism, is the spiritual father of socialism: the social question is a moral question, a political question, everything except a social question. The growing influence of money in democratic politics is an undeniable fact: whoever wishes to contemplate it at its apogee should study politics in the United States. Political choice in democracies is practiced in the sense of the elimination of true *abilities*. The credentials that accredit the new sovereign are base acts, the servility of characters. "Democracy is envy" (Proudhon), whatever the naïve and the optimists may want to say, they just do not realize. Logical democracy is collectivist; the democracy of the middle classes, a mere political label or scale in order to climb up to palaces, is a grotesque masquerade; when it is in good faith, it reveals incurable insipidness and inconceivable intellectual backwardness. The average kind of French parliamentarian is clearly inferior to the average kind of French citizen. None of the good or bad gentlemen elevated to the presidency of the French Republic were the most notable men in the Congress that elected them, nor even in the parties that voted for them, which *republican* theory demands. They were people of little prominence, with no initiative, prodigiously common, simple machines to sign laws and decrees. The latest poor man, Mr. Loubet, thinks he is giving a good example by not seeking reelection. In effect, he is renouncing a good salary, many comforts, and an infinity of satisfactions to vanity: this is a lot in a country in which he who can do nothing else writes on his card: John Doe, "member of the casino." My picture of the two Frances is on the dot!

siege; Great Britain trembled, threatened by the "the Invincible." The letters, sciences, and arts shone with names that no one could ignore, and that still pale by comparison to those that imply saintliness. The world is full of Spanish names and power, like a starry sky. At that time,

> Spain was the land of statesmen and of soldiers. The character which Virgil has ascribed to his countrymen might have been claimed by the grave and haughty chiefs, who surrounded the throne of Ferdinand the Catholic, and of his immediate successors. That majestic art, "regere imperio populos," was not better understood by the Romans in the proudest days of their republic, than by Gonsalvo and Ximenes, Cortes and Alva (Macaulay, review of *History of the War of the Succession in Spain*, historical study, by Lord Mahon).

A greatness, gentlemen, that lasted a little more than one century and that, in a little more than one century, collapsed. Philip II's eyes had barely closed when the decadence set in: palpable and obvious because the effective was beforehand; a decadence that, after being described in concise and striking phrases, a biblical expression came out of Lord Macaulay's mouth: "But how art thou fallen from heaven, O Lucifer son of the morning! How art thou cut down to the ground, that didst weaken the nations!" And with the aim of answering these questions, the celebrated English historian wrote the essay to which I refer for "Whoever wishes to be well acquainted with the morbid anatomy of governments, whoever wishes to know how great states may be made feeble and wretched."

Yet neither Lord Macaulay, perturbed by his triple passion of being a Protestant, a Whig, and an enemy of the House of Bourbon; nor Buckle, attentive to demonstrating the theses of his contemptible positivism; nor several others that followed and imitated them in the philosophical study of Spanish decadence, succeeded in discovering its causes. Because ascribing these to "the bad religion that Spaniards professed and they having stagnated in the ideas and sentiments of the fifteenth century," as does the former; or attributing them to the bond between the religious and the patriotic spirit, deriving therefrom "the blind spirit of respect, the shameful submission with regard to the Crown and the Church, the huge essential vice of the Spanish people that has been enough to ruin them completely," as does the latter, is worth as much as discovering the easiest and categorical refutation, since these causes preceded Spanish greatness. How, then, were they effective in destroying what they had not impeded being constructed? Other historians, specifically those in Spain, casting aside lofty philosophies, either fall into looking toward principles, or are content with enumerating subaltern causes: they insist on terrible administrative, economic, and political government, on the lack of men of state and eminent captains. Here is the crux of the matter: why were the governments terrible, the statesmen contemptible, the generals hopeless?

Note that the Spain of the sad Charles II era was identical to the Spain of the glorious Charles I. No substantial change in the political system and regime, no confrontation of religious beliefs, no replacement of one dynasty by another less imbued with national spirit had taken place: circumstances that, typically, are elevated to the category of causes when the history of Spain under the House of Bourbon is studied, especially in the modern period.

Yet the Spain of the two Charleses was only seemingly identical: the most active social combustion of the era of greatness had been reduced to a minimum number of eugenics, to the select elements. National decadence was an expression of ethnic decadence. Religious selection, military selection, had put up their natural obstacles to reproducing men of consistent energetic will; artistic and political selection, prepared for the coming of intellectual mediocrity through nervous *surmenage*. From the times of Charles II to the present, with the exception of some years of passing flourishing, the decadence continued its destructive work. I decline the nauseous task of describing it. A pair of features save many words: Spain is impotent when it comes to correcting the abuses that everyone denounces and castigates the powerful for. It has ministries, but it lacks government. It no longer produces sailors, or generals, or statesmen, or even bullfighters of any merit.

In vain the empiricists of law and those of the left extoll the specifics of their pharmacopeia. It is as impossible to restore the Spain of Philip II as it is to acclimate, without degenerating them, foreign institutions. We infect and corrupt everything. From American federalism we extract *cantonalism*; from the English parliamentary system, the brothel of the Spanish parliament. One does not heal the lungs of tuberculosis by changing the color and shape of one's clothes. The illness is diathetic, constitutional; one would have to regenerate blood, cure the nervous degeneration. I will characterize the situation with a familiar phrase: the pedigree dogs died, and the street dogs have invaded everything.

The Concepts of Race, People, and Nation Applied to the Basques

Forgive me, gentlemen, this most long digression. It flowed naturally from thesis that the large nationalities are made up of various ethnic groups whose social value cannot be identical. Let us resume once again discussion of this point.

The concepts of race, people, and nation, explained previously, are applicable perfectly to the Basques. There is a Basque race, individualized by its own, original, and persistent anthropological characteristics that distinguish it from others. This race, in eras remote from our own, combine with other gentilities, without losing because of that its ethnic supremacy, since is kind was maintained amid randomly gathered types that, in one way or another, served as a frame. It was maintained by virtue of its most compact mass, and by the laws of inheritance and atavism. This new compound elaborated a spiritual and cultural community, exteriorized energetically by the language, and arrived at the category of people that, through the indigenous name of the language, it termed itself *euskaldun*. The Basque people, through the vicissitudes of their history that we know directly, organized themselves into diverse nations, sovereign in themselves, politically and internationally objectified into just as many states. The Basque nations destroyed, the Basque people lasted without the adjectives French and Spanish, which, like dust and mud on clothes, have been collected along the way, altering the millenarian nature of the noun *euskaldun*.

The Basque Nations and the Spanish Monarchy

Yes; the fractions of the Basque people, historically organized in states, were truly nations. The land of Gipuzkoa, the Araba association of Arriaga, were incorporated into the Crown of Castile by means of solemn pacts; the Seigneury of Bizkaia, through inheritance and legitimate succession; Navarre, through the personal bond of a prince that wickedly and perfidiously usurped the crown from his relatives, the legitimate monarchs. Weighing up his services to the Catholic King, the Duke of Nájera, one of the principal actors in those events, wrote him: "I have thrown out of the Navarre the king that used to be from there." Of all the titles that the Spanish Monarchy can claim over the Basque states, the flimsiest is that belonging to Navarre, because at root it is corrupted by force, and law is eternal against this. The King of Castle, like the Seigneur of Bizkaia and like the King of Navarre, replaced the old lords and kings acquiring the attributes and prerogatives that they enjoyed, but nothing new, whether large or small. The four Basque nations retained their own internal sovereignty; they did not renounce their own constitution, nor the faculty to modify it according to how they saw fit, adjusting it to the changing times, nor did they subject themselves to other laws other than their own. There is more: it was not necessary for them to enter into forming part of another unitary state that did not exist, or for them to subject themselves to general legislation that was still to be established. This was reinforced by law. Thus the Catholic Monarchs classified Bizkaia as a "separate nation," and the fundamental laws of Navarre, sanctioned by the most powerful

Spanish monarchs, declared that those of that kingdom were so according to the "personal union." What Bizkaia and Navarre did lose, while their personal union with Castile lasted—which was not even tweaked by a common law of succession for the crown—what they did lose, by the nature of things, was external executive power, the quality of international juridical persons, transforming from active subjects in international law to being subjects of private international law. I am not saying the same thing for Araba and Gipuzkoa, because there is no documented evidence that they had possessed that quality. Whatever the case and within the frame of the restrictions indicated, the four Basque states remained, after their incorporation into Castile, independent nations like before.

The Spanish Monarchy was the group of kingdoms and states that obeyed the monarch of Castile. Common and technical language always distinguished the monarchy from the particular kingdoms. Monarchical power was the native body of the collective state, the Spanish compound state. The Basque nations formed part of the Spanish Monarchy, but they were not absorbed by any of the component kingdoms.

What I am telling you, gentlemen, is indisputable doctrine: history an legislation confirm it. But the modern tyrants, the political parties, those parties that, with their military uprisings, with their civil wars, with their riots and revolutions, with their slovenliness, administrative robberies, and the garrulous hot air of their great men, ruined Spain, leading it to the hospital of moribund nations; those parties, on hearing this doctrine, tear off their garments self-righteously in the name of the only idol they worship and revere sincerely, clearly because it reserves for them a field in which to lurk and provides them with a blank check in the name of the so-called *national unity*, are attempting to gag us and handcuff us. But we will not be quiet or stop shaking off the idol until we cast it over the other side of the Ebro, shouting that our grandparents did not know that so-called unity, nor do their grandchildren want to put up with it, and if they are so worried about its maintenance, let them show themselves to be men of heart, may they break free of the journalistic rabbit holes and go in good time to restore the rock of Gibraltar, the jungle of Cuba, and the boiling Bay of Cavite!

Historical Evidence of the Basque Nations

We are not speaking a new language or voicing criminal ideas, for all that those who confuse "national" unity with "political" unity may maliciously pretend otherwise and contend that when we propose stopping this or that at our historic borders we are entertaining the idea of destroying it. National unity, understood in the way that the old Spanish Monarchy understood it, ignites not hatred, but the loyalty of our hearts. We repeat now that or country always expressed before the throne of its kings and lords, respectfully and firmly, without attracting for that reason any threats or punishments. The examples are so abundant that we would need all night to enumerate them. I will copy some words that the provincial council of the Kingdom of Navarre aimed at her majesty the Queen Regent Doña Maria Cristina on June 16, 1834: "Navarre, Ma'am, has been and is an independent and separate kingdom since such remote epochs that they have been lost in the obscurity of the centuries. *This same independence was recognized at the Burgos Parliament of 1515, in which the happy incorporation into that of Castile was verified by means of a solemn obligatory pact between the royal power and the kingdom itself.*" Which is, more or less point by point, the same thing that the aforesaid provincial council had said on June 24, 1808, to Napoleon I, a somewhat more imposing character than the Count of Romanones, or even than the venerable Mr. Montero Ríos: "Navarre has been governed independently of the other kingdoms of Castile, even after its incorporation therein in the year 1513, having been done by means of principal union, Navarre maintaining its fueros and laws..." Words that are quite in harmony with that which, for its part, the Seigneury of Bizkaia put forward to the emperor of the French:

from the remotest antiquity, or rather from its primitive origins, Bizkaia has existed separate from the general government of Spain, with its own constitution and laws; and even later when, following inheritance, the Crown of Spain and Seigneury of Bizkaia came together, the same system was observed without any confusion, the Spanish monarch exercising his authority as king and seigneur independently.

Mr. Mella and Spanish Nationality

Mr. Mella asked in his beautiful parliamentary speech on the events in Barcelona whether Spain was a group of nations, and he answered negatively. If we look at historical formation, my thesis that Spain is a nation of nations seems to me irrefutable. At the very least, the Castilian nation, the Catalan-Aragonese nation, and the group of the four small Basque nations must stand out in that compound. The celebrated orator distinguished between national, political, and constitutional unity. His concept of nation matches that of many German treatise writers: a spiritual unity. He spoke to us of a community of beliefs and sentiments, of common traditions and customs and hopes; assuming that these are sufficient and in fact existed some time ago, he argued that Spain in the fourteenth century was a nation divided into different states. A most evident exaggeration that authorizes us to declare that Europe of the Crusades was also a nation. In modern times, the conservative politician Mr. Antonio Benavides said in the Senate: "We do not have a unity of race, or of territory, or of language, or of legislation." These words, as true today as they were in the year 1876 in which they were pronounced, demonstrate how little intimate is that national unity that Mr. Mella presumed was established in the fourteenth century: a unity that thereafter he equated with homeland, classifying it as "common." By virtue of national unity and common homeland, any political movement that proposes restoring the institutions of the historic nationalities in Spain would lack, perhaps against the intimate feeling of Mr. Mella, substance and nerve, being reduced to a mere modification of the unitary state, a mere modification of the governing internal political system, and the mere devolution of certain usurped functions, a tendency that some term autonomism and others regionalism; to the implantation, in sum, of a new general theory of government, applicable more or less symmetrically, but without producing a radical transformation, to the modern form of national unity, declared intangible by the unitarians. A form irreconcilable with Basque nationalism, but marvelously reconcilable with the Carlist principle: political centralization; administrative decentralization.

One can debate all one may want about national unity and common homeland. We are interested in demonstrating that the Basque states formed part of the Spanish Monarchy by means of pacts of incorporation; that the unitary Spanish state has destroyed them, and that we shelter in our chests the unflinching desire to restore them. The political denomination of these aspirations is Basque nationalism.

Nationalism and Foralism

A new expression, an old plan. In my youth, the term "nationalism" had not crossed the Pyrenees with the meaning it has today, and it was used less scientifically as a synonym for unitary ideas, looking toward the pretensions of the "Spanish nation" over us, the aspiration to reintegrate the Basque Country in its secular rights received the name of foralism. A word that had been passed from its traditional technical meaning onto our lips, with the same sense that had sounded in the mouths of the most upstanding lawyers of the councils and lords of the three states of the Kingdom of Navarre. We called ourselves foralists with pride in days of greater risks than the present. Given that there circulated a more graphic term, more intense and totally expressive, and did not allow for any shelter for the *Euskaros*, who sought things halfway, or sophisticated, which is worse, without repudiating even an ounce of my antecedents, or professing new dogmas, or adopting new attitudes, rather, continuing my modest history, I renounce the old description, and from today I call and will call myself a *nationalist*.

Nationalism and Related Tendencies

I do not belong, gentlemen, to the number of those that adjust their political conduct to that maxim that is like a symptom of the spirits that are idealists, not because they pursue and ideal goal (which those of this kind love all the noble spirits), but because they do not take charge of reality, and therefore rather than idealists, they are visionaries.

The maxim to which I allude is: those closest to us are those farthest away from us, and therefore they are those whom we must combat with the greatest might. This maxim is absurd. Save for the doctrinal integrity of nationalism, so that there is no place therein for deleterious principles that may weaken or distract it from its single objective, nationalism must possess a mobile scale of sympathies in order to apply it to the political forces that contact it, according to the degree of political and social *Euskarismo* they may contain. It is my theory of an accompanied stroll. If I suggest going to Andoain, and another person suggests going no further than Hernani, why should we not walk together? Would it be rational of me to strike them with my cane because their trip is shorter than mine? Now, if I may suspect rationally that the companion may cherish some plan to impede me from reaching Andoain or make me lose my way en route, I would have to refuse their company; and if this were not now possible, to spy on all their movements, and at the first signs of suspicion, break their ribs.

The Basis and Character of Nationalism

The bases of nationalism have to be legal and historical. It is not based on any general political theory. Its works of reference are not books by treatise writers and philosophers. In fact, it ignores them, and makes use only of the legal bodies, accredited traditions, and history of the country. Between nationalist and revolutionary aspirations, of any sort and color, there is an abyss. We propose reestablishing a legality, ours, without any other boundaries than those imposed by the possible. We do not disregard other institutions, except those which time has destroyed irredeemably: for example, the three wings of the Parliament of Navarre, which would today have to be replaced in another form, taking into account that that parliament was an expression of the then existent social classes and not an expression of modern-style inorganic suffrage. So long as institutions are restored wholly or partially, in their pristine form or likewise, they belong to the flag of nationalism.

The Monarchy and the Seigneury in Nationalism

For this, it is not worth noting the criticism that Mr. Mella aimed sharply at the famous bases of Manresa: "in those bases," he said, "a part of the Catalan constitution, of the Catalan tradition, was suppressed, because the Count of Barcelona, who formed part of it, was disregarded:" an error that, in turn, many nationalists stressed. We must not disregard the Seigneur of Bizkaia, the King of Navarre, Araba, and Gipuzkoa. The monarchy, gentlemen, is the only genuinely historical institution in the current Spanish Constitution: while it survives we should claim it as our own, since it has cohabited and coexisted with our institutions, and several of these are connected to it. Thanks to the Seigneur of Bizkaia and the King of Navarre, the independence of both nations is clear and undeniable; because they lacked their own kings and lords, that of Araba and Gipuzkoa shines less. I will add another important thing: that our claims must be made directly to the throne, above the political parties that occupy the ministries and the parliament, as Navarre did on solemn occasions in the modern era, and the Catalans themselves, turning to Alfonso XII and the Queen Regent. The king is, or should be, above the political parties.

If the monarchy were to disregard systematically the demands of nationalism, when the latter becomes the living incarnation of the opinion of the country, we would not give in because of that, and we would work within the fiction that the monarchy had been kidnapped by the parties on duty; just as our forebears, without disobeying the king or denying him his prerogatives, imagined that favorites captured the attention of kings. And I say that we would not give in or calm down, because on opening up the venerable Fuero of Navarre, the first words that we read therein are those that tell us "how the mountain people won over the lands of no kings."

The Legitimate Dynasty of Navarre

In certain nationalist writings—some of them famous—the contribution has been made that the legitimate dynasty of Navarre has disappeared; from which the consequence flows that royalty in my homeland cannot hold titles other than those of the conquest. Mistake: the last effective monarchs of Navarre beyond the Pyrenees, Catherine and John d'Albret, had a son, Henry II, who ruled Navarre beyond the Pyrenees, where the talons of the Catholic King did not find any prey. Henry II's daughter was Jeanne III, the wife of Antoine de Bourbon, Duke of Vendôme, and they were the parents of Henry of Bearn, IV of France and III of Navarre, from whom all the Bourbons that have reigned in France and Spain descended. Subject to strict law, the Bourbons of France have been the legitimate monarchs of Navarre, and the return of that crown to them was the object of many diplomatic negotiations, the reason for many wars, and the source, perhaps the most copious, of the enmity the Bourbons declared against the House of Austria, until they managed to break its power considerably and replace it in the Spanish Monarchy. The last beneficiary of the French house in the Kingdom of Navarre was the illustrious Count of Chambord. Once the primogenitary Bourbon branch had died out, the rights of the Angevin line increased, which began with Louis, the grandfather of Louis XV of France and father of Phillipe V, Duke of Anjou and King of Spain, from whom the rivals for the throne, Don Carlos of Bourbon and Alfonso XIII, both descend. Yet as the edict agreed in 1713, which established the new form of succession to the crown of Spain, goes against the laws in the General Fuero that regulated transmission of the crown of Navarre and the constant practice of the kingdom, and it has never been accepted as law in Navarre or inserted in the subsequent legal bodies, nor could it be without perpetrating a major anti-foral measure, the fact is that the pretentions of Don Carlos of Bourbon to the throne are null and void. As you see, gentlemen, it is not a legitimate king that is lacking: something else is missing, a legitimate kingdom!

Destruction of the Basque Nations

In a short time the independence of the Basque nations, which had withstood so many attacks and so many enemies, was destroyed. A catastrophe that it would be unfair to put down exclusively to externally enforced violence, overlooking their own faults, which were many. Faults combined with circumstances, with the "historical moment," and all that has produced the deplorable present situation: that the Basque nations are provinces in which the unitary Spanish state governs to its liking.

Causes of the Fall of the Basque Nations: The Absolutism of the Monarchy

I will point out quickly the main causes of this fall; feeling that I should limit myself to tracing out a line, when I have data to paint a picture.

First, the absolutist tendencies of the Spanish Monarchy, which increased insofar as it decadence was accentuated. The Count-Duke of Olivares offered three ways to King Philip IV in which to secure and stipulate the laws of the diverse kingdoms "in conformity with those of Castile:" violence, guile, and subornation. Advice that was repeated from that day on in the chambers of the royal palace, and that fell more pleasingly on Bourbon than Austrian ears, the former having been educated by that great despot who went by the name of Louis XIV. The founder of the Spanish dynasty, Philip V, wrote the dynastic program in his decree of July 29, 1707: "my royal intention is that every continent of Spain be governed by the same laws." His descendants have fulfilled this. The more the degradation of the system, so Godoy and Zamora plotted the destruction of the foral institutions in the shadows: "If this peace [that of Basel]," said Zamora to Godoy,

> is followed by the union of the [Basque] provinces to the rest of the nation, without the foral hindrances that separate it and make it an almost dead member of the kingdom, your excellency will have carried out one of those great tasks that we have not seen since that of Cardinal Cisneros for the great Philip V. These eras are those that should be made the most of in order to augment the foundations and the strength of the monarchy.

Court opinion at the time made the Basque provinces, following the military disasters in the Pyrenees, fulfil the same role that contemporary liberal opinion assigns to Fr. Nozaleda, after the disaster in the Philippines. The final blow was not struck; but the terrain was prepared with the publication of the Royal Academy's *Diccionario geográfico-histórico* [Geographical-historical dictionary]; of Llorente's *Noticias históricas de las Provincias Vascongadas* [Historical notes on the Basque provinces]; the *Documentos oficiales* [Official documents] relating to the Basque provinces, by González; the creation of the Reform Council on the Abuses of the Royal Treasury; and, especially, with the series of anti-foral measures in later years by Charles IV and Ferdinand VII: a series that began with the royal order of September 1, 1796, reproduced on May 14, 1829, abolishing the foral veto or right to review royal legislation, a firm bastion of the Navarrese Constitution. That is how the provincial council of the kingdom, in 1830, argued that, de facto, the fueros had been abolished, and it denounced the memorable document respectfully before the king.

The intrinsic tendencies of this later period of absolutism were abolitionist. Yet the struggle against liberal constitutionalism caused Ferdinand VII to come to an accommodation with this country, in which liberalism was justly despised.

This explains the ups and downs in our privative system; the inconsistency of the king, who abolished the foral veto and convened the parliaments of 1817 and 1818, of 1828 and 1829, authorized numerous tyrannical solutions, and declared in the royal order of February 15, 1824, "that, by means of the appropriate way, it is communicated to the aforementioned Kingdom of Navarre that, in possession of my sovereign authority, I will concede it, from and including this year, annual parliaments ... all with the aim of restoring the full practices of the fuero, etc.;" and on August 9, 1830, that "Navarre has its parliament, fueros, and privileges, which his majesty wishes to be respected." And however great the moral degradation of that monarch, a Neronian soul in the earth of Vitellius, discussions about him made some impression of the sort that can be observed in those of the province of Gipuzkoa on February 6, 1824: "His majesty has been disposed twice, with unspeakable scandal, of his inalienable rights of sovereignty ... and the province has been disposed of its idolized fueros the same amount of times."

Liberal Absolutism

Liberal absolutism, exotic and heterodox, outdid in intensity the destructive work of monarchical absolutism, from which it received its countersign: "Moreover," confessed Mr. Canovás del Castillo,

> for all that neither me nor anyone that my belong to the liberal school are proud of it, one cannot nor should one deny that fact that Godoy, his agents, and publicists were the true fathers of official liberalism in Spain. The Spanish Liberal Party continued, as in the whole Basque question, the traditions of Godoy, of Llorente, and of González Arnao.

The Cadiz liberals, without it causing them any shame or embarrassment having confessed that, the venerable fueros were a terrible protest and claim against the government, and an irresistible counter claim to the rest of Spain for its dishonest suffering, abolished them in its reworded constitution. And they abolished them again in 1820, in 1834, in 1837, and in 1841. They mutilated them in Navarre with the law of August 16, 1841, and in the Basque provinces, with the decrees of July 4, 1844, and February 22, 1847, and they erased their last vestiges with the law of July 21, 1876. Despicable work that makes them deserving of eternal execration!

The Spanish Envy

The third cause that led to the ruin of our national institutions was, to be sure, pointed out by Mr. de Marcillac in the year 1807, in narrating the events of the "Zamacolada." "Do you ignore," he asked the people of Bilbao, "the fact that the provinces in the kingdom to which you belong envy your privileges and that your very compatriots are your enemies?" An accusation that, without any rhetorical veil, Yandiola, a representative of Bizkaia in the Baiona Parliament, planted in his correspondence with the seigneury: "Yet, in honor of the truth, I must say that the Spanish are our greatest and perhaps only enemies." And it is as enemies, gentlemen, that they have behaved; without it being necessary to adduce proof in recent times, because it appears to me that you will have not been able to forget any of this.

The Error of the Basque-Navarrese

Yet the most profound, effective, and transcendental of all the causes is to be found in the modification of the Basque-Navarrese spirit, which began to ferment with the yeast of general ideas and spilled out of the vessel that had contained it for centuries. Encyclopedist ideas corrupted the mentality of the upper classes, predisposing them to acknowledging and accepting all kinds of new ideas, without the main body of society being contaminated. Then came the War of Independence, a popular and spontaneous movement that broke the legal framework with which the Italian genius Bonaparte had disguised his usurpation, impeding the initial explosions of resistance. This was the protest of ideas and sentiments of "friarly democracy" in Spain, against the revolutionary sentiments and ideas that the invaders personified, giving rise to the paradoxical spectacle that the "internal French," that is, the Cadiz constitutionalists, personified for their part the struggle against the "external French." The War of Independence was a giant bonfire in whose flames many particularist sentiments and ideas were founded and evaporated. This converted Basques and Navarrese into "militant" Spaniards, throwing them into the currents of Spanish political life.

Our national constitution demolished, de facto; the locals of this country mixed with those of elsewhere and obeyed the orders of foreign authorities: their own borders, which Navarre and Bizkaia had protected so carefully during the war against the Republic, refusing to go beyond them in the radius of their military action, were broken. The supporters of modern-style national unity owe Napoleon a statue; no one has worked more successfully than the emperor for its cause.

The French expelled, the mood of the Basques and Navarrese soon had occasion to be revealed. The struggle between liberals and royalists having begun, Basques joined one or the other side, subordinating the fortunes of the country to that of those parties, the maintainers of an implacable dispute, sometimes vile, sometimes barbarous. The Spanish parties in our land date from that time, the instigators of our ruin and agents of our moral disintegration, who would end up killing us if we did not kill them first. They were the liberal disciples of French philosophy and sectarians of the French Revolution; through both concepts, staunch enemies of historical tradition and of religious tradition, incapable of respecting diversity or practicing liberty if it did not serve as a catapult in order to attack the Church. The Liberals, during their initial fervor, absolutely hated our constitutions; later, by the natural dwindling of the virus through the passage of time and the demands of reality, they were inclined to a moderate foralism, an adulteration of liberal unitary values and Basque nationalism. Yet there was never a lack among them of those who maintained the brutality of the primitive denials.

The Traditionalist and Liberal Parties in the Basque-Navarrese Country

Such, gentlemen, are the psychological forces, that, unequally rationed out, they have taken possession of the Basque spirit and elaborated our contemporary history, a history that has produced our national decadence. The war with the French Republic already posited the old and new spirit face to face: it was like the prologue to the subsequent hideous tragedy. On the one hand, the general provincial council of Gipuzkoa that came to an agreement and understanding with the conventional side; on the other, the exceptional council of Arrasate-Mondragón, and especially the priest of Beizama, who, at the head of five hundred volunteers, his parishioners, took part in the Sasiola skirmish, waving the banner of the Virgin of Rosario and responding to the verses of the "Marseillaise" with biblical verses from the litany. Pay close attention, gentlemen, to the figure of Mr. Antonio de Anchutegui, the true representative figure.

Within him there are, like the acorn in the holly oak, the brigands of faith, the battalions of Zumalakarregi, the modern Carlists and ultraconservatives: people who pursued foral restoration, but within the Spanish general political formula, completely ineffective until now.

The opposing tendencies have been sketched out but have not acquired a definitive irreducible form. There was a period of vacillation, of doubts. The Basque-Navarrese provincial councils committed the error of sending representatives to the General Council of Baiona, where they had to address, according to the terms of the convocation, "the happiness of the whole of Spain;"

a task in which it was not feasible to intervene, under penalty of renouncing implicitly their own legislative power. The provincial councils accepted without any effective protest, years later, the Cadiz Constitution and constituted themselves peacefully. The Council of Bizkaia, presided over by General Mazaredo, ignored candidly "whether, having received said Spanish Constitution, it was necessary to renounce completely the Bizkaian one, or whether the advantages of both, in whole or in part, were reconcilable." Yet the country, indifferent to the new regime, and Ferdinand VII barely having returned from captivity, demanded and achieved the reinstatement of the old state of things. In the statement that, in the name of Navarre, the Elío brothers handed in, acceptance of the 1812 code was described as "a farce made between tumult and force."

The second constitutional era reproduced the conflict, aggravating t with the struggle of parties, which emerged defined and organized, and it provoked the uprising of the Basque-Navarrese royalists. This uprising was so Spanish that the Navarrese division abandoned its homeland on the insatiable rancor of the liberals, going to Catalonia to fight under the orders of the Regency of Urgel: a fact that would have appeared monstrous to the Navarrese that fought against the Republic in 1793, who always refused to leave their native land. And shortly thereafter, that division advanced into Spain, serving the vanguard of the Hundred Thousand Sons of Saint Louis.

Pro-Spanish, likewise, to its core was the uprising in favor of the prince Don Carlos María Isidro, as the Provincial Council of Navarre made it known in its motion of April 25, 1834, to the president of the council of ministers, speaking to him about "those unfortunate subjects that moan, even despite themselves, under the scourge of not a Navarrese but a Spanish uprising." A pro-Spanish stance that was not welcomed and helped the winner take as a consequence that contradiction, which was moreover an infamous folly, of seeking to intervene directly in the internal arrangement of things in Spain while keeping us separate from the laws of Spain. A pro-Spanish stance that not without apparent logic was able to disfigure furious passion, when the government, in the year 1875, rebuking this country, said: "People that dispute even the sovereignty of the nation and the legitimate king, are attempting, in the height of insolence, to impose on the nation a monarch, as if he were a gift, a service, the only tribute they were obliged to lend their brothers..." These are words that should be part of the record of the services to the country that Carlism has carried out, and that, whatever the case, confirm how the people of Yanguas always beat Don Quixote, whether he was from La Mancha or the Basque provinces.

The Basque-Navarrese Liberals

The Basque-Navarrese Liberals did not just take part in the pro-Spanish politics of the royalists, but they followed the directions of the most radical anti-foral and unitary ideas. They consented to and applauded several laws drawn up by their coreligionists against the system of the Basque states, and externalized the patricidal spirit that encouraged them with their own personal acts. I will cite just two events. Here, in the public square of Donostia-San Sebastián, they attempted to burn the sacrosanct book of the fueros. There, in Navarre, on one particular day when the rumor spread that the government was trying to end the civil war by means of a transaction, founded on maintaining the foral system, the provincial council turned to the Spanish Parliament, on March 5, 1838, asking it to abolish the Navarrese Constitution, which it painted so negatively that it was slanderous. Basque-Navarrese liberalism was a traitor to its homeland.

From this anathema, which the impartial study of events reveals, there is no cleansing despite the good faith with which many liberals would adopt the sophism whose origins are to be found in the fact of the constitutionalists of Cadiz having praised the foral system and some of its institutions (for example, the permanent provincial council of the parliament that existed in Navarre) at the same time as they abolished them. The General Council of Bizkaia patronized his sophism plainly in accepting the 1812 Constitution: "after considered examination," it said, "in which it revealed by demonstration the marvelous uniformity that existed by the essentially constitutional principles of the political constitution of the Spanish Monarchy and those of the constitution that, from remotest times, has governed and governs in this province, etc." However complete the parity pointed out, greater still were the reasons for maintaining the special constitution that, in unexpected ways, came to coincide with the general one, affirming their mutual compatibility. Yet the Basque-Navarrese liberals, who were happy to see the principles of their special constitutions incorporated into the Spanish Constitution, had lost the feeling of Bizkaian, Araban, Navarrese, and Gipuzkoan nationality; and on account of having lost it, or through sacrificing it to the modern Spanish national unity, deserve precisely the title of traitors. But not everything was a hallucination in the reasoning of the liberals. For all that they shouted about the parity of principles, they knew very well that in the Catholic foral constitutions, preserved and applied by the dominant Catholic opinion in the country, there was no room for the liberal spirit, and this is what at all costs they sought to enthrone. Once this was achieved, the total eradication of the fueros was of less importance to those that were not fanatic revolutionaries; and even for the aspect of economic advantages and administrative freedom, they were sympathetic to their partial maintenance.

Foralist Liberalism

Here you feel, gentlemen, the origin of the dissidence that was developed within Basque-Navarrese liberalism, and that to some extent matches the "moderate" and "frenzied" split that came along then to Spanish liberalism. The constitutional foralist tendency assumed timidly the leadership, in a report emitted on March 25, 1820, of the commission appointed to rule on the analogy between the Bizkaian and the Spanish Constitution: "Nevertheless," it states, perfect accordance is not observed, without that of the monarchy having adopted the wise Bizkaian institutions that organized the provincial internal system and that have been viewed justly as a bastion of the liberty and happiness of their natives . . . In this way [with the consent of the council and the approval of the seigneur] some of the general measures dictated for the other provinces of the kingdom could be adopted, adjusting them to the particular circumstances of this uneven and thankless country . . . In order to obtain, then, explanations and adjustments that may be compatible with the general happiness in the monarchy and of that in the seigneury, the general provincial council may be charged with explaining to the government whatever may be conducive to preparing the transactions and measures that may be necessary, without the foral system being updated in the interim.

The Jacobins of Navarre, who, through their hatred of the Church, rejected the constitution of their homeland in the statement to the Spanish Parliament, it has not often been recalled, had laudatory words for the Basque institutions, declaring that their possessors "can preserve a useful system reconcilable with all the known systems."

The seed of reconciling the general interests of the nation and the particular ones of the so-called provinces would bear fruit. It was an idea predestined to walk a long way. The form could be debated, some believing the consent of the country necessary, others declaring the will of the Spanish parliament enough; but most of the liberals coincided on the fact that the full maintenance of our constitutions was impossible or inconvenient, and that such maintenance had to be attributed to institutions of an administrative kind and economic advantages or benefits, except the obstinate progressives, of which those of Donostia-San Sebastián, who lit up their homes to celebrate the traitorous Espartero for his tyrannical decree of October 29, 1841, a violation of the Bergara Agreement and the law of October 25, 1839, and who ordered representatives of the city on the general council to not add their votes to the protests raised as a result of anti-foral measures of the government, but instead to accept what the government had decided.

The Law of October 25, 1839, and its Consequences

With maintenance of the fueros having been used as bait to achieve the pacification of the country, and the Bergara Agreement having been reached, the time came to give legislative shape to the promise. The government was inclined toward confirming them without any reservation: the progressive party and quite a few Basque-Navarrese liberals disagreed with this. The Gipuzkoan Claudio Antón de Luzuriaga, the embodiment of the spirit of Donostia-San Sebastián at the time, asked the Spanish Parliament to not confirm them flatly and fully. Finally, with the introduction into the confirmatory article of the perfidious postscript, "without detriment to constitutional unity," which, in the end, as the Count of Ezpeleta feared, was "a deception, a ruse, to say that something had been yielded that had not." The Navarrese liberals used the circumstances to carry out their attack on the constitution of the kingdom, and came to an agreement with the government, without any power or mandate, over the famous law of August 16, 1841.

It is not something, gentlemen, that I would repeat now, that which in the years 1887 and 1888 I wrote in my articles in *La España Regional* about foralism, regionalism, and federalism; nor what I said in my parliamentary speech of July 28, 1893, defending Navarre against Mr. Gamazo, on the original invalidity of the law of 1841 and the tremendous sacrifices we were putting up with at the time. More still, being null and burdensome over any growth, and worthy of us classifying it as a crime of high treason and loathing it and cursing it with all our soul, and classifying it as a calamity, the greatest to ever befall Navarre in the course of its long history, a thousand times worse than suffering the invasions of Romans, Goths, Carolingians, Arabs, French, and Castilians, because we expelled them and preserved our independence, while that ill-fated law has snatched us away; despite everything I am saying, that law had one good part: it retained the pact principle, an expression of which was the principal union idea of 1513. For that reason, we patriots cannot find in the Navarrese institutions it preserved, or in those it sacrificed for the future, or in those it introduced by way of compensations for consideration, any satisfaction that calms us, or iron shield that defends us, or any weapon that may sparkle in our hands; but the pact principle provides us with shield and weapon, although imperfectly except at the time, by virtue of which we are not a dead body in the Spanish Monarchy, laid out on the dissection table of the unitary idea. For that reason, because it represents a pact, we have defended the law, not just those who declare themselves satisfied with it, but also those of us who cast our sight out to wider and more glorious horizons, knowing that the anti-foral and de-foralizing measures of the government will always include the an open petition to introduce, whenever appropriate, a counterclaim of our full rights. That law is a wrong, but it is a minor wrong, less than absolute leveling out. Within its shadow we could regroup our forces, preserve the salient features of our personality, exercise some fraction of our sovereignty, withdraw to some extent from the corrupt and inept despotism of the state, if the inexcusable weaknesses of the foral judiciary and the perversion of the Navarrese public spirit, consecrated stupidly in the evil hailstorm of the new parties, do not transform it into a slope down which our honor and our rights slip… Ah, Navarre, my homeland, idolized mother of my soul! Leave the slaves' prison of political parties! Rip up the deceitful slogans of their foreign banners and wrap yourself in the red flag of Navarrese nationalism! Only that way will you be great once again and will you fulfill the promises that you made to your own history from the heroic crags of Orreaga-Roncesvalles!

Out of the law of 1839 and out of the royal decree of July 4, 1844, which in part repealed Espartero's irascible decree, was born an anomalous legal state for the Basque provinces, without any firm base, which Mr. Canovás del Castillo termed the "state of things" when he used the catastrophe of the second civil war to apply rigorously the, in his view unfulfilled, law of 1839: a state that I described years ago in the newspaper *Lau-Buru*, noting that it only left standing, "the exemption from the draft and general taxes, that is, speaking non-hypocritically, instead of a set of rights, a couple of revocable privileges *ad nutum*." That state of things deserves the same judgement as that of Navarre; that of the least wrong, that the Basques were perfectly right to defend, ensuring to derive from it the previous, truly legal, state. And if there were anyone today in the country capable of reviving it, far from insulting him with the name of nationalism, I would applaud him in a big way and would believe that full foral reintegration was close. From that "something," perseverance, good judgement, the gift of opportunity, and other guarantees, one could draw "everything." The issue is to save the principles and not stop until assuring the triumph.

Nationalism and Separatism

The fifth essence of nationalism consists, in my opinion, of reinstating our country with its legislative power, which would involve caring for adapting our historical constitution to current needs, and introducing into the pacts of incorporation and sovereignty clauses that both parts may agree on. I would not be one of those to advise then a politics of the closed hand, of egoism, and intransigence; rather, I would hope that the size of the concessions matched the Basque heart, which is very big. This nationalist demand was defamed by stubborn and insidious spirits with the term separatism: other much more modest enterprises received it. On this point I would like to say something, gentlemen, with the frankness of my character; I do not like mistakes or opacities. Insincerity disgusts me, and I want to say so in order to bring an end to this talk that, I suspect, you will fear never-ending. Having considered the situation in the serene light of principles, set out before the court in which pure truth informs and absolute justice rules, the sentence of separation "by cruelty," would have been passed years ago. We had a pact; we have fulfilled it loyally, often surpassing it in its fulfillment; we have been loyal and honorable. The powers that destroyed our constitutions never dared to deny this most patent fact. They out forward against us doctrines of public law: national unity, constitutional unity; theories about political progress: the integration of modern nationalities, the concentration of unitary power against feudal and federative disintegrations, etc. etc., doctrines and theories that we have the right to not share and reject; and in the final case, they put forward the reason of force, which excused all the rest. On bidding farewell to the army that had triumphed over the Carlists, King Alfonso XII said to his soldiers: "the constitutional unity of Spain founded by your heroism, the fruit and blessings of your victories will be felt by even the most distant of generations." The punishment or warning of God: before those distant generations should find out, the perfection of "constitutional unity" in Spain followed the destruction of national unity in Cuba and the Philippines. The victory over a pernicious party, elevated to victory over the country: this is the only and true title. The current state, a logical derivation of the previous state, opened up by the law of 1839, is not a legal state, it is a state of force. Juridically speaking, we are separate.

I ask now, gentlemen: what should the tendency of nationalism be? With what aim should nationalism direct its propaganda? To ensuring that that juridical separation descends from the abstract sphere of principles to the concrete world of deeds, taking shape in reality, and leading to a secessionist movement such as in Spanish America or that of Cuba? Or on the contrary, should efforts be aimed at reestablishing the broken unity, to covering the cracks through which anti-Spanish separatism may seep, and to renovating what were in their day the old and venerable pacts with the Spanish Monarchy? I do not know whether secessionist nationalism exists; but I declare with the greatest possible solemnity that mine is unionist. I take things as they are presented to me from the hands of several centuries of history: the Spanish Monarchy, and within it, attached to it, but with their own life guaranteed by solemn pacts, the Basque nations, the Basque states. I do not want to loosen any of the ends of this golden chain. Those that infringe our rights, those that destroy our institutions, those that proclaim the compatibility between these and national unity, are the separatists. To affirm national unity and deny our constitutions is to proceed iniquitously. I protest against that and put forward, contrary to the uniform ideal of contemporary political scoundrels, the authentic tradition of our public law, respected by monarchs so jealous of its authority and so capable of glorious enterprises as Charles I and Philip II.

Difficulties of the Nationalist Enterprise: Motives for Hope

What a great, lofty, and most noble aspiration is that of nationalism, gentlemen! And in the same way, arduous and difficult. A summit that one does not reach with the wings of lyrical enthusiasm and the puerile intransigence of an imagination ignorant of life, but by practicing the most virile, austere, and judicious virtues: that of prudence, that of fortitude, and that of perseverance. It is necessary to lift the heart beyond all reverses and place intelligence at the level of all difficulties. The means that serve to gather proselytes are not those that supply the triumph. At a certain point in time the "school" must transform into a political party, that is, into a coherent group of people and doctrines in which an ideal aim may shine, served by practical means. That moment has not yet arrived for nationalism. The first thing is to uproot the Basque people from Egyptian servitude and the worship of false gods. False prudence, pusillanimity of will, and the egotistical contentment for the present material wellbeing will shout to us of stubbornness: you are chasing a chimera; you are knights drifting into the impossible; the Basque nations, the Basque states died. Are you trying to resurrect the miracle of Lazarus?

Such dismissals, *a priori*, do not impress me. The day that the Basque people consecrate nationalism with the ardor and resolve that it squandered in the service of exotic ideas and parties, the moment will have arrived to take the pulse of that premature impossibility... I would be filled with greater discouragement by reasons that would demonstrate the decadence of the race, the depletion of its eugenic sources, the apathy of its will! Nor do I fear them, gentlemen. A people that in its political life demonstrates such an extraordinary phenomenon as the Carlist Party, which covered its native mountains with battalions and for seventy years resisted the depression of defeats, the flattery of corruption, the hostility of power, the diverting of the Church; a people that knows how to sacrifice the blood in its veins and the gold in its arches of triumph of an idea, and to repeat in these positivist times the messianism of the Hebrew prophets, that people is not degenerate or moribund: the thing is to change the ideals. This, although difficult, is not impossible. We should know how to, gentlemen, under the sweet imprint of hope, repeating the poet's verses:

Ezagutzen dot denporak chandan
Char eta onak dirala,
Gure munduak burpillak legez
Jira egiten dabela;
Gabak urrengo dakar eguna,
Neguak uda barria,
Oriek atzetik uda loratsu
Eder ta zoragarriya...

I know that times change
for good and for bad,
our world turns around
like a wheel;
night leads to day,
winter to spring,
behind that the beautiful and amazing
florid summer...

I have spoken.

Chapter 14

The Tree of Gernika
Speech at the Solemn Evening Event held in
Donostia-San Sebastián on July 11, 1906

On the Occasion of the Basque Festival and
Organized by the Council of the Floral Games

My honorable gentleman, ladies, and gentlemen:

I would have liked courtesy and gratitude not to forbid me to decline the invitation of the illustrious Council of the Floral Games. This is the fourth ties my words have been spoken in the meeting room in which those who cultivate Basque letters gather, and while I do not doubt the benevolence of the audience, which has always been prodigious and liberal with me, I doubt my own performance to deserve it truly, as it is not on the terrain of intentions, which has never thought of itself as a territory subject to the jurisdiction of art, in contrary to what happens in morals: here intentions, being pure, save, and there they highlight the disparity and dissonance between the aspiration and the work of the author, provoking and justifying his failure.

The council has always given me ample freedom in choosing a topic. Making use of that, I was able in Azpeitia to respond to several erroneous assertions, and still less patriotic than truthful, in a certain raucous speech by Miguel de Unamuno, with whom I continue to shake hands after refuting him, a case in truth not very typical during these times of brutal controversies; and in Oñati I was able to proclaim quite early, and not without vehemence, the necessity of including in the order of the day of intense questions in the derisory Spanish politics, including Basque politics, *velis nolis*, the Basque question, the supreme question of our national reintegration, managing to break into pieces the funerary stone laid down by centralism, today corralled in its supreme ignominies, on our immemorial liberties, a glorious Passover whose brightness will dry the tears in which pain and rage blurred our eyes; and I was also able, in Irun, transformed by the exoticism of people and ideas, by the border of Gipuzkoa into the border of Spain, I was also able in Irun to resume my "hand to hand combat" with the enemies of the Basque language, shielded by the demands of their "culture," generally so distant and external that, on hearing them extoll their excellence, the image comes to my mind of a bear dressed up as a lady.

Yet with all this freedom of matters and subjects that the council offers me, I understand, ladies and gentlemen, that I have traversed most of the circle of ideas and sentiments that I have been capable of sketching out for these solemn ceremonies; I understand that mothers are withering and that the arid rock does not even secrete the faint stream of yesteryear; I understand that the melancholy and fatal hour of self-repetition is ringing almost in my ears; that the persistent work of winter is turning into the cerebral fatigue of summer, and that he who worked like an ant cannot sing among the cicadas.

Such cerebral fatigue and depression advised me to decline the council's invite, not to interrupt the intellectual repose that is prescribed to me temporarily. But I confess that one of the acts in the current Basque Festival dominated my understanding, enthused my heart; it made me think, it made me feel; it unfolded before my eyes a magical world of memories and, in a concerted harmony of movements, another magical world of hopes. I heard the distant murmur of sources of inspiration... Will their torrents penetrate my dry jaws? God knows; not I, on starting to fulfill my difficult mission with the burdensome idea. If they do penetrate, be thankful to God, ladies and gentlemen; and if not, forgive me in the grace of the love that made me reckless.

The act to which I am alluding is the planting of a sapling of the tree of Gernika, associated with the school holiday of Gipuzkoan children. That tree is our whole past; those children are our whole future. The future destinies of the Basque Country depend on the tree growing, on it extending its branches like a canopy decreeing honor and liberty; on the children, captivated by the voices that reverberate among its leaves, should never wish to leave the holy circle of its shade. The tree of Gernika, in reality more than the most famous one of Dodona, as the English poet Wordsworth observed, speaks. On raising it to a symbol of history, the ages filled it with the gift of language. In its branches nest the migrating birds of tradition; from its branches hang the harps of poets that eulogized it. Beneath its sonorous tip, children that venerate the tree will hear as a reward not murmurs but words.

The tree guards a secret tenaciously: that of its origin. It refuses to let science date it or point out where it comes from. It observes the identical discretion as the race that is personifies politically. It does not constitute a Basque "specialty;" there have been many other trees linked to historical events and social institutions. King Abimelech was proclaimed under the shade of a holly oak. The elm of Astudillo trimmed with its foliage the close-fitting crown of Ferdinand the Saint. Beneath one of the most corpulent beech trees in the forest of Vincennes, Saint Louis, King of France, administered justice. In the dark groves of Domremy, Joan received visions that transformed her shepherd's stick into the fleur-de-lis standard. If I had to demonstrate the importance of trees in the natural forms of worship in antiquity, it would occupy all the time of which I dispose. The gentilic religions, of course, evoked the white theory of the druids that surrounded the ancient oak in order to cut with golden shears the sacred mistletoe, a ceremony nowhere else dramatized with such mysterious solemnity as on the coasts of Armorica, when the ocean breeze brought with it the orgiastic moans of virgins on the island of Sen. Trees, and especially the oak, play such a key role in the poetic traditions and historical tales of peoples termed Celts, linked so closely to their popular customs, to their beliefs, and to their superstitions, that it is impossible nowadays to

deny a copious infiltration Celtic blood in that of the Basque, and
the subsequent social influence that ethnic blending implanted, with
some being able to see in that path the origins of the meeting of the
Bizkaian national assembly under the tree of Gernika. I believe that
the hypothesis is more ingenious than solid. The idea of meeting
under trees, or of taking this or that tree as a milestone or boundary
marker in territories in which certain tasks had to be fulfilled, or
carrying out distinguished events in the shade of a certain particular
tree, for being famous in the district, is an idea very much befitting
of peoples who still live close to what I would dare to term a state
of nature, so long as no pernicious error were to infect the phrase,
and along the same lines that could never be classified properly as
Celtic, Basque, Germanic, etc., but human. Aymeric Picaud, a twelfth-
century pilgrim, called Navarre "wooded" when crossing it on his
way to [Santiago de] Compostela. I do not believe Bizkaia was any
less deserving of the epithet in ancient times when we may assume
the oak of Gernika began to be used, one of the five foral trees of
the seigneury. And Bizkaia being "wooded," and the Bizkaians of
that time a rough people, living in dispersed farmhouses around the
forest, who did not even possess any churches of a monumental
nature, and still less palaces for the incipient needs of the political
and administrative order, should we be amazed that they designated
an oak tree as a meeting place for their assemblies? We will never
unearth the reason it was that of Gernika designated, and not another;
it had to be one, and probably reasons of local convenience or of
the fortuitous renown of the tree itself would have intervened in
the designation. With the reasons that at the time influencing the
decision unknown, data about the Bizkaian "mentality" at that time
on such matters are provided by the reasons that the people of
Durango put forward when it was proposed to change the location
of its council, under the oak of Gerediaga, to the field of Astola:
"From Gerediaga," said those in favor of the traditional oak, "most
of the representatives see materially their homes, and therefore see
more devotedly that touching the possessions of their land, and
others see Gerediaga as worthy of veneration for having conferred
in it since time immemorial the representatives of the republics."
The good sense of the honorable councilmen of Durango flowed

with the profundity with which the political will would flow; the real reason that, from the perspective of the happiness of peoples, condemns the large nationalities radiates in the aforementioned words: the government found itself too distant from the governed in order to function with the intimate love of the common good of the land. The large nationalities can boast about their glory; on the smaller ones can achieve such happiness. It is the recompense that God concedes to the humble.

Of all the symbolisms that decorate the oak of Gernika, the most beautiful and transcendental, in my opinion, is that which attributes it with the personification of the Bizkaian constitutional body. Consider what an oak is in itself. It originates in a tiny seed and develops slowly, more or less seven millimeters every year. In order to raise and sustain its bulk and resist wintry hurricanes, it must bifurcate in the soil numerous roots and its nourishing core must supply it with the appropriate chemical elements; the climatological and seasonal conditions should be suitable for the botanical species to which it belongs; in a word, that the environment should be favorable for it, thereby establishing its internal and external movement, constitutive of life. In this way, that seed that fell on the earth where chemical agents decomposed it, preparing it for its future transformation; that appeared buried in an imperceptible mound, shaped by its own enlargement; that in search of light and oxygen raised to the surface, making use of the porous nature of the earth, a small delicate plant that the vaporous wings of the most minute insect made vibrate; this was the stem, a defenseless sapling that the paws or teeth of herbivorous animals at any moment could uproot; that insignificance, that trifle, that atom of buried organic life, stretches out, gets wider, covers itself with a woody shell, rises up in the form of a trunk, today slender, tomorrow stocky, sprouts branches and more branches in an indefinite bifurcation, always upward, looking for the sky, getting covered with foliage and its verdant tip unfolding into the blue sky: with such majesty that eagles are stopped in their flight, and with such fortitude that it will resist the brutal jolt of gale force winds and the overwhelming grief of snow.

The Bizkaian Constitution was born and developed in the same way. It was not elaborated by any constituent assembly in an ordinary, nominal, or any other kind of vote; nor was it prepared by any commission of notables, supplied with their manuals translated from English or French; nor was it discussed solemnly by philosophers of political nonsense; and by no means did the clamorous mob, beating at the doors of Congress, demand its promulgation. No one embroidered a prologue of rights, founded on the derogation of duties, for it. It was something done the other way around from those done in the French Revolution. It began to take shape one day when some shepherds and woodcutters, from a small district, met to discuss their common business, with an ease of spirit that betrayed the choice of place for the particularity of a tree. The remedies that were reached responded to the needs they felt. This was the formula of their legislative science, which was the same, in sum, as that employed by Rome and England, by peoples blessed with personality, with juridical sense, and, what is less frequent, with common sense, which is an everyday temperament. A legislator that, before dictating a law, understands what the governing legislative "fashions" are, would have appeared in the proclamation against the foolish, by Quevedo, with the accessories of stupid and silly fools. The "famulus" Wagner sums it up in *Faust*: "*Was man an der Natur Geheimnisvolles pries / Das wagen wir werstandig zu probieren / Und was sie sonts organisieren liess / Das lassen wir krystallisieren.*" "The thing in Nature as high mystery prized, this our science probed beyond a doubt, what Nature by slow process organized, that we have grasped and crystallized it out." The ridiculous Homunculus, who exists precariously and was procreated by Wagner in a glass vial, is the pure image of constitutions created in one piece, according to the canons of rational reason. The Revolution made a deductive science out of political science, which is an inductive science. The master of the Bizkaian legislators was a tree; from it they learned the secret of successive adaptations, of measured progress, of transformations in chain, of a force that lasts, that is, of *tradition*. And when, through the multitude of legislative acts verified in the shade of the tree, it became their "symbol," and on seeing it reach continually for the sky, they got accustomed to measuring the beauty of its tip by how far it extended upward, the Bizkaians understood its profound meaning and planted a cross on the oak, linking religion and homeland.

The specific note of Bizkaian legislation (and whoever says Bizkaian, means Basque, since the Basque people coincide in all this) is the spirit of tradition. In order to delve into and address the life of beings whose nature is as alien to our own as that of the stars, plants, and animals, there is just one key: experience. With people similar to us, on the contrary, we both possess common life. Between us and them *consent* constitutes at the same time a need and a principle of action. Therefore, when we leave that relation with nature and enter into relations with men, the main rule that drives us through that new world of life is consent. Yet this same consent is conditioned, and constantly and invariably fed, by *tradition*, which is no deadweight that humanity is condemned to drag along, the unconscious slave of an unknown owner. The idea of perpetual movement, the base of revolutionary systems, is radically absurd. Living is not just about changing: living is continuing. Our life participates in change and in persistence. Changing through persistence and persisting through change, this is what truly constitutes the normal life of society and the law of its progress. Without tradition, social or collective will would be similar to the inconstant, incoherent, and capricious will of a child. It is what one observes in revolutionary peoples, in peoples that have reneged on and apostatized from tradition. And as religion forms a substantial part of this, and with religion comes morality, the elimination of these traditional principles turns puerile will into perverse will, and governments, deprived of discerning bad from good, come to resemble a gang of bandits, destined fatally to create iniquity. For that reason one must understand their words in the opposite way to what they mean literally. And when they say fraternity, understand a class war to the death; and when they say liberty, understand the persecution of virtue and of science, and the breaking of the chains with which the old society restrained error, vice, and crime; and when they say equality, erase from your memory that most beautiful image of the president of the United States, Garfield, who compared the democratic movement to a current that lifts a humble drop of water from the dark uniform depths of the ocean and mounts it on the rolling tails of waves. And understand that what perverted democrats pursue is to plunge it once more from its resplendent heights into murky depths.

The tree of Gernika is a tree of tradition, and in the same way, a tree of stable and healthy progress. Wherever Basques experience the dep sadness of a lost possession and cherish the immortal hope of recovering it, they externalize their feelings by means of a sapling from the tree of Gernika, which, as well as personifying Bizkaian liberties, symbolizes those of all the tribes, separated nationally, of the Basque people. For that reason, you will find their offspring or descendants in Navarre, in Araba, in the Americas, and until recently here in this city of Donostia-San Sebastián, which, just as Shulamite to the daughters of Jerusalem, for its beauty eclipses all the daughters of the Basque Country.

Reference to the all the reasons for this personification is an analytical task not befitting of this act. It is suffice to enunciate one of them, which, although it is the case that it may not be the main one, it is without doubt that which best fits the kind of solemnity we are celebrating. Of course you will have understood, ladies and gentlemen, that I am alluding to the popularization and glorification of the tree of Gernika in poetry.

Poets are those that, with the greatest foresight, perceived the symbolism of the tree, and in demonstrating it, transforming the effect into a cause, they completed it with new touches. It is impossible for me to speak to you about all of them as I would like: I will choose two, since they demonstrate in different ways the two crucial phases in the poetic life of the Gernika tree: the epic and the lyrical.

The first of them in order of time is, likewise, the most famous. There, in those days when the Spanish Monarchy was reneging on its principles and demonstrating the degrees of its decadence with Caesar-like usurpations, a mercenary friar, the master Téllez, better known in the immortality of letters under the pseudonym Tirso de Molina, slapped the face of Austrian absolutism with sticks extracted from the oak of Gernika. The concise and sculptured strophes put in the mouth of Don Diego López de Haro, express with absolute fidelity the intimate and total sense of Bizkaian history. That marvelous friar saw everything, and knew how to say so in the briefest of ways; each of his words is a concept; each phrase, a description; each description, a maxim. He saw the pristine independence of the country, maintained impenetrably by a handful of heroes; he saw a nobility founded on original nature, on what the Romans termed *ingenuity*, of which the letters of nobility freed by the monarchs were but cheap parodies; he saw the brusqueness of customs, the coarseness of civilization, the scarcity of fruits of the land, the austere lifestyle of the mountains, the virile industriousness of the women; he saw the biblical indigeneity of the race, the uncontaminated purity of its Catholic faith, its generous participation in the defense of Spain; and, dominating the highest of mountains, above the sparse snowy summits, which any figure summarizes by means of a synthesis it sums up, he saw the blessed oak, whose leaves were never sullied by the sludge of traditions, nor cut by the knife of tyranny!

The second of the poets was not a monk; but if in his epoch there had still been monks in Spain, I suppose I would have been drawn by the soup of the monasteries: such were the unfortunate! The crown of poets, before the laurels, is made of roses: people see the roses; the poet feels the thorns. He called himself "the great mess," expressing all his miseries in just one word. I met him in the year 1879 at the Basque festival in Elizondo. He stood there, coming from the heart of Gipuzkoa, its lofty crags, with his old guitar slung over his shoulders and his staff in his trembling right hand. The color of his modest black suit had disappeared in the mud and dust of the journey. His dignified posture, still upright; his lion-like mane of hair and copious beard, coarse, uncombed, and gray; the expressive look in his eyes, sometimes as soft as idyll, other times as iridescent as a storm, illuminated by the legendary halo of his name, left an impression. I met him some months later, even more intimately than in Elizondo, in Etxarri-Aranatz, where I had gone to give him four thousand *reales* with which the provincial council of Navarre had come to his aid. The deception, the disillusionment, of those first meeting was then intensified. I judged him, and alongside me many others, with the cruel criticism of youth. We thought of him as a one-song man, a single-sentiment man, the bard that, having celebrated the glory of the tree of Gernika, would not contemplate any fall without extracting from inspiration a shout to make the people rise up, or an curse to defame the tyrant. The reality was otherwise. Seated at a table, with a bottle and glass of wine before him, de deplored expansively not the miseries of the Basque Country but the many that were afflicting or had been inflicted on him; he argued about endless, and not always edifying, memories of his adventurous life; he made references to anecdotes, jokes, bawdy tales; he sang French, Italian, Spanish ditties; he only appeared to recall that he was the composer of "Gernikako Arbola" [Tree of Gernika] when this memory served to qualify his anguished postulation, among bitter and most just complaints for having been exiled to the Americas, where he lived forgotten even by himself, and bringing him to die of hunger among his countrymen... Poor Joshe Mari! The mess, not even great any more, filled the stage; the bard disappeared as a hazy image, as a fantastic whole perhaps... but if the fluttering course of personal feelings, or the suggestions of fellow guests, provoked the rekindling of Iparraguirre's truly immortal essence, and put in his mouth the anthem that we had always wanted to hear, the dross of the old mess disappeared and he was transformed into the symbol, into the representative man of the Basque Country and its freedom!

One should apply to Iparraguirre, too, the splendid term that Donoso Cortés applied to O'Connell and to Olano, man of the people. The Basque people have not sung the odyssey of their pilgrimages, the epic of their battles, or the drama of their history: we know nothing about that which he himself transmitted it to us. They are a silent people. They loved their institutions madly, ended up running the risk of losing them, they have lost them, several times already... and with all that, their affection remained locked away in their consciousness under seven seals. Iparraguirre broke them and detached the centuries-long clipped language. On listening to him, the Basque people heard themselves. The "Gernikako Arbola" is the least poetic poem that has been able to inspire such a matter; its rhyme is poor, its images, thoughts, and comparisons poor; but it is rich, rich in sentiment, summarized in the lines "*adorantzen zaitugu / arbola santuba...*" [we adore you / holy tree]. Internal worship became external. For this reason, Iparraguirre is great, because he gave shape to what we all felt and no one expressed; and he is great, moreover, because he made the most of a unique moment that time offered in order to do things well. Other poets would surpass him easily in purely literary contests; critics would easily evaluate him and demonstrate that the words and the *zortziko* music were not penned by the same hand, taking away from him paternity of the artistic element that most contributed to propagating the work as a whole. It does not matter: the memory of the tree of Gernika and that of Iparraguirre are legitimately inseparable, and posterity will determine that the statute in Urretxu was well erected, because that is not the statute of a poet, it is the statute of foral love; and like the Penitent Thief, Joshe Mari, the mess, in a brief instant would have gained mortality.

Since Sunday, this civilized city of Donostia-San Sebastián, known by so many pleasant titles, has possessed a sapling from the tree of Gernika. I ask God that the tree take root, not just in the earth, but in hearts, and that the branches of the oak celebrated because it refused its shade to the converted and traitors, should not shrivel but instead extend beyond the gamblers and harlots that some wretches seek to compete with Ostend and Monte Carlo. If the destiny of the sapling were that of presiding over the apotheosis of vice and the systematic de-Basquization of the people, I would propose to you, ladies and gentlemen, that we should leave here to uproot it.

Clearly, its destinies must be more glorious: it will serve as a labarum that leads to the victory of the spirited patriots of Donostia-San Sebastián who wish to link the legitimate progresses of their beloved city with the perpetuation of its Basque character. The recently planted little tree will be the monument that marks the resurrection of the national spirit, destined, with the grace of God, to reestablishing in their entirety the immemorial rights of Gipuzkoa

I have spoken.

Notes and Commentaries

Speech of Thanks Read at the Floral Games of Barcelona on May 17, 1891

It was translated into Catalan by my good friend, the eloquent Catalanist orator Don Narciso Verdaguer y Callís.

For personal reasons I did not have a lot of time to compose this speech. I restricted myself to expressing my enthusiasm for Catalonia and encompassing my different notions about that country in oratory form, but without going into detail on any of the points that my rapid enumeration entailed. Hence the many omissions from which it suffers. I want at least to make up for one: in speaking about epic poetry I did not mention the celebrated Mallorcan poet Calvet.

It also seems to me opportune to rectify something about what I said about Don Jaime the Conquerer: this egregious monarch was not, strictly speaking, the *creator* of the Catalan Parliament, but its organizer. He gave seats to the representatives of cities and towns (see *Llibertats y antich govern de Catalunya*, by Pella y Forgas, pages 111 and ff).

Lecture on the Origin and Development of Navarrese Regionalism

Some *bizkaitarras*, great friends of arguing about words, criticized that of "regionalism," assuming that on using it we rejected the substantial right of the Basque-Navarrese Country to reacquire its historical national personality. A region is part of a whole—they said; thus, those who call yourselves regionalists assume that that portion must be subordinate to the whole, and you are opposed to its individuality, etc., etc.

The important thing is to understand what the name designates, instead of imbuing with overly deductive reasoning. The dictionary of the Royal Academy defines region in these terms: "the extension of a larger or smaller country, which can only be established according to the cases in which this word is used." The Basque-Navarrese Country being part of the Iberian Peninsula, and in fact forming part of the Spanish nation, it is evident that all movements demanding change that may emerge in Navarre, Araba, Gipuzkoa, and Bizkaia, even if they end up at separatism, could be classified correctly as "regionalist," given that they do not emerge throughout the territory of the peninsula. This is the geographical sense of the word.

When I gave my lecture at the Lliga de Catalunya, and when I wrote certain works, the word "nationalism" had not acclimated in Spain. Mr. Arana Goiri imported it into the Basque Country and, in doing so, provided a great service to the calls for change, refining the terminology and clearing up the situation, which had been rather distorted by the errors that the word "foralism" had introduced.

I called myself a foralist because this was the name that the political tradition, the typical political vocabulary in our land, supplied; and as in recent times our rights had been denied or unknown in the name of the rights of the Spanish nation, the epithet of "national" was reserved for the unitary tendency, the enemy of the country's own constitutions. In many passages in my writings, "national" is equivalent to "pro-Spanish," and that is how it should be interpreted. Yet I have never discounted the concept that Navarre was a perfect nation united to another nation, as the reader will observe in several of my speeches.

Now I am going to explain my political concept of regionalism, used on certain occasions and less correctly as a synonym of foralism.

In my study titled "Foralism, Regionalism, and Federalism," which *La España Regional*, in Barcelona, published in the years 1887 and 1888, I defined foralism as "the tendency or political aspiration that proposes reconquering the fueros of which the Basque-Navarrese Country has been dispossessed, and in the meantime retaining those that it still maintains" (volume 21 of the aforementioned journal, page 766). And I understood regionalism as a "political doctrine that, holding the unitary concept of the modern Spanish state to be false and detrimental, recognizes and proclaims the right that befits regions and nationalities, differentiated historically and today constituting our Spanish nationality, to enjoy an autonomous life, but coordinated within a common national goal" (volume 23, page 1). This definition took into account the mixed aspect of the philosophical and the historical that the regionalist movement embraced.

I said then that I could not be indifferent to the Basque-Navarrese foralism that the concept of the unitary state had modified through the activity of regionalism; but as regards this, that we should consider it a new doctrine of state, that is, in its philosophical sense, I repeated and adopted the words of Don Fidel de Sagarmínaga: "the Basque provinces are not strictly regionalist, nor do our particular circumstances suggest that we should be." Rejecting this regionalism, which was just like "a new doctrine of general Spanish politics," he adopted a very different attitude with regard to historical regionalism, understanding it as "activity in favor of change carried out by components of the Spanish nationality." According to this latter regionalism, which was dominant in Catalonia, the regions demanded their own constitutions, claiming imprescriptible titles; and Basque-Navarrese foralism should, in my opinion, take this regionalism into account, without losing its own personality, in order to combat the unitary state (volume 23, pages 2 and ff). And with the exception of the coexistence of national unity, understood correctly, and the reestablished rights of the regions, by means of the federalist system, equally applicable to monarchies and republics (volume 26).

The statement (page 61), inadvertently printed in this lecture, that the first Basque-language poetry competition held in Spain was in Elizondo is incorrect. In 1879, I myself published in the *Revista Euskara*, in Pamplona, a note that was titled "A historical precedent in Basque-language poetry competitions," revealing that it had been sponsored by the Bishop of Pamplona, Don Antonio Venegas de Figueroa. I took the data from a curious article by the distinguished Basque scholar Mr. Julien Vinson, titled "Le basque navarrais espagnol á la fin du XVIe siècle" [The Spanish Navarrese Basque at the end of the sixteenth century]. The bishop justified the Basque competition with the following words: "…holding here in the Kingdom of Navarre the solemnity of this festival, *there is no reason that the original language of the kingdom should be disadvantaged.*"

Speech at the Traditionalist Regional Circle of Pamplona

At the beginning of this speech, I ratify my concept of regionalism expressed in Barcelona.

The citation of Donoso Cortés (page 78) reproduces his thought, but not his exact words.

See the allusion to the recognition of new powers (page 89).

Today, unfortunately, my observation about the most extreme opinions, transplanted in Navarre, being toned down (page 91), is not true. Although few, anti-Catholic sectarians here are as audacious as those in any other place.

In this speech I reclaimed publicly the reestablishment of Navarrese legislative power (pages 91 and 92).

Parliamentary Speech, Intervention in the Debate on the Message

I think I was the first representative, after 1876, to protest in Congress against the anti-foral abuses of central government (page 98).

Likewise, I presume I was also the first to wave the regionalist flag (page 98), detached from any other party ideal.

If that were really thus, these initiatives would constitute the only merit of this most modest essay.

Today, thanks to the path taken, to the power of Catalan solidarity, and to the oratory value that many of its representatives possess, the supreme question to which I could but allude, inhibited by isolation, inexperience, and the reasonable mistrust of my own powers, would have acquired the resonance it deserves. From my retreat I will take part in the grandiose battle, like an invalid commenting on the combats and victories of his brothers-in-arms. I know that some of them recall the obscure soldier that went out to reconnoiter...

Parliamentary Speech about Power and Legislation

This speech heralded the most distressing period of my political life, whose resumption has been impossible.

Said speech is a chapter in the history of the reception that Spanish Catholics accorded the politico-religious ideas of the great Leo XIII. It is not befitting of the nature of this collection to recall the antecedents that preceded the speech, nor specify the circumstances that sterilized it. I may write a book about that: it is a witness that I wish to share with a public audience on the day that the scandalous disunion among the Catholic forces in Spain should come to an end.

Although this speech, on account of its principal subject matter, is detached from the rest that accompany it, I have included it in my collection. Any other way, suspicion would have questioned whether I repudiated it, or whether it sat well with the maintenance of other ideas that I love, or whether I had tended discreetly toward ensuring the overlooking of an act that had imprisoned me in a leper hospital. There is no such incompatibility, nor do I repudiate acts when they are good in themselves.

My speech is an homage of submission and respect to the authority of bishops and the pope. Of absolute submission and respect, without distinctions, excuses, or feints.

During the disagreements that arose among certain Catholics at the time of my speech, my good faith did not experience any brief eclipse; thereafter, in public and in private I proposed to my contradicters that they should reduce our discrepancies to written propositions and elevate them to the decision of Rome, committing ourselves, on both parts, beforehand to venerate and respect the verdict. The response I received was jeering and ridicule.

In my speech, I followed the steps of the Spanish bishops and applied to Spain the celebrated doctrine of Leo XIII on power and legislation, a proposal to French Catholics in memorable circulars.

Why did I follow the bishops? The following texts answer this:

"It is often the case that those who investigate what is the most convenient method to defend the Catholic cause do not do so out of the authority of bishops, as would be fair and just. What is more, sometimes if a bishop has given advice about something, and even ordered something on the basis of his authority, there is no shortage of those who would be offended by that or openly reprimand him, interpreting it as if he were trying to please some, and insult others" (*Cum multa* circular). "Therefore, just as the union of bishops is necessary in the running of their Episcopate with the Holy See, likewise it is also befitting that both clerics and lay people should live and work in close harmony with the bishops" (*Sapientiae christianae*). Spanish Catholics "should ease the political passions that unsettle and divide them and, leaving God's Will to oversee the destinies of nations, work entirely in accordance with, guided by the Episcopate, in order to encourage by all means laws and fairness to allow for the interests of religion and the homeland, and together resist the attacks of the impious and the enemies of civil society" (Address by His Holiness to Spanish pilgrims). "… it is worth knowing: that all Catholics, heeding the word of their pastors and putting to one side all mundane interests, vigorous of spirit, worthy of the faith of their elders, and with an extremely close union of wills, should throw themselves into the race, etc." (Letter from His Holiness to the Bishop of Urgel).

> "…it is necessary on all accounts that even the last vestiges of the discords that have, miserably, divided Catholics in Spain should disappear, and that the forces that have been divided should join together and combine, willingly and in agreement, not under the leadership of men lacking authority, who attend above all else to the interests of current life and party passions, but under those whom God placed front and center to defend and preserve the religious and moral order … one must postpone temporal interests and whatever is of private use, all of us making an effort so that, in the current struggle, the triumph of the Church is complete. But this must be carried out in effect, not according to the prudence or whim of whoever, but with the approval and mandate of those that received this task from God. Any other way of proceeding suggested to Catholics, if it is contrary to or diverges from this, would produce not happy but deplorable effects, since it would not be the work of God" (Letter from His Holiness to Cardinal Benavides).

These texts and others that I omit as a courtesy to brevity suggest, if I am not mistaken, a model and guide for politico-religious action to their excellences the bishops; and even taking for granted that the faithful are not obliged to imitate them in everything, at least no reasonable person would contend that imitation constitutes an intrinsically bad thing, as, in fact, and covering the severity of the concept, was argued against me.

Yet I would not have decided to work on my own initiative on matters in which Catholic preoccupations, the daughters of almost a secular mentality, appeared to be so deeply rooted, had it not been on the understanding that the Holy See wished that the doctrinal principles in the circular to the French, of February 16, 1892, be applied everywhere, and that these principles dispelled the lightest of shadows of danger that could emerge from the appearance of the new powers. A thousand unequivocal signs and a thousand unequivocal testimonies, corroborated in the interviews that I had the honor of holding in Madrid with Monsignor Cretoni, the Nuncio of His Holiness, and later, in Rome, with the Cardinal Secretary of State, Monsignor Rampolla, convinced me that the policy of Leo XIII with regard to the new powers was identical in France and Spain, although here it was limited to indirect means, suggestions and exhortations, without the imperative tone of the circular to the French, through respect for the dynastic rights disputed by Don Carlos de Borbón and the history of the Carlist Party.

Leo XIII's satisfaction at seeing the principles consigned in the aforementioned circular to other countries was demonstrated officially in his reply to the clergy of the Archbishop of Braga, who, in a message proclaimed to the Pope, declared: "If this circular, in fact and in form, is for France, its doctrine, its material, and its essence is also for us, Portuguese Catholics, and as a consequence we embrace it with all our heart and consider it a rule of politico-religious conduct, the only one capable of establishing and affirming solidly the desired union and agreement between the faithful in the great Portuguese family." His Holiness deigned to respond in the following terms:

The sentiments that, in this noble text, we have admired and estimated greatly, sentiments of distinguished loyalty and supreme respect for Us and for the documents emanating from Us, are recommended to you everywhere before Us, no less than the previously cited beloved children ... Therefore, we confess to a great extent that that evident and opportune testimony of filial courtesy imbued us, amid the present bitterness, with pleasant consolation, so that we honor with deserved praise all those who subscribed to it with their names and the rest that adhered to the same wishes and sentiments. We of course are greatly encouraged by the certain confidence that their piety and their zeal will invigorate others to follow them (Letter from His Holiness to the Archbishop of Braga, September 26, 1893).

The criterion of the Braga Catholics was that which naturally took possession of serene and docile perceptions. I will cite two or three testimonies. The Bishop of Vich, on inserting in his *Boletín eclesiástico* the famous declaration of the five French cardinals, which was a solemn acceptance of the circular, accompanied it with a commentary, in which one reads: "It turns out from here that, in large measure, and at root at least, this doctrine, so magisterially explained in the cited document, applies to us; and it is for that reason that we call attention strongly to our faithful and especially to our beloved clergy, so that, insofar as the occasion occurs, they may know how to lead their people along the true path." Mr. X (Don Félix Sardá y Salvany), in an article that was published in May 1892 in the *Diario Catalán* and that was titled "Cuestión resuelta" [The question resolved], reproduced the following concepts:

Heaven has just sent sovereign and most opportune reinforcement to our both embattled and glorious flag, by means of the latest circular from His Holiness to French Catholics ... This question having been ruled on and resolved by he who has the unique, supreme authority to resolve it without any form of appeal or recourse. As far as France is concerned, the sentence is direct and decisive; for the other nations that find themselves in an analogous case, it will at least be a most important rule of jurisprudence and of an orientational value that all sincere Catholics of good faith will not be able to help but abide by.

El Criterio Tridentino wrote an article that *El Fuerista, El Diario Catalán,* and *El Gorbea* (ultra-conservative newspapers) reproduced. It said, among other things: "We understand that these duties that, according to the Princes of the Church of France, were imposed there on the conscience and patriotism of Catholics, mostly after Leo XIII's latest most sapient circular, are imposed today equally on the conscience and patriotism of Catholics in Spain and the other nations."

Without fear of being mistaken, I can state that there was a time during which non-Carlist Spanish Catholics believed that the doctrine in the circular to the French, of February 16, 1892, was applicable to Spain; at the very least, none of them was capable of imagining then that its application may have infringed on the integrity of Catholic principles.

These three antecedents combined, 1. The role of guides and teachers of Catholic action assigned to the bishops; 2. The distinction between power and legislation introduced by the aforementioned circular; and 3. The plausibility of applying it in Spain; the most logical solution to how many I could adopt in these matters seemed to me to be that of accepting, insofar as it was Catholic, constituted power. Working in this manner, I presumed to share the sentiments of "distinguished loyalty and supreme respect" that Leo XIII praised among the Catholics of Braga.

So as not be erroneous in such a grave matter, I wove the formula of my acceptance with phrases taken textually from the bishops' messages, which in the message of Zaragoza offered H. M. the Queen Regent public testimony of their "loyalty," in that of Valencia, of their "love, fidelity, and unflinching adhesion," and in that of Tarragona, of their "loyal submission, respect, and high consideration." The words of Leo XIII, which I cited immediately thereafter, were pronounced in an address aimed at Spanish pilgrims on September 23, 1891, responding to the Bishop of Tortosa.

My acceptance of constitutive power, covered by such venerable guarantees, led in the militant Catholic field to furious reprobation: I believe sincerely that if I had apostatized from the holy Catholic faith, the fuss and violence would not have been greater. All the resentments that the Poe's policy, seconded by the bishops, had deposited in their hearts were satiated then so much that there was not even a shadow of respect for such sacred figures to call for a reduction in the attacks. I was at the time the Turk's "great head" on which the blows of swords fell without flagrant impiety.

A few years later things got worse; furious passions were not held back, not even before the cardinal's purple. The Most Eminent Cardinal Cascajares having published a pastoral in which he advised Catholics to accept the new power, he was attacked bitterly. This is what I was told by the distinguished Archbishop of Valladolid in a signed letter he sent me on October 28, 1896; I call the attention of readers to the passages I highlight: "*I have fulfilled, Mr. Campión, a sacred duty, I have been to Rome, I have spoken to His Holiness, I see the Queen frequently, and it is clear that I have not spoken for the sake of speaking;* yet without hope, and I have not been mistaken: no one is more deaf than he who does not want to hear, that is a truth. There is a lack of humility, and this explains everything. *There, in the court of God, how will the blind volunteers be able to respond?*"

The tremendous bitterness that my speech of January 14 led to was softened with undying consolation. His Holiness Leo XIII deigned to award me his apostolic blessing. The communication in which he transmitted to me the news took the number 22,474 in the Register. Here is the translation of the Italian text:

Scarcely had Monsignor the Nuncio of Madrid sent me, in His Excellency's name, the two copies of the speech pronounced by him recently in the Spanish Parliament, I hastened to deposit one in the hands of the Holy Father, together with the letter that His Excellency intended for His Holiness. The august pontiff accepted with particular gratitude the tribute of His Excellency, and, taking pleasure in the renewed sentiments of devotion to the Holy See, has deigned to award him, with the effusiveness of paternal affection, an apostolic blessing. While I am glad to make this known to him, I am grateful for the other copy of his speech that he favored me with courteously, and with feelings of much distinguished esteem, I proceed to make myself available to His Excellency. Rome, January 28, 1895. Honored to serve you, Monsignor Cardinal Rapolla.

It seemed to me that a reprinting of this, my speech, demanded a brief comment, mostly documentary on format; I have the duty of safeguarding my tarnished Catholic honor.

The position that I adopted in this speech is that which, by the grace of God, I must maintain forever. Wherever the Pope indicates or orders Catholics to go, I will go without hesitation or wavering. It is sad that such complete submissiveness provokes, sometimes, the ire of excellent Catholics. But being with the Pope, and not even being with him matters, if such absurdity were fitting.

Lecture on the Basque Personality

The greatest number of diatribes that have been written against individualism confuse it with "egoism" and attribute it with qualities that only befit the latter. In general terms, I would say that any doctrine that bases the perfection of society on the perfection of the individual is "individualist;" and "socialist" that which seeks it via the perfection of the state.

Basque democracy, the political expression of a social fact, like everything produced by Nature, responded marvelously to the dominant circumstances. The modern error consists of assuming that societies profoundly differentiated and hierarchical in their structure, as contemporary societies are, can adjust without any serious risks to a system that requires a little less than homogenous matter. Rousseau, the father of all revolutionary errors, did not diffuse what he pointed out: "democracy [suits] States that are small and poor" (*Social Contract,* bk. 3, chap. 8). Yet his countless disciples did not warn of the restriction in the text, and "political" democracy, democracy founded on *a priori* principles, is at ease in large and rich states, embroiled in the folds of the Rousseauian flag. Its triumph depends on the degeneration of the leading classes, a clearly ethnic phenomenon: degenerates, as is known, always capitulate; those generously imbecile nobles on the night of August 4, 1789 began, and now the *bourgeoisie* follow them, imbeciles too, yes, but without any generosity. Nowhere does the triumph of "political" democracy produce an improvement in public customs; in using the word in its everyday meaning, not that which Montesquieu assigned it, no one, unless in a sarcastic way, would write today that the principle of democratic government is "virtue."

If democracy triumphs on the terrain of deeds, it is completely banished from the world of ideas. No thinker of any note supports it at the current time. One must belong to an "advanced" party to consider certain fossils of thought stupendous novelties. Democratic ideas are the passkeys with which career politicians, more or less models of the classic demagogue, open the doors of the palaces in which they, in the name of the people, settle. They will still serve for a long time, causing ruin and disaster. The cruel Jacobin proconsul, a demagogue first and duke second, described the entire "species" with these words: "We used to speak about equality, but within the internal fuero we were all aristocrats. Yes! More aristocratic than any other. Our system must propose halting the course of a revolution now without any objective, after obtaining several gains they could try." Oh Fouché, the eternal democratic figure, you called yourself . . . give the reader names!

The democratic phenomenon was so salient and intense that it intruded like a veil before the eyes of the most sagacious observers. Tocqueville believed that, "The gradual development of the equality of conditions is therefore a providential fact" (*La Democratie en Amerique* [Democracy in America], introduction). Those that adored democracy and those that cursed it and those that merely supported it coincided in considering it an overwhelming universal occurrence. The reaction was initiated in the very field of moral and political sciences. Sumner Maine, an Englishman, that is, someone resistant to the deductive method, to *a priori* ideas, to generalizations, combatted that providential nature of democracy (see *Popular Government: Four Essays*); he noted that observations were limited to a small number of nations and that, even within these, no importance was given to a force that works in the opposite direction to democratic leveling out: science. One of the conclusion sin the book was that, instead of popular governments being presented with an indefinite future, these governments in Europe were characterized by their extreme fragility. And when few people discerned the antinomy that appears today in all spheres of thought, he pointed it out sharply: "there is a marked antagonism between democratic opinion and scientific truth as applied to human societies . . . This theory [of Population] has now been generalised by Mr. Darwin and his followers, and, stated as the principle of the survival of the fittest, it has become the central truth of all biological science. Yet it is evidently disliked by the multitude" (page 37).

It seems inconceivable, but it is true; for several years Darwinism and the democratic doctrine, those two implacable enemies, shook hands. Supposing the composition of democratic parties, battering rams that struck against the walls of the old regime, the inexplicable case is explained. Let us listen to Mr. de Lapouge (a Darwinist that considers a series of doctrinal consequences with an imperturbability that is frightening): "In Darwinism, one saw, above all, the argument that could be in opposition to religions, in our country especially, to the Church, creationist and chained to the text of Genesis" (*L'Aryen* [The Aryan], page 513). Darwinism was one of many anti-Catholic ingredients that militant democrats used. But the old alliance is broken and the new intelligentsia destroys without mercy the articles of the democratic creed. Democracy is now an anachronism, good for the fossils of progress and the pretentious parliamentary left. "Liberalism, socialism, are forms of clericalism, that is, of politics based on the postulates of the Church..." (Ibid., page 513). The time has come for us to laugh a little.

Lecture on the Basque Language

An old infirmity of the history of philosophy is that of restricting or refuting the rule of free will in the course of human events. As liberty is demonstrated in the moment and history only knows past events, the historian studies the circumstances that influence such moments and establishes a completely causal relationship between them. This tendency has become stronger on a daily basis with the application of the methods of the natural sciences to their moral and political counterparts. Today the dominant concept in history and in sociology (to a certain extent, the brand-new philosophy of history) is determinism: the law of continuity, the evolutionary development of organisms. Each historical era is the fatal result of a previous and procreative one, and equally fatal for the subsequent one. Europe today has gone *a fortiori* through revolutions, the great monarchies, the Reformation, the Renaissance, feudalism… history is a chain of links; if one of them were to be missing or occupy a different position there would be no chain.

These depressing theories, which proclaim the inanity of voluntary effort and advise the conquered to accept defeat, are refuted by a resonant fact, by a glaring fact. Japan entered into the era of current European civilization without having passed through its previous stages; it arrived at that conclusion without the need of any premises. The refutation is absolute: race, climate, religion, social state, everything seemed profoundly different and indicated a profoundly immovable obstacle to the Europeanization of the Orient. The obstacle was a phantasm, and the blindest people can see that the best actor in the world is free will.

Lecture on the Restoration of the Basque Foral System

To the Bizkaian case alluded to on page ??? I would add another one from Navarre. In 1440, King Don Juan II wanted the people of the Baztan Valley to pay a tax for grazing their pigs in the mountains. Those levied turned to the king, telling him: "The nobles and minor nobles in Navarre . . . will not consent to settle the frontier territories of the king, they being distributors of the land and producers with the present king of their fueros and agreements; those present do not consent nor will consent to said declaration, preferring beforehand to leave the land and go and settle elsewhere."

In the writing these notes and commentaries I do not now agree with the Bizkaian example alluded to in the text. It is possible that when I prepared my lecture without books to hand I may have attributed to the Bizkaians words that were written by the people of Baztan. I seem to recall that the event that I sought to allude to was that in one of the famous letters that mediated between Philip III and the Seigneury; yet in this letter there was no threat to go and settle other lands, but instead the Bizkaians declared themselves obliged to defend their beloved homeland to the bitter end, and to seek whoever may support them and treat them well. Mr. Sagarmínaga questioned the authenticity of such letters (*El Gob. y reg. foral del Señorío de Vizcaya* [The government and foral system in the Seigneury of Bizkaia], page 194).

My lecture on foral restoration fell on deaf ears. A few newspapers published extracts from it, but they did not comment on it and even less did any support it.

A few days later, on October 13, the representatives Don Juan Santo Domingo, Don José de Itarte, Don José María Alberdi, Don Joaquín Pavía, and Don Vicente Loidi presented a patriotic proposition to the provincial Council of Gipuzkoa; gaining strength from the fact that the council had met for the first time since the king had been declared of legal age and had sworn an oath of allegiance to the constitution, and inspired by the most pulsating yearnings of the country and the agreement of the general councils, adopted on account of the law of July 21, 1876, they demanded: that, the provincial councils of Araba, Gipuzkoa, and Bizkaia being in agreement, they should take collectively to the highest powers of state a respectful and rational message, maintaining a current and permanent protest against the law of July 21, 1876, and that they should remain firm, resolved, and united as one single entity, working tirelessly, effectively, and by all legal means, until achieving the abolishing of that law and the just return to Basque ancestral home of its foral state with its own secular institutions.

This most noble proposition by the Carlist, ultra-conservative, and independent Catholic representatives was unsuccessful; eleven votes by Liberal and Republican representatives rejected it and defeated its five signatories together with Mr. Carrión, who joined them. Nor did the press deign to give any news about the event, making it a preferred topic for its debates and publicity.

Later, on the occasion of the alcohol tax and the renovation of the fiscal pacts, one could observe a certain resurgence in the Basque spirit: there were enthusiastic demonstrations, fiery words were pronounced, a league was founded in Gipuzkoa for the first time, after many years, elements in the left agitated in favor of the rights of the country... That wave was approaching the shore without being followed by any others, and it seemed like the sterile sand would break and undo it. The latest state of things is the agreement that the provincial councils took to solicit the reestablishment of foral bodies. We are still waiting.

اللّٰه

Lecture on the Worst Enemy of the Basque Language

Borther Luis de León, in divine speech, in his immortal treatise "De los nombres de Cristo," discussed the relationship between knowing and doing. In another and most excellent way, and rising to the high peaks of wisdom, demonstrates H. Spencer's lesson:

Yet Christ, our true Redeemer and Legislator, although it is true that in the doctrine of his Gospel he laid down some mandates, and he renewed and improved some others that had been understood mistakenly through bad use, but the main thing is his law, and that in which it differed from all those who had laid down laws in times gone by was that, deservingly on account of his works, and for the sacrifice he made of himself, the spirit and the virtue of heaven for his people, and He creating it himself in them, it addressed not just our understanding, but also our will; and spreading therein this spirit and divine virtue of which I speak, and curing it thus, it sculpted therein a law both efficient and powerful in its love, making everything that one would want to be deemed fair by the laws, and on the contrary everything that one may abhor to be prohibited and refuted by the laws . . . Moes only established a law of precepts, which could not provide justice because they spoke with understanding, but did not heal the soul: of which the burning bush in Exodus is an image, how it burned but did not burn, because it was the quality of the old law, which illuminated understanding, but did not give warmth to will," etc. (book 4, section 3).

According to the data that Mr. G. Berry read out before the French chamber of deputies in his interjection of the past February 28, in the previous fifty-eight days there had been eighty-eight murders in Paris—Juvenile delinquency has continued to rise since 1903 (the date of my lecture) there. This is not a question of crimes of passion: these agreeable youths murder merely to steal. The bloody wave is so formidable that many trials by jury, on finishing their sessions, demand of the public authorities the maintenance of the death penalty. Because this is the occasion that Clemenceau and company have chosen to abolish the guillotine, making pariahs of some ideas that were "progressive" there around the year 1840. Take note of my prescription readers; whenever you want to find out which ideas were elaborated a century ago, read the discourses of orators on the left and you will find them all.

The proposal was to abolish all defensive measures in society in order to destroy it with the least possible risk. Nor would I would swear that crime, in itself, is odious to all the elements that figure in the French parliamentary majorities. It was not long ago, even, that a certain socialist congress, held in Amiens, declared that, "crime, given the current society, indicated a superior mentality."

The bankruptcy of schools as instruments of morality is a proven fact.

The data in a recent *enquete* or survey, conducted among French soldiers who had attended school, speak very eloquently about its "useful" effect as a means of effective illustration. The results are stupendous. The seed fell on live rock in most cases. The ignorance produced by instruction, still free and obligatory, is incredible. Historical knowledge for example, reached such heights that most did not know who Joan of Arc and Louis XIV were, and, if I recall the percentage rightly, one third of them could not provide a specific detail about the Franco-Prussian War of 1870! It was, in their report, something akin to an earthquake that had hit the Antipodes; they remembered the name of the catastrophe, but nothing else. This is the characteristic feature of popular education: the rapid and almost complete extinction of learned notions.

Apparently, the democratic H. M. is very thick-headed.

The topic of these speeches was often common to several of them in certain passages: hence the inevitable repetitions, which extended in the same material way in my thoughts when I believed to have finally succeeded in expressing them.

Pamplona, May 25, 1907.

Roldán Jimeno is associate professor of legal history at the Public University of Navarre (UPNA-NUP), where he is currently the provost. He holds degrees in law from the UNED and history from the University of Navarre. At the latter, he was awarded the end-of-degree extraordinary prize and he also came third in the Spanish national prize. He holds a doctorate in philosophy from the University of Navarre, a doctorate in philosophy and educational science from the University of the Basque Country (UPV-EHU), and a doctorate in law from the University of Deusto. He has been a visiting research scholar at universities in the United States, Ireland, Venezuela, Italy, and France. He is the author of more than twenty books, a couple of hundred journal articles, and has collaborated in numerous multiple-authored works.

Made in the USA
Middletown, DE
18 March 2020